D0205469

ART, ENTERPRISE AND ETHICS
The Life and Work of William Morris

ART, ENTERPRISE AND ETHICS

The Life and Work of William Morris

CHARLES HARVEY
and
JON PRESS

FRANK CASS
London • Portland, OR.

First Published in 1996 in Great Britain by
FRANK CASS & CO. LTD.
Newbury House, 900 Eastern Avenue
London IG2 7HH

and in the United States of America by
FRANK CASS
c/o ISBS, 5804 N.E. Hassalo Street
Portland, Oregon 97213-3644

British Library Cataloguing in Publication Data:

Press, Jon
    Art, enterprise and ethics : the life and work of William
Morris
    1. Morris, William, 1834–1896 2. Designers – Great Britain –
Biography 3. Artists – Great Britain – Biography 4. Art,
British 5. Art, Modern – 20th century – Great Britain
I. Title II. Harvey, Charles
709.2

ISBN 0-7146-4712-8 (cloth)
ISBN 0-7146-4258-4 (paper)

Library of Congress Cataloging-in-Publication Data:

Harvey, Charles, 1950–
    Art, enterprise, and ethics : the life and works of William Morris
    / Charles Harvey and Jon Press.
        p.   cm.
    Includes bibliographical references and index.
    ISBN 0-7146-4712-8 (hbk) – ISBN 0-7146-4258-4 (pbk.)
    1. Morris, William 1834–1896. 2. Businessmen – Great Britain –
– Biography. 3. Artisans – Great Britain – Biography. 4. Designers –
– Great Britain – Biography. 5. Socialists – Great Britain – Biography.
I. Press, Jon, 1953–   . II. Title.
HC252.5.M65H367   1996
338.7'61245'092–dc20
[B]   96-18659
                                                                       CIP

Typeset by Vitaset, Paddock Wood, Kent
Printed in Great Britain by
Bookcraft (Bath) Ltd, Midsomer Norton, Avon

Contents

List of Plates and Figures

PLATES

FIGURES

Picture Credits

Preface

THE LIFE AND work of William Morris continue to excite the imaginations of fresh generations of scholars working in many traditions, from the history of art and design, to literary criticism, and the history of socialism and socialist thought. More recently, the authors of this volume have added a new dimension to Morris studies through their writings on his career in business. In our earlier book, *William Morris: Design and Enterprise in Victorian Britain* (Manchester, 1991), Morris is revealed to be an original and accomplished man of business, effectively dispelling the persistent notion that this part of his life was somehow tangential and of little consequence. We have since explored various dimensions of our thesis in greater depth and we believe that the essays presented in this volume make a further original contribution to our knowledge of one of the greatest figures of the Victorian era.

Chapter 1 surveys the writings about Morris from Vallance and Mackail at the end of the nineteenth century to Fiona MacCarthy in 1994. We focus on those writers who have made a significant contribution to the understanding of Morris's life and work, and discuss the ways in which that understanding has changed over the course of time. Inevitably, the choice of works is highly selective, and readers may query the inclusion of some and the omission of others. On a personal level, those included have helped to inform and shape our own work on Morris. We also seek to set our own contribution in the general context of Morris scholarship.

Chapter 2 examines Morris's early life and family background. Through an investigation of sources frequently used by business historians, but not previously used by Morris scholars, new evidence is provided which deepens our understanding of Morris's formative years. We stress that Morris's background was commercial rather than artistic or literary, and consider the influence of his early experiences upon his later career in business.

Chapter 3 provides an overview of Morris's career in business. It examines the motivation for setting up the partnership with Webb, Burne-Jones, Rossetti, Madox Brown, Faulkner and Marshall in 1861; the early history of the firm and its successes in ecclesiastical markets; its re-direction towards the middle-class secular market; the re-establishment of the firm under Morris's sole ownership; and the emergence of the mature firm in the 1880s. It concludes with a reassessment of the Kelmscott Press, which is seen not as an indulgence of Morris's last years but as another well-run and profitable business. This essay provides the core of our interpretation of Morris's business affairs.

Morris scholars have for long recognised the importance of his visits to Iceland in 1871 and 1873 to the reformulation of his world view. Chapter 4 takes up the theme, and, based upon a close reading of Morris's translations, journals and letters, reaches a number of signifi-cant conclusions – some of which reinforce established ideas, others of which challenge conventional wisdom. In particular, we question whether the 'horrors' from which the first visit to Iceland saved him were purely matrimonial. Rather, we argue, the cathartic influence of Iceland had more to do with his intellectual coming of age, so laying the foundation for his great period as designer, businessman and social critic.

Chapters 5 and 6 are based upon the writings of George Wardle, which are colourful, factually rich and full of insights. Wardle's 'Memorials' were prepared in 1897 for J.W. Mackail, Edward Burne-Jones' son-in-law, who was then at work on his two-volume *Life of William Morris*. They contain fascinating descriptions of Morris's work practices and the operation of his firm. Though used by a number of Morris's biographers, the only printed version is difficult to obtain and contains numerous errors. The Society of Antiquaries has kindly allowed us to reprint the entire text, together with a brief introductory note on its provenance and importance. In 1883, Morris & Co. had a stand which comprised six rooms at the Boston Foreign Fair. It showed a wide range of products, including fabrics, carpets, tapestries and wallpapers. The catalogue (written by Wardle, who attended the Fair to advise clients) is a remarkable document. As well as describing the products on show, it provides a detailed statement of the firm's use of colour and approach to interior design, and reveals the methods which it used to gain a foothold in overseas markets. The Boston catalogue is possibly the most important document on Morris (and Morris & Co.) never to appear in print. We reproduce it in full, together with a brief introductory note.

In Chapter 7, we examine 1 Holland Park, the home of a leading member of the Greek émigré community. As well as being one of Morris & Co.'s most important commissions in the 1880s, it is also one of the best documented. Correspondence between the firm and its client survives in the Victoria & Albert Museum and it was also widely reported in contemporary journals, bringing the project to the attention of a wide and appreciative middle-class audience. In 1893, for example, Lewis F. Day wrote an account of a visit to 1 Holland Park for the *Art Journal*. Other articles appeared in the *Building News*, the *Studio* and the *Architectural Review*. Additionally, many of the objects in the house – such as the *Holland Park* carpet, the *Forest* tapestry and fabrics by Morris & Co., survive in national or private collections. Together with contemporary drawings and the photographs of Harry Bedford Lemere, they allow us to reconstruct a vivid impression of the house in its late Victorian heyday.

By the early 1880s, William Morris's reputation as a successful businessman and an expert on the decorative arts was firmly established. He was called before the Royal Commission on Technical Instruction of 1881–84 to give evidence as an accomplished and well-informed witness. The Royal Commission was one of several which examined the state of Britain's education system in the course of the nineteenth century. They were a response to rising concern over international competition and the perceived superiority of French, German and American scientific and technical training. Most concern was expressed about training in the applied sciences, but there was also anxiety about the lack of educational opportunities for artists and designers, and about the standards of industrial design. Chapter 8 considers Morris's views on the role of the designer, the commercial importance of originality and beauty, and the role of museums in technical education. It concludes with an assessment of the extent to which his views were heeded by the Commission, and their influence upon the subsequent development of technical instruction in the UK.

In *Unto this Last* and other works, Ruskin appealed to the business leader to behave in a socially responsible, paternalistic fashion according to his own moral prescriptions. In this way, he believed that British society might be regenerated. Chapter 9 examines the ways in William Morris sought to give practical expression to Ruskin's ideas on business ethics. There is no perfect correspondence between the business notions of John Ruskin and the practice of William Morris. Yet it is evident that

Morris stuck to many of his mentor's ideas with remarkable tenacity; and the operation of the Morris business, especially those aspects relating to design, craftsmanship, work organisation, working conditions, scale and the market, owed much to Ruskin.

Finally, Chapter 10 draws together many of our more general thoughts and perspectives on Morris. We look at the influences upon him – real world and intellectual – and the ways in which they shaped his feelings towards life. His emotions, his aesthetic sensibility, underpin his thoughts and actions, and account for his transformation from political liberal to revolutionary socialist. Carlyle, Ruskin and Marx are all seen to have contributed to the Earthly Paradise of *News from Nowhere*. But much more came from Morris himself than it did from any of these other giants of the Victorian stage.

We are indebted to many friends, colleagues and associates for their assistance in preparing this book for publication. They have given generously of their time, explaining their research in detail, identifying key sources, and helping us to clarify our thoughts on various matters. In particular, we would wish to record our thanks to Peter Cormack and Norah Gillow of the William Morris Gallery, Walthamstow, for their support and encouragement. Their knowledge of Morris archives and sources is a vital asset to all those researching in the area. We also wish to thank Linda Parry, Deputy Curator of Textiles at the Victoria & Albert Museum and organiser of the 1996 William Morris Centenary Exhibition, whose unparalleled knowledge of nineteenth-century textiles has been enormously valuable to us; Ray Watkinson, formerly the President of the William Morris Society, who has read most chapters in draft, and suggested numerous improvements and lines of enquiry; Bridie Dorning and Katie Williams, who have helped us to identify and locate important sources; and Martin Will, who generously shared with us his knowledge of old Icelandic. As always, however, any errors or deficiencies which remain are ours alone. We should also like to record our gratitude to the Scouloudi Foundation (formerly the Twenty-Seven Foundation) and the Research Committee of Bath College of Higher Education, which kindly supported our research through the provision of funds for travel and other expenses.

For help with illustrations, we would particularly like to thank Anne Woodward, Liz Churchman and John Greenacombe of the National Monuments Record (Buildings), London; Nicola Gordon Duff and Joanna Ling (Sotheby's); Isobel Sinden and Glenys Evans (Victoria &

Albert Museum Picture Library) and Peter Cormack of the William Morris Gallery.

Earlier versions of several essays in this book have previously appeared in scholarly journals. We are grateful to the editors and publishers of the *Journal of the William Morris Society*, the *Journal of Business Ethics*, and the *Journal of the Decorative Arts Society* for permission to reprint them here. Where a chapter has previously appeared (either in an identical or similar version) in a journal, the full reference is given as the first endnote to the chapter. We are also grateful to the Society of Antiquaries for permission to reprint in full George Wardle's 'Memorials', and to the William Morris Gallery for permission to reprint Morris & Co.'s catalogue for the Boston Foreign Fair of 1883. Finally, we would like to thank Robert Easton, Jacqueline Lewis and their colleagues at Frank Cass & Company for their consideration, patience and warm support throughout.

Charles Harvey
Jon Press   April 1996

— 1 —

Morris and his Biographers

NEARLY A hundred years after its publication, John William Mackail's *Life of William Morris* remains essential reading for Morris scholars. Mackail was an Oxford classics don[1] who married Margaret, the daughter of Morris's closest friends, Sir Edward and Lady Georgiana Burne-Jones. He remained a valued friend and advisor to Morris's younger daughter May until her death in 1938. As an intimate of the Morris circle, he had access to key people and sources, and his detailed knowledge of Morris's private and public life enabled him to weave a detailed and attractive chronological narrative. His account of Morris's early life, for example, draws upon the reminiscences of Morris's sister, Henrietta, and brother, Stanley, and from Oxford friends like Richard Watson Dixon.[2] Further information was provided by the friends and associates of Morris's mature years, like his publisher and executor, Frederick Startridge Ellis. Particularly valuable was the detailed description of Morris and the firm compiled by his former manager, George Wardle, which is reproduced in Chapter 5.

It is a truism that biographies often reveal almost as much about their authors as their subjects, and it is not surprising therefore that Mackail's biography reflected many of his own interests and predilections. There are some areas for which he pulled together sufficient details for the purposes of his narrative, but little more. For example, he has little to say upon the operation of the Morris business – a theme to which we return later in this chapter. Nor did he claim expertise in many of the fields in which Morris had made a mark, such as the design and manufacture of textiles. Moreover, at times there are errors in the detail of Mackail's story. Ray Watkinson has pointed out the inaccuracies in the account of the work done at Red House, Morris's home at Upton, Kent from 1860 to 1864 – inaccuracies which led him to doubt whether Mackail had ever visited the house.[3] Evidently, at times Mackail rearranged details and selectively drew upon his sources to 'maintain his flow of description and keep it stylistically consistent'.[4] Such errors, though perhaps relatively minor in themselves, are significant because of the way that Mackail's account has for long held sway as the 'standard story', repeated in numerous books and articles over the years.

More seriously, Mackail's freedom for manoeuvre was constrained and determined by his relationship with those who had commissioned the biography. He was to produce a celebratory work, a tribute to a great man, something not just for public consumption but also directed at the surviving family and friends. In doing so, he was to contribute to what Fiona MacCarthy has termed a 'conspiracy of memory'[5] about his subject. It is now well known that there are significant lacunae in the narrative woven by Mackail. For example, Morris's contribution to socialist thought and action, though not ignored, does not occupy the central place it deserves, because neither Mackail nor his father-in-law sympathised with Morris's political beliefs. The impression Mackail tends to convey is one of a temporary aberration, rectified towards the end of his life when working on the Kelmscott *Chaucer* with Burne-Jones. Likewise, having close ties with the Morris family meant that Mackail could not speak out about the difficulties of Morris's private life – his wife Jane's prolonged affair with Rossetti and the illness of his elder daughter, Jenny. Only on rare occasions did he give readers a hint of the true state of affairs, such as when he remarked that an auto-biographical element might be found in Morris's poetry. In reading through Mackail's correspondence and research notes, one sometimes glimpses the frustration which he felt at the constraints placed upon him: 'how extraordinarily interesting one could make the story', he once remarked, 'if one were going to die the day before it was published.'[6]

The general acceptance of what may be termed the 'Mackail story' was encouraged by Sydney Cockerell, who had been appointed Morris's secretary at the Kelmscott Press in 1894. He became Director of the Fitzwilliam Museum in 1908, a post he held until 1937, and was knighted in 1934. Despite his careful and dedicated work as one of Morris's literary executors, Cockerell's influence was not always a beneficial one. He was generally doubtful of the value of Morris scholarship, believing that all the best letters had been published in Mackail – 'the only life of Morris worth anything at all'. He once told Philip Henderson that 'unfortunately other people are now taking it upon themselves to pry into matters which do not concern them', by which he meant Jane Morris's relationship with Rossetti. He described Morris as a 'giant', quoting Ruskin's remark that 'Morris is beaten gold'. Henderson commented that 'from the low reverent tone of Sir Sydney's voice and the hushed atmosphere of his study, I felt as though we were both taking part in a religious ceremony, an act of devotion to his beloved friend and master'.[7] Cockerell believed that mere business records would be of no interest to succeeding generations of scholars, and in the same spirit discouraged May Morris from including the unpublished Socialist lectures in her 1910–15 edition of Morris's *Collected Works*.

Not surprisingly, May herself followed a similar line, though she did in fact publish a few of the lectures. In 1938, shortly before the end of her life, she wrote a letter to Cockerell in which she spoke of the acrimony which surrounded the break-up of Morris, Marshall, Faulkner & Co. in 1874–75: 'W.M. however hurt would never want gossip-mongers to pick up anything in the future, so I always took care to write nothing that might go counter to Mackail's statements.'[8] At the William Morris Gallery in Walthamstow there is the text of a speech written by May Morris in 1934 (and edited by Mackail), which she delivered to celebrate the centenary of her father's birth. She began by conjuring up a happy image of Morris and his young friends beautifying Red House: 'All the friends must help ... the rooms were alive with happy workers, the garden gay with flowers and altogether Red House was slowly being made as Burne-Jones said "the beautifullest place on earth".' She recognised that 'youthful days cannot last', but characterised the 1870s as 'a peaceful life for some years, with the same friends round him: and the work of the firm of Morris & Co. growing in fame'. Then she described the way in which he came to question the contradiction between his hopes of 'an art made by the people and for the people as a joy to the maker and the user' and the restriction of his wares to a relatively small and privileged middle-class market. She noted his commitment to socialism and the drain on his physical and mental resources which this entailed. Yet she concluded that 'Morris lived a life of work unhindered by disappointments and enriched by generous and unclouded friend-ships: surely, though he died before his time, he may be called a *happy* man, leaving as he did such a memory in the hearts of those who knew him'.[9] No one would present such an interpretation today; on the contrary, most would agree with Fiona MacCarthy's assessment of his personal life: 'the full extent of his unhappiness, and his fortitude and generosity in facing it, is only now being revealed.'[10]

In retrospect, the unbalanced and incomplete picture presented by Mackail, Cockerell and May Morris is neither reprehensible nor

difficult to understand. After the passage of a century, and secure in the
knowledge that Morris's influence and reputation has survived, we can
afford to see him as a whole. This was not the case in the 1920s and
1930s, when his family and friends were struggling against the odds to
keep his memory alive. In 1934 Mackail noted sadly that 'now, nearly
forty years after Morris's death, his work has been superseded in favour,
fallen largely into neglect, even in certain quarters into contempt'.[11]
Mackail's biography remains a work to be admired and respected; the
shortcomings of his story are by no means as large as his critics have
sometimes assumed. We should be grateful to those who sought to
preserve Morris's memory during the early decades of the twentieth
century – not least for their efforts in ensuring the survival of many
documents and artefacts essential to later research.

There is a good deal of evidence of a decline in interest in the man
and his work after the First World War. The waning of the Morris firm
was no doubt partly due to poor management and lack of vision on the
part of Morris's successors, but equally it was indicative of general
trends in design and interior decoration. Meanwhile, the number of
publications about Morris's life and work fell to an all-time low between
1913 and 1932.[12] Few books from that period have proved of enduring
worth. Compton-Rickett's *William Morris: A Study in Personality* (1913)
and Clutton-Brock's *William Morris: His Work and Influence*, published
in the following year, are worth dipping into, though they do not add
very much to our knowledge of Morris.[13] More valuable is Henry
Halliday Sparling's *The Kelmscott Press and William Morris, Master
Craftsman* of 1924. Though Sparling's own connections with the Morris
family had long been severed – his disastrous marriage to May in 1890
had lasted just four years – and he was writing long after the events he
described, his reminiscences nevertheless contain important insights
into Morris's work practices and the operation of the Kelmscott Press
in the last years of his life.[14] John Bruce Glasier's *William Morris and the
Early Days of the Socialist Movement*, published in 1921 with a foreword
by May Morris, demonstrated that there were those in the labour
movement who continued to treasure Morris's memory. However, it
was written in the last months of his life when under the influence of
narcotics, and the accuracy of Glasier's interpretation is regarded as
suspect by later writers.[15]

The task for succeeding generations has been to identify and fill in
the gaps in Mackail's story. Over the years, Morris has attracted the

interest of many scholars who have sought to add to our understanding. Some have tried, like Mackail, to portray the whole man, and do justice to his multi-faceted talents; others have drawn upon their specialist expertise to illuminate particular aspects of his life and work. The process may be said to have begun with the celebrations to mark the centenary of Morris's birth in 1934, which included the first exhibition of Morris's work at the Victoria & Albert Museum. However, the interest which this engendered soon ebbed away, and it was not until the second half of the 1950s that a growing enthusiasm for Morris became evident. In the 1960s the stream of Morris studies swelled to a veritable flood, which shows no sign of abating. The average number of publications on Morris appearing each year roughly doubled in the 1970s, and doubled again in the 1980s. By 1985, when Gary L. Aho's *William Morris: A Reference Guide* was published, the volume of books, articles and catalogues relating to William Morris ensured that this comprehensive bibliography would immediately become an essential research tool.[16]

Of course, numbers are not everything. Most of the books and articles which appeared in Morris's centenary year have not stood the test of time. However, a few of them did make a significant impact upon the course of Morris scholarship. *The Studio*, though it had long ago made a shift away from the decorative arts, produced a large format special issue by Gerald Crow to mark the centenary. Crow provided a reliable and detailed account of Morris's work, and, unlike most previous writers, he recognised the 'inevitability' of his adherence to socialism. Particularly valuable for later readers, however, are the many illustrations; Crow reproduced many of Morris's working drawings, which at that time were still held by Morris & Co. at Merton Abbey.[17]

Most important of the 1934 crop of publications were those of G.D.H. Cole and Robin Page Arnot. Cole had been a member of the Labour Research Department before moving to Oxford to take up a distinguished career in academia. His *William Morris: Selected Writings* was published in Bloomsbury by the Nonesuch Press. It includes a wide and well-chosen selection of Morris's stories in prose and verse, and the lectures and essays on social criticism and socialism. There is also a chronology of Morris's life and a 14-page introduction. The prose stories which Cole chose were *A Dream of John Ball* and *A King's Lesson* of 1888, *News from Nowhere* (serialised in the *Commonweal* in 1890, and published in book form the following year), and, less predictably, the early and little-known *Story of the Unknown Church*, which Morris published in the *Oxford and Cambridge Magazine* in 1856. Under the heading 'Stories in Verse', Cole included *The Pilgrims of Hope* of 1886, and followed it with a goodly selection of shorter poems: half a dozen or so from *The Defence of Guenevere and Other Poems* (1858), one from *The Earthly Paradise*, and a number of later works. Cole commented that he could happily omit the rest of Morris's poetry with the exception of *Sigurd the Volsung*, which was too long for inclusion and defied abbreviation. *Sigurd*, he believed, was unlike anything else in the English language, revealing a side of Morris which was not to be found in any of his other poetry. Along with the *Iceland Journals*, which Cole considered to be 'one of the most revealing things he wrote', it demonstrated the essential contribution which Iceland and Icelandic literature made to the development of Morris's ideals. One short poem which Cole did include, *Iceland First Seen*, had to stand 'for all that vital part of his work'.[18] The volume concludes with a large and judiciously chosen selection of lectures and essays, including 'The Lesser Arts' (1877), 'The Beauty of Life' (1880), 'A Factory as It Might Be' (1884), 'Useful Work versus Useless Toil' (1884), 'How We Live and How We Might Live' (1884), and 'How I Became a Socialist' (1894). Cole made no apology for including so many of Morris's lectures and essays, stressing their importance in charting the development of Morris's thought from social criticism to socialism. Though most of Cole's selections were already available to those who could afford May Morris's edition of Morris's works,[19] the Nonesuch collection made them widely accessible for the first time. Reprinted several times during and after the Second World War, *Selected Writings* was be found on the shelves of many university and public libraries, affording many people the opportunity to hear Morris's authentic voice for the first time.

Arnot's work was not so widely known but arguably it has had an even more significant impact upon the development of Morris studies. He helped to establish *Labour Monthly*, in 1921, and was a founder member of the Communist Party of Great Britain, serving on its Executive Committee between 1924 and 1938. Throughout the 1920s and 1930s he acted as a British representative to the Communist International (Comintern). He sat on to the Marx Commemoration Committee for the celebration of the fiftieth anniversary of Marx's death, and was appointed Principal of the Marx Memorial Library in Clerkenwell when it opened in 1933. Arnot was particularly incensed by the anti-communist tenor of the celebrations which marked the Morris centenary in 1934.[20] The Victoria & Albert Museum's exhibition, for example, was planned by a committee consisting of J.W. Mackail, May Morris, Sir Sydney Cockerell, H.C. Marillier (one of the directors of Morris & Co.), C.H. St John Hornby (the Poet Laureate), and four members of the Museum's staff. Not surprisingly, the emphasis was on Morris the creative artist. Mackail himself chaired the committee and contributed a brief introduction to the catalogue. He acknowledged the appropriateness of the description 'poet, artist, manufacturer and socialist', but largely ignored Morris's socialism.[21] The opening of the exhibition was noteworthy for a speech by Stanley Baldwin, Georgiana Burne-Jones' son-in-law, which omitted any reference at all to Morris's political thought and action.

In his 32-page pamphlet, *William Morris: A Vindication*,[22] Arnot was really the first person to challenge the 'Morris myth'. In fact, he attacked not one but two myths which he believed distorted our understanding of Morris. The first of these was the bourgeois myth of the 'harmless saint', typified by the Victoria & Albert's celebrations. 'Of course Morris was a great artist and a great craftsman', argued Arnot; 'but neither his art nor his craftsman's work can be truly understood, nor can the whole man be understood, unless he is seen as he truly was, as a revolutionary Socialist, fighting for the overthrow of capitalism and for the victory of the working class.' The Labour Party and the ILP, on the other hand, sought to portray Morris as a reformer and 'gentle socialist'. Because they were anti-Marxist, they did not want to admit that Morris was a Marxist; 'so that in essence the fight over the body of Morris was a fight against the influence of Marx inside the Labour movement.' In support of this line, Arnot argued that even old associates of Morris had asserted that he had not studied – or not understood – *Das Kapital*. For example, he noted Bruce Glasier's claim that *Socialism: Its Growth and Outcome*, co-authored by Morris and Belfort Bax in 1893, did not represent Morris's true views – this despite the authors' declaration in the preface that 'the work has been in the truest sense of the word a *collaboration*, each sentence having been carefully considered by both the authors in common'. Then he turned to the way people had read *News from Nowhere*, claiming that, under the influence of the ILP myth, they had all glossed over the fact that '*the essence of "News from Nowhere" is the insistence on the necessity of an armed and bitter civil war as the only path to socialism for the working classes*' (authors' italics).

In short, Arnot urged, neither capitalists nor ILP members should be

allowed to canonise Morris. 'Many this centenary year will be turning
to read *News from Nowhere*', he concluded. 'As they do it, they should
realise that the poet, once "the idle singer of an empty day" in the
'sixties, had developed by his great period of the 'eighties into the full
revolutionary artist ... It is high time that the Morris myth was
destroyed; for the real Morris belongs to us, belongs to the revolutionary
working classes of Great Britain.' The intemperate nature of the
language makes *William Morris: A Vindication* something of a period
piece,[23] but there is no doubt of the legitimacy of Arnot's arguments, nor
of its impact on other scholars. In later years he continued his studies on
Morris. They culminated with the publication of *William Morris: The
Man and the Myth* in 1964, which drew together and expanded many of
the ideas in his 1934 pamphlet as an introduction to 49 letters written by
Morris to his socialist colleagues J.L. Mahon and John Glass between
1884 and 1895.

Robin Page Arnot was one of the small group of people responsible
for the establishment of the William Morris Society in 1955. The group
also included Edward and Doris Hollamby, the owners of Red House,
Graeme Shankland, Stanley Morison, Nikolaus Pevsner and John
Brandon-Jones. Sir Sydney Cockerell was invited to become the first
President of the Society, and Graeme Shankland the Honorary Secretary.[24] In 1966, it merged with the Kelmscott Fellowship, founded by
May Morris in 1918. From its headquarters at Kelmscott House,
Hammersmith (formerly Morris's London home), the Society organises
lectures and trips and publishes a *Journal*, books and pamphlets. It
embraces all those interested in Morris, both academic and non-
academic, and currently has a membership approaching 1,700. A brief
description of the work of the Society is given at the end of this book.

Arnot also did much to encourage younger researchers; both E.P.
Thompson and Philip Henderson were directly stimulated by him, and
many others, including Paul Meier, have recognised the extent to which
they are in his debt.[25] Edward Thompson's superb *William Morris:
Romantic to Revolutionary* may be claimed as the greatest product of
Arnot's influence upon others.[26] The essence of Thompson's view is
that Morris 'was not a muddle-headed convert to Marxism', but someone
who made a genuinely original contribution to English socialism. In his
lectures and writings, Morris repeatedly asserted that the creation of a
genuinely socialist society demanded a moral revolution, not just an
economic one:

Morris's claim to greatness must be founded, not on any single contribution to English culture, but on the quality which unites and informs every aspect of his life and work. This quality might best be described as 'moral realism'; it is the practical moral example of his life which wins admiration, the profound moral insight of his political and artistic writings which gives them life.[27]

Since Mackail was likely, in Thompson's view, to remain the standard chronological account of the main events in Morris's life, he did not set out to write a comprehensive biography, but rather a study of those aspects of Morris's life which contributed to his emergence as a leading figure of the socialist movement. Part one of *Romantic to Revolutionary* surveyed those who reacted against 'Gradgrindism' – the utilitarianism and political economy which made up the dominant creed of mid-nineteenth century Britain. They included John Keats, Carlyle and Ruskin, and Rossetti and the Pre-Raphaelites. Thompson considered each in turn before demonstrating how Morris drew upon their influence. In part two, 'The Years of Conflict', he takes us through the period from the building of Red House and the establishment of Morris, Marshall, Faulkner & Co. up to 1882, when Morris crossed the 'River of Fire' and determined that he was 'ready to join any body who distinctly call themselves socialists'.[28] Thompson charts the success of *The Earthly Paradise*, which confirmed Morris as one of the leading poets of the Victorian era, and the personal crisis of the late 1860s and early 1870s. Great importance is attached to Morris's Icelandic experiences in 1871–73, and, later in the decade, to his participation in the Eastern Question Association, which revealed to him 'the depth of cynicism of the Tory Party; the opportunism and moral cowardice of professional politicians; the power of the working class, even when only a mere fringe are organised'. In a similar vein, Thompson argued that the Society for the Protection of Ancient Buildings, largely created at Morris's instigation, 'quickened and deepened his insight into the destructive philistinism of capitalist society', and 'urged him forward from a passive to an active view of history'.

Part three, 'Practical Socialism', forms the core of the book. It provides a detailed account of the organisations and individuals who contributed to the development of socialism in Britain in the 1880s. Morris's participation in Hyndman's Social Democratic Federation is carefully analysed, as is his secession in 1884. The Socialist League, which Morris established with fellow secessionists like Belfort Bax, the Avelings, Frank Kitz, J.L. Mahon and Joseph Lane, receives particularly detailed attention. Thompson emphasises the importance of *Common-weal*, the journal Morris edited for the Socialist League, arguing that it provides impressive evidence of Morris's emergence as an important socialist theorist. Morris's eventual departure from the League in 1890 is analysed in detail, and Thompson concludes the section by stressing that Morris did not stop working for socialism in his last years, though of necessity his role became a less active one. Nor was he ever reconciled with the parliamentarian or opportunist approach, though he recognised its growing strength as the nineteenth century drew to a close. As Morris told the Fabian Sidney Webb in the year before his death, 'the world is going your way at present, Webb, but it is not the right way in the end'.

Part four, 'Necessity and Desire' continues the process initiated by Arnot of debunking the myths and misconceptions about Morris which had become entrenched over the years. It is a process which Thompson returns to in one of the appendices, an essay on 'William Morris, Bruce Glasier and Marxism'.

The first edition of *Romantic to Revolutionary* is a remarkable book. The breadth of Thompson's scholarship is truly impressive, and he provides many insights into Morris's life and its importance to early socialism. With the passage of time, its imperfections have of course become more evident – as its author later said, 'I wrote it in an embattled mood, from a position of strong political commitment, addressing an audience in the adult education movement and the political movements of the Left rather than a more academic audience.' It was also too long. Some sections deserved to be trimmed or omitted altogether – for example, the digressions into 'minor episodes of the early Socialist movement'. The revised edition, which eventually appeared in 1976 with a long 'Postscript' surveying the development of Morris writings in the 21 years since the publication of the first edition, is accordingly a more measured work, but in some respects a less exciting and challenging one. Its predecessor is still worth consulting.

Since Thompson, as Leslie Morton has remarked, 'the wilfully ignorant alone can continue to repeat the old mistakes'.[29] The recent publication of Morris's letters in Norman Kelvin's carefully researched and annotated edition[30] confirms the centrality and authenticity of Morris's socialist beliefs. In the words of Fiona MacCarthy, the letters 'finally disprove the Mackail/Burne-Jones confection that Morris's Socialism was a temporary madness. Read through in their long sequence, they show convincingly that, far from being an aberration, Morris's progression from the heart of the mercantile establishment to the forefront of late Victorian Socialist agitation in Britain had a grand inevitability.'[31]

This is not to say, of course, that after Thompson nothing remains to be said about Morris's socialism and political thought. The work of Paul Meier, amongst others, is worthy of note. A lecturer at the University of Nanterre from 1962 until his retirement in 1976, he first came to prominence through his translation of *News from Nowhere* into French (1962). In 1971, he obtained his doctorate for his thesis, *La Pensée Utopique de William Morris*, which was published in Paris the following year. It attracted a good deal of attention from British and American scholars, and in 1978 it was published in English by Harvester Press under the title *William Morris: The Marxist Dreamer*. It stresses the originality of Morris's ideas, but also the extent to which they were rooted in those of Marx and Engels. Though the argument is rather overdone in places it provides, as Aho has remarked,[32] by far the most comprehensive analysis of *News from Nowhere* ever attempted. Particularly interesting are the sections in which Meier identifies links with Marx's early work, and summarises the other authors upon whom Morris had probably drawn.[33]

More recently still, Morris's contribution to early English socialism has interested a new generation of scholars. Foremost amongst them is Nicholas Salmon, who has undertaken an in-depth study of Morris's contributions to *Justice* and *Commonweal*.[34] Between 1883 and 1890, he contributed almost 500 signed articles. Salmon argues that they represent the least well-known aspect of Morris's propagandist activities, and he sets out to remedy the situation. After a substantial introduction, in which he summarises the political career of Morris, almost 150 of Morris's articles are reproduced in full. The range of topics covered is very broad. They include, *inter alia*, many aspects of domestic politics; law and order in Ireland; issues of free speech in America; education under capitalism; impressions of the Paris Trades' Union Congress; and reviews of works like Bellamy's *Looking Backward*. Salmon omits most of the brief notes and *A Dream of John Ball* and *News from Nowhere*, which, though originally serialised in *Commonweal*, are well known and widely available. Important lectures like 'How We Live and How We Might Live' which are available elsewhere are also left out. Most of the pieces included have not been reprinted before, though they do include the series of articles with Belfort Bax entitled 'Socialism From the Root Up', which were published in a revised and expanded form as *Socialism: Its Growth and Outcome* (1893). As Adam Buick has noted in a recent review, Salmon's selections 'confirm Morris as having been not only an eloquent advocate of pure Socialism (which was already evident from his previously published lectures), but also as a skilful socialist journalist, ably analysing contemporary events with a fine knowledge of socialist theory and tactics.'[35]

Over the years since the centenary of Morris's birth, other writers have examined Morris's personal life and his wife's relationships with Rossetti and Wilfrid Scawen Blunt. The first writer to probe the mystery surrounding Morris's private life was Oswald Doughty, in *A Romantic Victorian: Dante Gabriel Rossetti* (1949). Doughty dealt at some length with Gabriel's infatuation with Janey, recording that Morris 'kept silent about his private sorrows', and speculating on the importance of *The Earthly Paradise* both as a consolation to Morris and as a vehicle through which he could express his private thoughts. Philip Henderson's *William Morris: His Life, Work and Friends* (1967) (2nd edn, Harmondsworth 1973) is an important biography, partly because it is accessible and well written, but also because of its treatment of Morris's personal crisis of the late 1860s and early 1870s. Henderson was able to draw upon new material, notably the 114 letters from Rossetti to Janey which were first made available to scholars in 1964. They contain numerous references to Morris in the period 1868–81, many of them far from flattering. The letters were subsequently published, along with 37 letters from Janey to Rossetti, in a fully annotated edition by John Bryson and Janet Camp Troxell.[36] Henderson also used many other Morris letters, which were published in his earlier *Letters of William Morris to his Family and Friends* (1950).

One of the most important developments of the last decade is that Morris's wife and daughters have been emerging from obscurity, as Norman Kelvin has put it, 'like a latent photographic image'.[37] Bryson and Troxell's collection of Janey–Rossetti letters began the process. The work has been ably carried forward by Jan Marsh, who notes that while women were important in Pre-Raphaelite circles, and their faces are seen everywhere, their voices have not been heard. It is no longer satisfactory to discuss women in terms of their importance to the men in their lives – no matter how fascinating and influential those men might be. With the publication of Marsh's *Pre-Raphaelite Sisterhood* (1985) and

Jane and May Morris (1986), the women in Morris's life have moved centre-stage. Jane Morris's emergence from obscurity continues with Peter Faulkner's fascinating account of her affair with Wilfrid Scawen Blunt. He makes effective use of her letters, revealing her as a highly complex person, very different from the silent and forbidding woman of earlier accounts.[38]

What about Morris's contribution to the history of textiles and the decorative arts? Aymer Vallance was the earliest contributor of note: his *William Morris: His Art, his Writings and his Public Life* was published in 1897, predating Mackail's biography by two years. Particularly good use is made of contemporary sources such as *The Studio*. As noted earlier, Gerald Crow's centenary edition of *The Studio* is also of value. Once again, though, a fuller assessment of Morris's work was long in the making. Peter Floud's 'Dating Morris Patterns', published in the *Architectural Review* in 1959, provided the first serious analysis of his textiles. Using records of design registrations, he sought to locate them in their chronological order, and thus identify stylistic trends and developments. In this way he was able to point to the shift towards a more rigid and repetitive style from 1876, caused by Morris's research into weaving and woven fabrics. Floud also drew attention to Morris's extensive use of historical examples, illustrating the way in which his knowledge of the South Kensington Museum's collections influenced his designing.[39]

Floud's work was sadly curtailed by his early death, and there were few willing and able to carry on his pioneering work. Then, as now, publications on Morris textiles were generally intended to grace the coffee table rather than to illuminate minds. Exceptions include the books of Barbara Morris, one of Peter Floud's colleagues at the Victoria & Albert Museum. Her 1962 book on Victorian embroidery contains numerous references to Morris and evaluates his part in the development of 'art needlework', which superseded the earlier craze for Berlin wool work.[40] She was responsible for the 1961 Arts Council exhibition to commemorate the centenary of Morris, Marshall, Faulkner & Co., thus turning the spotlight from Morris himself to the Morris firm. The catalogue provides a brief though invaluable introduction to those who contributed to the firm from its inception up to its demise in 1940, and recognises its role in the transformation of interior decoration – a revolution neatly summed up by Walter Crane as 'in the main a revival of the medieval spirit (not the letter) in design; a return to simplicity,

to sincerity; to good materials and sound workmanship; to rich and
suggestive surface decoration and simple constructive forms'.[41] More
recently, she has researched Morris's relationship with the South
Kensington Museum (now the Victoria & Albert Museum), which
began in 1864, when Morris, Marshall, Faulkner & Co. sold stained
glass panels to the Museum, and continued until his death. In an oft-
quoted passage, Morris once remarked that he had probably used the
Museum more than any man alive.[42]

Another important contributor on Morris as a designer is Ray
Watkinson, whose *William Morris as Designer* (1968) deservedly remains
in print nearly 30 years later. Watkinson asserts that William Morris
designed the finest fabrics and wallpapers of the nineteenth century;
mastered half a dozen diverse crafts; and wrote some of the finest poetry
of the age. More than this, he belongs to our own time as much as
his own, and 'nobody of his time is more worth the trouble of re-
examination'. It is an assertion which has now become almost a truism
as many have come to recognise Morris's relevance to the last years of
the twentieth century. Though quite brief, *William Morris as Designer*
manages to provide many insights into the principles upon which
Morris worked and how his thought developed. Watkinson argues that
'it was Morris's historical understanding of what he was doing that
made him so potent a force'. In similar vein, it is Watkinson's own
historical awareness which gives potency to his interpretation. One of
his strengths has always been his ability to contextualise and make
connections, and the chapters on precursors of Morris and the firm, and
on the Arts and Crafts Movement which drew so much of its inspiration
from Morris's example, effectively complement those on Morris's own
work. It is perhaps to be regretted that Watkinson has not produced the
really substantial account of Morris and his world which would properly
do justice to the breadth and depth of understanding which he has so
often demonstrated in his many talks and lectures. Yet *William Morris as
Designer* is not his only contribution. As well as his work on Ford Madox
Brown and the Pre-Raphaelites,[43] he has served the William Morris
Society over many years, latterly as Vice-President and President; and
he has generously shared his knowledge and understanding with many
scholars, including the authors of this book.

Apart from Barbara Morris and Ray Watkinson, few added much to
the understanding of Morris as designer between the 1960s and the
early 1980s. On Morris designs generally, Fiona Clark's *William Morris:*

Wallpapers and Chintzes of 1973 is worth a look, though marred by a number of errors and the generally poor quality of the (mostly black and white) illustrations. So, too, is Fairclough and Leary's *Textiles by William Morris and Morris & Company, 1861–1940*, the catalogue of an exhibition at Birmingham Museum and Art Gallery in 1981. As the title indicates, it conscientiously covers the whole period up to the demise of the Morris firm, though the late designs are not impressive.

Two years later, in 1983, however, came the publication of Linda Parry's *William Morris Textiles*. It is an essential source for anyone interested in Morris textiles. Parry is rightly regarded as one of the leading experts on the topic. She is currently Deputy Curator of Textiles and Dress at the Victoria & Albert Museum, and is responsible for the Museum's 1996 Morris Centenary Exhibition. Her research, for the most part, has not invalidated Floud's pioneering work, though it has shed new light on the subject. In particular, she has demonstrated that Morris created relatively few new designs in the last ten years of his life, and that many designs attributed to him – by his daughter May amongst others – were in fact by J.H. Dearle. As Barbara Morris wrote, 'The fact that all the designs for textiles with repeating patterns are reproduced in chronological order in Linda Parry's book means that one can quickly see which are Dearle's designs and discern the difference between his and those of his master. Dearle's designs are flatter, less intricate, more widely spaced and broader treated, with less intertwining of the elements of the design. But Dearle emerges as a more original designer than had hitherto been realised, and some of his most masterly designs such as the *Compton* of 1896, previously thought to be Morris's last design, show that he was no mere imitator.'[44] The only real problems with *William Morris Textiles* are that the colour illustrations of each design are rather small, and continuing research on Morris textiles over the last decade – much of it by Parry herself – has added to, and in some cases modified, the content of her book. A revised version is urgently needed.

What of Morris's literary reputation? Though it was as a man of letters that he was best known to his contemporaries, it was a reputation that has not proved durable. Few people nowadays would claim familiarity with his poetry or romantic novels. Part of the problem is that Morris is difficult to anthologise; as Burne-Jones once remarked, 'you cannot find short quotations in him, he must be taken in great gulps'.[45] Nevertheless, the work of Peter Faulkner has done much to re-establish Morris's literary reputation. Faulkner's first major contribution came in 1973, with the publication of *William Morris: The Critical Heritage*. Like the other volumes in Routledge's 'Critical Heritage' series, it focuses on the reception given to Morris as a writer by his contemporaries and near-contemporaries – though some contributions do address his work as a designer. A wide range of reviews and essays have been selected to demonstrate the diversity of opinion which existed about Morris's literary work. Faulkner's introductory essay provides a valuable summary of his career as a writer, and sets the context both in terms of 'the market' for literature and Victorian reviewers and reviewing practices.

In 1980 Faulkner published *Against the Age: An Introduction to William Morris*. As the title suggests, it is a relatively brief introduction to Morris, and has to cover a lot of ground, but it is the treatment of Morris's literary work which sets it apart from its competitors. There are useful commentaries upon his writings, from the well-known like *The Defence of Guenevere* and *News from Nowhere* to lesser-known works like *Love is Enough* and his classical translations. Faulkner draws upon his earlier research, and makes effective use of contemporary responses and reviews. Throughout, he stresses the extent to which Morris, in his writings, his design work and his political thought and action, remained 'against the age'. It remains the only brief introduction to do justice to Morris's literary work, and it is unfortunate that it has long been out of print.[46]

The process of re-evaluation continues with two recent books by Isobel Armstrong and Jerome McGann on Victorian poetry. Armstrong's in particular seems set to become a major reference work. Together, they claim a major place in the Victorian canon for Morris's early poetry – and in particular, *The Defence of Guenevere and other Poems*.[47] In a similar fashion, Morris's prose romances are again attracting critical interest. Among a growing array of publications, both on specific works and those of a more thematic nature, Amanda Hodgson's *The Romances of William Morris* (Oxford, 1986) is of particular value to the general reader. She provides a critical text which, though closely argued, is both accessible and readable. The essence of her argument is that the romances are not 'escapist', but should be taken seriously, as they 'reflect Morris's progressing attitudes towards society and towards the place in it of art and imagination'.

Morris's career as a publisher and book designer at the Kelmscott Press has also been the subject of renewed scholarly interest in recent years. The upshot is that he is now properly seen as pivotal to the revival of the small-scale private press in late nineteenth-century Britain. Duncan Robinson sees the Kelmscott *Chaucer* as the pinnacle of the Morris–Burne-Jones relationship. He is particularly interesting on the many illustrations designed by Burne-Jones, and the efforts of Kelmscott Press employees to turn them into wood blocks.[48] Needham, Dunlap and Dreyfus draw upon the many holdings of the Pierpont Morgan Library in New York for their *William Morris and the Art of the Book*.[49] The most valuable research on the history of the Kelmscott Press is that of William Peterson, whose publications include *The Ideal Book: Essays and Lectures on the Arts of the Book* (Berkeley, CA, 1982); *A Bibliography of the Kelmscott Press* (Oxford, 1984); and *The Kelmscott Press: A History of William Morris's Typographical Adventure* (Oxford, 1991). *The Ideal Book*, which is attractively presented and illustrated, includes a number of lectures and essays by Morris on printing, including 'Printing', 'The Ideal Book' and 'A Note by William Morris on His Aims in Founding the Kelmscott Press'. Also reprinted are several interviews with Morris about the Kelmscott Press. Peterson's *Bibliography of the Kelmscott Press* contains a wealth of detail on all aspects of the books produced by Morris. It began as a history of the Kelmscott Press, but soon changed into a exhaustive account of all the 52 books printed by Morris, together with notes on those which were projected but never realised. It is intended to supersede Cockerell's *Annotated List of All the Books Printed at the Kelmscott Press in the Order in Which They Were Issued* (1898). Peterson's latest book is the culmination of his work on Morris's adventure into book production, the history which he began over ten years earlier.

Peterson covers every conceivable aspect of Morris's printing and publishing, from the way in which his theories were based on fifteenth-century examples, and the way in which he sought to turn theory into practice, to the technicalities of choosing inks and paper and marketing his books. He identifies the key role of Emery Walker, noting that it was not confined to exciting Morris's interest in book production; throughout its life, the Kelmscott Press benefited from his enthusiasm and technical expertise, and Peterson concludes that the full extent of his activities may never be known.[50] In one important respect, however, Peterson's interpretation seems unsatisfactory. Drawing upon Sparling,[51] he argues that the Kelmscott Press was in essence non-profit-making, an 'amusing diversion' which Morris expected to cost money.[52] We refute this interpretation in Chapter 3, arguing that though Morris's primary objectives were artistic, not financial, the

Press ran on sound financial lines, and most of its publications, including the *Chaucer*, were profitable.[53]

Enough has been said to establish that over the years many scholars have set about the task of investigating the many facets of Morris's life and work, filling the gaps in Mackail's incomplete story. It has only been possible to refer to some of the most important works in this chapter. All this, however, had until quite recently left one major lacuna – the conduct of the Morris business. Few writers have paid much attention to Morris's business affairs, though Henderson and Watkinson are worth consulting, as is Paul Thompson's book *The Work of William Morris*.[54] Parry also provides useful information regarding Morris's relationships with his suppliers. Most writers, though, in focusing their attention on Morris the political writer and activist, Morris the artist and designer, or Morris the man of letters, have generally been content to relate the brief details provided by Mackail. The problem here is that Mackail, as a classics don, was neither very interested in business affairs, nor expected that his readers would be. One of the consequences of this is the emergence of a 'standard story' which assumes that Morris was woolly minded in his business affairs, and that Morris & Co. was a casual, amateurish organisation, whose success could be put down to good fortune, rather than to good management.

Nobody had conducted a systematic enquiry into his career as a businessman. The products of his firm have been much written about – as art. Where the organisation of that firm was touched upon, however, what was on offer was generally second-hand at best, and often superficial, not to say misleading. We found nothing that suggested that anyone had been sufficiently interested to do the research needed for a realistic and in-depth account. The consequence was that the loose, second-hand vagueness of the 'standard story' had become the norm; inaccuracies, unchallenged, had become accepted as facts, while their number had been added to by mere speculations, often groundless. We believed that sufficient evidence existed to challenge this view, and that, logically, Morris & Co. could not have flourished in a highly competitive field without good management and organisation. Furthermore, we felt from the beginning of our researches that Morris's business career would prove to be a profoundly interesting area for study in its own right, and deserved better than to be treated as a mere footnote to accounts of his other accomplishments: an understanding of his business methods does, in fact, add enormously to an understanding of his life as a whole. A man's job, after all, is usually taken to be the very thing that defines him as a public figure. The results of our investigation are to be found in our previous book, *William Morris: Design and Enterprise in Victorian Britain* (1991) and in the essays which make up this volume.

To some extent, our work has been based upon the reassessment and reinterpretation of well-known sources such as those at the British Library, Victoria & Albert Museum and William Morris Gallery. This is a favourite occupation among Morris scholars, and there is no doubt that it can be a valid and worthwhile undertaking as succeeding generations of researchers and writers address new questions. We certainly hoped that a new perspective on Morris's business career would make fresh insights possible from even the most familiar of sources. However, we also searched for new material. Here again we were aided by the fact that our priorities differed from those of earlier researchers. Although often enough our questions would have been familiar and obvious to business historians, they had not previously been asked of William Morris and the Morris enterprise. *Inter alia*, we needed to know about business organisation and management; profitability and growth; the development of the product range; marketing strategies; the nature of competition; and human resource management.

Although the firm's own production and financial records are no longer available, the picture was not entirely bleak. The survival of the minute book for 1861–75, together with the account books of three of the partners, was particularly important; although not as complete as one would have wished, these are documents which will always come high on a business historian's 'shopping list' of useful sources. Other business documents have also survived; Morris & Co.'s invoices, for example, reveal much about terms of trade and pricing policies, while the firm's brochures provide invaluable information about its product range and advertising strategy. Some of the major projects carried out by the firm are well documented; notably the decorative work carried out at St James's Palace in 1866–67 and 1880–82, for which records exist in the Office of Works series at the Public Record Office.[55] Another example is the redecoration and furnishing of 1 Holland Park for one of the firm's wealthiest clients, the Greek merchant Alexander Ionides. (The firm's work at Holland Park is the subject of Chapter 7 below.) Morris & Co. worked on the house from 1879 until 1888, and its progress is well documented in the Victoria and Albert Museum's archives and in contemporary accounts.

The discovery of other records previously unknown to Morris scholars was due reward for a long and arduous search. At the Public

Record Office, for example, there is an Inland Revenue series entitled Selected Death Duty Accounts of Well Known People (IR59). It is replete with information about Victorian artists and men of letters. The series includes Thomas Carlyle, John Ruskin, John Stuart Mill, Sir Edwin Landseer, Joseph Mallord William Turner and Frederick Engels, as well as Morris, Rossetti, Burne-Jones and many others prominent in Pre-Raphaelite and artistic circles. The records contain valuations of real estate, stocks, furniture and other personal property, statements of debts and funeral expenses, correspondence with executors, and calculations of death duty payable. There are sometimes estimates of the value of business interests (including goodwill), or newspaper cuttings and catalogues giving details of auctions or sales of effects. In Morris's case, the records were particularly useful because they included financial statements and estimates for the last six years of his life, and thus shed light upon the Kelmscott Press as well as Morris & Co. They also included the partnership agreement which Morris concluded in 1890 with two of his managers, Frank and Robert Smith.

As a result of our research, we have been able to examine the 'standard story' which has been repeated in numerous books about Morris, and have been able to focus on certain periods in Morris's life which were crucial to the development of his thinking and his business activities. In all of them, we believe that we have been able to present new evidence, and offer a significant reinterpretation of the standard story. The result, we hope, is a more accurate and more logical representation of Morris's business activities, and their contribution to his life as a whole.

First, our new evidence is vital to a proper understanding of Morris's early years, the commercial circles in which his family moved and the formative influences to which he responded. If we fail to understand the environment in which he was born and grew up, we may also fail to understand his thoughts and actions in later life. Secondly, we have reassessed the early history of the Morris enterprise. What we found amply justified our initial suspicion that the firm turned out to be a much more professional organisation than the conventional view of it has allowed. It became clear that the collapse of West of England copper mining, and the consequent loss of his substantial income from his inherited shares in Devon Great Consols, forced Morris to treat the firm as, in effect, his only source of income, and to ensure that it would satisfy his by no means negligible financial needs. The result was a period of adjustment as he sought to widen the firm's horizons and secure the custom of the prosperous middle classes. Thirdly, we set out to examine the mature firm of the 1880s and 1890s. Morris, of course, was far from being a conventional businessman. To a remarkable degree, the identity of Morris & Co. was a reflection of his own personality, thought and aspirations. The originality which was the hallmark of Morris & Co. was largely the originality of Morris, and in this he was more a medieval master than a modern capitalist. Yet, while Morris & Co. may have looked to the past for technology and inspiration, we argue that the commercial side of the business was very much of the present. Due attention was paid to costs, prices and profit margins, and in many ways Morris & Co.'s approach paralleled that of the newer types of retailers, like multiples and department stores, which rose to prominence in the last quarter of the nineteenth century. Morris came to exert a powerful influence upon Victorian ideas of design and taste, and developed a 'house style' which was instantly recognisable not just to interior designers but also to the public at large. Finally, as noted earlier, it has been possible to reassess the Kelmscott Press, which has sometimes been viewed as the indulgence of a wealthy man's last years. It was undoubtedly a remarkable creative adventure; but it was also a commercial concern with orthodox financial aspirations.

The essential purpose of our work has been to emphasise that William Morris was neither an unprofessional businessman nor a reactionary idealist. He was a man of clear thought, of powerful intellect, whose business success was firmly grounded in his deep understanding of the rules of capitalist enterprise. Certainly, it is true that his thinking was very different, wider in scope and more profound than that of the average businessman. In examining Morris's dealings and thought, we have been confronted with the unorthodox: unorthodox organisation, strategies, products, technologies and managerial behaviour. In particular, we are faced with a quite different view of the social purpose of business, which draws on the ethical pronouncements of John Ruskin, and anticipates in many ways modern concerns about the destruction of the environment. Yet although Morris's dealings and perspectives were unorthodox in important respects, it must also be recognised that Morris & Co. was not entirely divorced from the conventional business world: it had to cope with very similar problems to those confronting any firm operating in a competitive environment. And, in fact, it was the ever-present tension between practical necessity and ideals which made the firm unique in character and influence, and which makes it so interesting to the historian of the nineteenth century.

In researching and writing business biography – like any biography – there is a need for empathy; to get inside the person as best one can, and gain an understanding of his psychological make-up, his ideas and his working habits. Usually, this will lead the writer to develop a degree of sympathy for his or her subject. At the same time, though, there is a need for objectivity. One must take care not to stray from biography into hagiography. Morris at times may impress with the clarity of his thought or the breadth of his achievements, yet at the same time he was not by any means faultless – he was himself well aware of his own limitations and weaknesses. The attempts of his daughter, May Morris, and some other early biographers, to present a sanitised portrait of Morris by ignoring or suppressing unfavourable evidence about his marital problems, business affairs or less attractive personal traits can in retrospect be seen to be unnecessary. Morris no longer needs the services of self-appointed guardians of his reputation.

Of course, in our work we have not sought to re-examine the whole Morris. There are facets of his life and work, notably the socialism and the poetry, where we have little or nothing to add. Yet, if we are correct in our assertion that we have filled the last major gap in the 'standard story' – and that is an assertion which will probably be challenged by subsequent generations of Morris scholars – this suggests the need for a fresh interpretation of the whole man. Surprisingly, perhaps, no one had attempted a general biography since the publication of Jack Lindsay's *William Morris: His Life and Work*. This, though engagingly written, met with a mixed reception. In parts Lindsay follows Mackail and Henderson closely, though the debt is not always acknowledged. Elsewhere, he goes rather too far in his attempts to read meaning into the evidence. His treatment of Morris's psychology is challenging and provocative. So too is his suggestion that Morris's relationship with Georgie Burne-Jones was more physical than other writers have allowed. Reviewers have also noted that he did not seem to be aware of the correspondence between Janey Morris and Wilfrid Scawen Blunt, though this was available by the time Lindsay was writing.

Towards the end of 1994, however, came the publication by Faber & Faber of Fiona MacCarthy's biography, *William Morris: A Life for our Time*. More than five years in preparation, it has been eagerly awaited by Morris scholars. Expectations will always be high when a major new biography – in this case running to over 750 pages – is published about a figure like William Morris. In some ways, of course, the task has become easier over the years, with the publication of specialist research on many aspects of Morris's life and career. The ready availability of Morris's letters is a particular boon, which incidentally makes one appreciate all the more the scholarship of earlier writers like E.P. Thompson. At the same time, though, the sheer wealth of material and potential themes to explore make the task an increasingly daunting one. Moreover, expectations are particularly high in the case of a writer like MacCarthy, whose previous work, especially her biographies of Eric Gill and C.R. Ashbee, has been accorded a generous reception.[56]

She has not disappointed us and *William Morris: A Life for our Time* has generally been well received by its reviewers. She has made effective use of a wide range of sources, and, as she says in her preface, in the case of someone like Morris there is a need to research places and things as well as words.

Much of the research ... has taken the form of voyages around the places where Morris lived and worked and travelled. ... There is no real way of understanding Morris until you can see, almost with his eyes, the particular pattern of a landscape, the relationship of buildings, the precise lie of the land. Without tramping around Kelmscott, finding the hidden churches that so delighted Morris, the glimpses of the river, the mediaeval barns, it would be difficult to comprehend the hold Kelmscott had upon him. Without tracing his journeys around Northern France and Iceland it would be hardly possible to see how the places he returned to, in his imagination, lasted all his life.[57]

The results of these travels permeate the book, and differentiate her from earlier biographers. Indeed, they form the basis for a highly effective organisational device, for each chapter identifies a place which had an impact upon Morris's personal development – not just northern France, Iceland and Kelmscott Manor, of course, but also the places where he studied and worked: Marlborough, Oxford, Red Lion Square, Queen Square, Leek, Merton Abbey, to name a selection.

MacCarthy examines many of the issues which Mackail glossed over. The handling of Morris's personal relationships with friends and family is a particular strength, and her interpretations are often original and credible – for example, her description of his compelling urge to act the buffoon and become the butt of practical jokes. Morris's own health problems are considered in some depth, although George Bernard

Shaw's opinions should probably be treated with some caution. She is on safer ground in her descriptions of the ill-health of Morris's wife and elder daughter, which affected him deeply. The relationships between Morris, Janey and Rossetti are handled with particular sensitivity, as is Janey's later affair with Wilfrid Scawen Blunt.

Like any biography, it has its weaknesses as well as its strengths. Even in a work of this length, we will always find aspects of the Morris story that deserves fuller treatment. For example, there is relatively little on the conduct of Morris's firm – the business affairs which took up such a large share of his adult life – or on the experimentation and craftsman-ship which were so crucial to his business success. Though the chapters on Morris's socialist thought and action are carefully considered and well crafted, MacCarthy does not do much to add to or modify the story. The author would no doubt respond that her emphasis is very much upon the man, rather than seeking to catalogue all his activities. Some readers may also question whether the subtitle is deserved. A life for our time, it says, and surely no generation has found more of relevance in Morris's example than our own. Yet the theme is not explicitly developed, and it is only as we follow MacCarthy through her account that the relevance of Morris's life and work begins to be revealed. Perhaps we might have expected a fuller treatment in the concluding chapter. Certainly, though, this relatively low-key approach is preferable to some of the rather agonised attempts to spell out Morris's relevance which have appeared in the past.

After the publication of Mackail's *Life* in 1899, Jane Morris remarked that 'Mackail was not an artist, so did *not* understand such a man'. She might equally have remarked on Mackail's lack of understanding of Morris's socialism. Fiona MacCarthy both understands and sympathises with her subject. The Morris she portrays is not just the Marxist Morris, the artistic Morris, the green Morris, or the entrepreneurial Morris; it is an intensely personal interpretation of the whole man, and one from which we can gain understanding and inspiration. With the centenary of Morris's death in 1996, we can no doubt expect a spate of publications, ranging from the specialist to the more general, and from the trivial to the substantial. A number will add something, be it little or much, to our understanding; others will leave us merely hoping for factual accuracy. All of course are welcome, if they help to bring Morris's life and work to the attention of a wider readership. It is unlikely that any will equal the breadth and the ambition of Fiona MacCarthy's *William Morris*, and it will be some while before another hand feels the need and the desire to attempt a biography of the whole Morris.

NOTES

1. He was a very good Virgil scholar. His translations are not often used nowadays, but are accurate and attractive.
2. Mackail's notes of Dixon's reminiscences are preserved at the William Morris Gallery, Walthamstow, J189.
3. R. Watkinson, 'Red House Decorated', *Journal of the William Morris Society*, Vol. VII No. 4 (Spring 1988), pp. 10–15.
4. Ibid., p. 11.
5. F. MacCarthy, *William Morris: A Life for Our Time* (1994), p. x.
6. British Library, J.W. Mackail to Sydney Cockerell, 7 Dec. 1897.
7. P. Henderson, 'Visiting Sir Sydney', *Journal of the William Morris Society*, Vol. 1 No. 2 (Winter 1962), pp. 12–13.
8. Hammersmith & Fulham Archives Dept., DD348/14, May Morris to Sir Sydney Cockerell, 11 May 1838.
9. William Morris Gallery, Walthamstow, J191.
10. MacCarthy, *William Morris: A Life for our Time*, p. xii.
11. J.W. Mackail, 'Introduction', in Victoria & Albert Museum, *Catalogue of an Exhibition in Celebration of the Centenary of William Morris* (1934), p. 8.
12. G.L. Aho, *William Morris: A Reference Guide* (Boston, MA, 1985).
13. A. Compton-Rickett, *William Morris: A Study in Personality* (1913); A. Clutton-Brock, *William Morris: His Work and Influence* (1914).
14. Sparling also reprinted 'A Note by William Morris on his Aims in Founding the Kelmscott Press' and Sydney Cockerell's 'An Annotated List of All the Books Printed at the Kelmscott Press in the Order in Which They Were Issued'.
15. See, in particular, E.P. Thompson, *William Morris: Romantic to Revolutionary* (London, 2nd edn. 1977), pp. 747–50. On the circumstances in which the book was written, see L. Thompson, *The Enthusiasts: A Biography of John and Katharine Bruce Glasier* (1971), pp. 224–5.
16. Aho, *William Morris: A Reference Guide* covers the period 1897–1982. More recently, David and Sheila Latham have published *An Annotated Critical Bibliography of William Morris* (1991) for the years 1854–1990. The Lathams' updates are published biennially in odd-numbered years in the *Journal of the William Morris Society*; for 1990–91, see Vol. X No. 3 (Autumn 1993), pp. i–xxvii. Both sources add value through the authors' careful summaries of each work listed.
17. G.H. Crow, *William Morris, Designer* (Special Winter Number of *The Studio*, 1934).
18. G.D.H. Cole (ed.), *William Morris: Selected Writings: Stories in Prose: Stories in Verse: Shorter Poems: Lectures and Essays* (1934).
19. There were some notable exceptions, such as 'A Factory as It Might Be'.
20. On Arnot's career, see H.E. Roberts, 'Commemorating William Morris:

Robin Page Arnot and the Early History of the William Morris Society',
Journal of the William Morris Society, Vol. XI No. 2 (Spring 1995), pp. 33–7.

21. Mackail, 'Introduction', in Victoria & Albert Museum, *Catalogue of an Exhibition in Celebration of the Centenary of William Morris*, pp. 7–8.

22. R. Page Arnot, *William Morris: A Vindication* (1934). The essential sections were reprinted in *idem*, 'William Morris versus the Morris Myth', *Labour Monthly* (March 1934), pp. 178–84.

23. See, for example, the reference to 'the unspeakable Cripps and his crew of faint-hearts'.

24. R. Cavendish, 'The William Morris Society', *History Today*, Vol. 40 (June 1990), pp. 62–3; E. Hollamby, 'Address at the William Morris Birthday Party, 1993', *Journal of the William Morris Society*, Vol. X No. 3 (Autumn 1993), p. 12; Roberts, 'Commemorating William Morris'.

25. R. Watkinson, editorial, *Journal of the William Morris Society*, Vol. V No. 4 (Winter 1983/84), p. 2.

26. E.P. Thompson, *William Morris: Romantic to Revolutionary* (1955; 2nd edn. 1977).

27. Ibid. (2nd ed., 1977), p. 717. On Thompson's views, also see *idem*, 'The Communism of William Morris', in S. Nairne (ed.), *William Morris Today* (1984), p. 135; W. Wolfe, 'A Century of Books on the History of Socialism in Britain', *British Studies Monitor*, Vol. 10 No. 3 (1980), pp. 23–5.

28. W. Morris, 'How I Became a Socialist', *Justice*, 16 June 1894.

29. A.L. Morton (ed.), *Three Works by William Morris* (1986), p. 12.

30. N. Kelvin (ed.), *The Collected Letters of William Morris*, Vol. I (Princeton, NJ, 1984); Vol. II (Princeton, NJ, 1987). Volume I covers 1848–80; Volume 2 (in two parts) covers 1881–88. Volumes III and IV, covering the remaining years of Morris's life, appeared as this book went to press.

31. MacCarthy, *William Morris: A Life for Our Time*, p. xi.

32. Aho, *William Morris: A Reference Guide*, p. 333.

33. For a critical review, see A. Buick, 'William Morris and Incomplete Communism: A Critique of Paul Meier's Thesis', *Journal of the William Morris Society*, Vol. 3 No. 2 (Summer 1976), pp. 16–32.

34. N. Salmon (ed.), *William Morris: Political Writings: Contributions to Justice and Commonweal*, 1883–1890 (Bristol, 1994).

35. A. Buick, *Journal of the William Morris Society*, Vol. XI No. 2 (Spring 1995), pp. 42–3, review of Salmon (ed.), *William Morris: Political Writings*.

36. J. Bryson and J. Camp Troxell (eds), *Rossetti and Janey: Their Correspondence* (Oxford, 1976).

37. Review of P. Faulkner (ed.), *Jane Morris to Wilfrid Scawen Blunt: The Letters of Jane Morris to Wilfrid Scawen Blunt together with Extracts from Blunt's Diaries* (Exeter, 1986), in *Journal of the William Morris Society*, Vol. VII No. 3 (Autumn 1987), p. 24.

38. Faulkner (ed.), *Jane Morris to Wilfrid Scawen Blunt*.

39. P. Floud, 'Dating Morris Patterns', *Architectural Review*, Vol. CXIII No. 750 (July 1959), pp. 14–20. It was a reworked version of a lecture given in 1956 under the title 'William Morris's Designs: Some Controversial Points Reconsidered'. Also see *idem*, 'The Wallpaper Designs of William Morris', *Penrose Annual*,

Vol. 24 (1960). *Victorian and Edwardian Decorative Art*, a Victoria & Albert Museum exhibition catalogue edited by Floud in 1952, is also of interest.

40. *Victorian Embroidery* (1962, reprinted 1970). Also worth a look is her introduction to early Victorian textiles; 'Textiles', in R. Edwards and L.G.G. Ramsey (eds.), *The Early Victorian Period, 1830–1860* (1958), pp. 113–28.

41. B. Morris (ed.), *Morris & Company, 1861–1940: A Commemorative Centenary Exhibition* (1961); *Scribner's Magazine*(July 1897).

42. Barbara Morris's 1985 Kelmscott Lecture has been published by the William Morris Society as *William Morris and the South Kensington Museum* (1987). Also see *idem, Inspiration for Design: The Influence of the Victoria & Albert Museum* (1986). See Chapter 8 on Morris's relationship with South Kensington.

43. See R. Watkinson, *Pre-Raphaelite Art and Design* (1970); T. Newman and R. Watkinson, *Ford Madox Brown and the Pre-Raphaelite Circle* (1991).

44. B. Morris, review of Parry, *William Morris Journal*, Vol. V No. 4 (Winter 1983/84), p. 71.

45. Quoted in MacCarthy, *William Morris: A Life for Our Time*, p. 205.

46. Also see, however, the introduction to his more recent *William Morris: Selected Poems* (Manchester, 1992).

47. I. Armstrong, *Victorian Poetry: Poetry, Poetics and Politics* (1993); J. McGann, *Black Riders: The Visible Language of Modernism* (Princeton, NJ, 1993). They are reviewed by Simon Dentith in *Journal of the William Morris Society*, Vol. XI No. 2 (Spring, 1995), pp. 43–7.

48. D. Robinson, *William Morris, Burne-Jones and the Kelmscott Chaucer* (1975, expanded edn. 1982).

49. P. Needham, J. Dunlap and J. Dreyfus, *William Morris and the Art of the Book* (New York and Oxford, 1976).

50. For a brief account of his work, see D.A. Harrop, *Sir Emery Walker, 1851–1933* (Nine Elms, 1986).

51. H.H. Sparling, *The Kelmscott Press and William Morris, Master Craftsman* (1924), pp. 75–8.

52. W.S. Peterson, *Bibliography of the Kelmscott Press* (Oxford, 1984), p. xl.

53. For a review by Richard Pearson which, though generally favourable, is critical of other aspects of Peterson's work, see *Journal of the William Morris Society*, Vol. IX No. 4 (Spring 1992), pp. 38–41.

54. P. Thompson, *The Work of William Morris* (1967, 2nd edn. 1977, 3rd edn. Oxford, 1991).

55. Public Record Office, WORK19 19 and 20. Also see E. Shepherd, *Memorials of St. James's Palace* (1894), pp. 128–32, 364; C. Mitchell, 'William Morris at St. James's Palace', *Architectural Review* (Jan. 1947), pp. 38–9.

56. Her previous publications include *All Things Bright and Beautiful: Design in Britain, 1830 to Today* (1972); *British Design Since 1880: A Visual History* (1982); *The Simple Life; C.R. Ashbee in the Cotswolds* (1981); and *Eric Gill* (1989).

57. MacCarthy, *William Morris: A Life for our Time*, pp. viii–ix.

— 2 —

The Origins of the Morris
Family Fortune[1]

IT IS A COMMONPLACE in biographies to stress the significance of childhood and youth as a formative period which critically determines the subject's later actions, beliefs and intellectual development. Yet Morris's family, and the commercial world in which it moved, is not a subject which has attracted much attention from Morris scholars, most of whom have been content to recount the 'standard story' as told by Mackail. Enough evidence survives, however, for an examination of his father's career, of the business community of which he was part, and of the making of the Morris family fortune. Lacking in glamour these subjects may be, but if we fail fully to appreciate Morris's pedigree and financial circumstances, we may also fail to understand his thoughts and actions at a number of key points in his life. Morris became acquainted with business at an early age, and over the course of his adult life he wrestled almost constantly with business problems and financial dilemmas. His personal knowledge of Victorian capitalism was one factor which makes his critique of modern industrial society so powerful and influential.

At the time of William Morris's birth in 1834, his father was already a prosperous financier, with his own business and an office in Lombard Street at the heart of the City of London. William Morris Sr was then 36 years old. He had been born in Worcester in June 1797, the second of four brothers, and had moved to London with his parents around 1820. What little we know of him is suggestive of an ambitious man, anxious to secure the financial fortunes of his family and to make a mark in the world. Drawn by the prospect of good financial rewards, he made his way to the City where he joined the firm of Harris, Sanderson & Harris, discount brokers.[2]

Discount broking (or bill broking, as it was also known) played a vital role in the development of a national economy in late eighteenth- and early nineteenth-century Britain. Nowadays the use of bills of exchange is confined to specialist transactions, principally international transfers, but at that time they were of great importance in commercial life because the loan and overdraft facilities offered by banks were very limited. They were orders to pay a specified sum at a given date, and a payee could obtain cash immediately by selling a bill for something less than its face value. The purchaser of the bill could collect the full amount when it became due, or sell it on (rediscount it) to another buyer. Bill or discount brokers, therefore, were vital intermediaries between the City and the provinces, putting bankers, manufacturers and merchants who held bills in touch with those who had money to invest. They made their living from the commissions paid by clients. It was certainly a risky business, but very profitable for firms surviving the periodic crises which shook the commercial and financial world.

Bill broking had its origins in the 1780s, and grew rapidly between 1797 and 1815. It was pioneered by Thomas Richardson, a Quaker, and by 1810 his firm, Richardson, Overend & Co., was the largest broking firm in Britain.[3] The period from 1810 to 1825 saw steady growth in bill broking and the formation of several new broking firms.[4] Sanderson & Co., established in 1812 by Richard Sanderson (1784–1857), was one of them. Sanderson had learned the business as a clerk at Richardson, Overend & Co. and he left to specialise in 'discounting the bills drawn by the Cheapside wholesale houses upon their customers in the provinces'.[5] Sanderson opened an office at 2 Laurence Pountney Hill, and in 1816, as the business grew, he went into partnership with two brothers, Joseph Owen Harris and Robert Harris. The Harris brothers were bankers who had founded the Reading bank of Micklem, Stephens, Simonds & Harris in 1790. The firm became known as Harris, Sanderson & Harris, and new premises were acquired at 32 Lombard Street, where the firm was based until 1836, when it moved to 83 King William Street.[6]

The banking crisis of 1825 led to the collapse of many broking firms, but provided new opportunities for the strongest. A few of the most successful brokers began to act as principals rather than intermediaries, assembling portfolios of bills and deriving their profits from the margin between buying and selling prices.[7] This was made possible by a change in policy on the part of the London banks; instead of investing surplus funds in government securities, they increasingly placed them on short-term deposit with the more secure bill brokers. Buying and selling bills was a far more lucrative prospect than commission work, but for some time only Richardson, Overend & Co. had the reputation and connections needed to deal on its own account. Sanderson & Co., however, by virtue of its extensive business with the Cheapside wholesalers, was a rising force, and the firm soon attracted the funds needed to enter the market.[8]

For a young man newly arrived in London and setting out to make his way in the world, a position with such a prestigious firm must have seemed the epitome of success. Evidently, William Morris Sr was well favoured. His good fortune may have been due to some extent to his own abilities – subsequent events indicated that he was both able and hardworking – but, as was so often the case, personal connections formed the basis of a successful career. The Harris brothers offered Morris a post because they were distantly related to his family by marriage. Religious affiliations may also have played a part in bringing him to their attention. Robert Harris (1763?–1840) and Joseph Morris (1733?–1806) were both members of the Society of Friends in Reading, and in 1794 Joseph Morris's son Richard (1770–1825) married Robert Harris's sister Anna. Unfortunately, however, it has not been possible to determine the exact relationship between Richard Morris and William Morris Sr Quaker records are mute on the subject because at some point towards the end of the eighteenth century both Robert Harris and Joseph Morris were disowned by the Reading Monthly Meeting 'for opposing the rules of discipline' – voluntarily paying tithes and church rates. Perhaps their families had already adopted the 'rich establishmentarian puritanism' to which William Morris referred in his oft-quoted autobiographical letter to the Austrian socialist Andreas Scheu.[9] Certainly, though, they continued to maintain close links with the Quaker community, which was strongly represented in banking and bill broking circles. Thomas Richardson and the Gurney family were Quakers, and Lloyds Bank (then Taylors & Lloyds), which made large loans to Sanderson & Co. in its early years, was also run by leading members of the Society of Friends.[10]

William Morris Sr must have impressed the Harris brothers as a man of sound judgement and dependable character, as from an early stage in his career he was groomed to take over the business. The problem of succession in business partnerships, as Martin Daunton has shown, was often a serious one for City firms.[11] If the right man or men could not be found, dissolution would result, and in this event the retiring partners or the heirs of dead partners frequently lost capital. It was preferable for new partners to be found who might build up their capital while retired (sleeping) partners gradually withdrew funds from the enterprise. This was the procedure favoured by the Harrises. Joseph Owen Harris retired in 1824, and his brother Robert joined him two years later. They were replaced in January 1826 by William Morris Sr, then only 28 years of age, and Richard Gard, another young employee of the firm. The partnership continued trading as Sanderson & Co.[12]

Soon after becoming a partner, Morris married Emma Shelton, one-time neighbour and the daughter of a prosperous Worcester merchant. For several years they lived in Lombard Street, above the office, where their two eldest children, Emma and Henrietta, were born. In 1834, the family moved to Elm House, a plain but spacious building at Clay Hill, Walthamstow, and it was here that William Morris was born, followed by four brothers and another two sisters. At the time, Walthamstow was a suburban village on London's north-east periphery. It was a pleasant spot, close to Epping Forest, and had not yet become 'cocknified and choked up by the jerry builder'.[13] One of its attractions was that it lay within easy reach of the City, and thus was popular with the wealthier members of London's financial and business élite who travelled daily to the office by stage coach.

Sandersons prospered, and with it the Morrises. Only the most creditworthy houses could act as bill dealers rather than brokers, and to all intents and purposes there were only four discount houses of any significance: Overend, Gurney & Co., Sanderson & Co., Alexander & Co., and Bruce, Buxton & Co. Gurneys was much the biggest, with deposits exceeding £6 million in the mid-1840s, but those of Sandersons and Alexanders were not inconsiderable at around £2 million. Sandersons had accumulated a capital in the region of £180,000.[14] Bill dealing, it can be seen, was both prestigious and profitable. Richard Sanderson sat as MP for Colchester from 1832 to 1847, and was described as 'a large East India proprietor'. Increasingly, the day-to-day running of the business fell to William Morris Sr. He became managing partner in the mid-1840s on the retirement of Richard Gard.[15]

The reward of success in business was a very comfortable lifestyle. In 1840, the Morrises moved to Woodford Hall, a large Georgian mansion in the Palladian style, which stood on the edge of Epping Forest in its own 50-acre park and surrounding farmland. Three years later William Morris Sr obtained a grant of arms from the College of Heralds, to mark

Plate 2.1 Morris's parents, William Morris senior (1797–1847) and Emma Shelton Morris (1805–94); miniatures by T. or J. Wheeler (fl. 1817–45).

his standing in society. His eldest son, who was six at the time of the move to Woodford Hall, later told the Austrian socialist Andreas Scheu that his family had lived 'in the ordinary bourgeois style of comfort'.[16] It may indeed have felt 'ordinary' to the young William Morris, but the standard of living at Woodford Hall was, we might deduce, way above that enjoyed by most members of the Victorian middle class, let alone the majority of the population. Only with a large income from the partnership could the Morrises have afforded to rent a house at £600 a year.

A comfortable home and a substantial income might have satisfied the ambitions of many businessmen. But this was not the case with William Morris Sr Sandersons had developed an extensive network of business connections, both in the City and the provinces, and he began to speculate in the flourishing share market of the 1840s with a small group of like-minded men. Amongst them were his brothers, Thomas and Francis. Thomas was a coal merchant in Camberwell with interests in South Wales. Francis, who lived in Denmark Hill, was a member of the Coal Exchange. Closely involved with the Morris brothers were William Alexander Thomas and his brother John, whose family stock-broking business, P.W. Thomas & Sons, had been founded in 1820 with offices at 50 Threadneedle Street. Railway shares were a favoured speculation in the 1840s, especially during the 'railway mania' of 1844–47. West of England copper mining ventures, which were increasingly seeking capital in London, also drew the attention of the Morris and Thomas brothers. The first half of the nineteenth century was the apogee of copper mining in Devon and Cornwall. Some well-known mines, like Consolidated Mines, Cook's Kitchen, or the great Dolcoath mine, had been in production for many years, earning substantial profits for their proprietors. The problem of drainage had been solved through the application of powerful, fuel-efficient steam engines, and existing mines were being worked deeper and deeper. Many new ones appeared. Between 1800 and 1850, copper ore raised by West of England miners realised over £13 million, and by mid-century there were over 100 mines in production, of which about 70 had earned more than £100,000.[17]

Copper mining was invariably a very speculative business. For every successful mine there were dozens of fruitless or abandoned workings. But much of its attraction lay in the possibility of earning big returns for a small outlay. West Country mining 'adventurers' had for a long time organised the industry, but their access to capital was quite limited, and most mines operated on a relatively small scale. By the 1840s, however, the industry, impelled by the higher capital requirements of deep level working, was beginning to draw upon the City of London as a source of finance. In the second half of the nineteenth century, and especially after the 1870s, London emerged as the financial centre of the mining world, and promoters of mining ventures – abroad as well as in Britain – looked naturally to the City for capital. But in the 1840s and 1850s participation in West Country mining ventures by City men was still relatively rare. There was a good deal of local hostility to outsiders, or 'out-adventurers', who were looked upon as mere financial speculators, lacking in mining expertise. And London men were equally suspicious of Cornish adventurers. Their lack of familiarity with local conditions and customs had caused a number of outside investors to fall victim to unscrupulous promoters during the speculative booms of 1823–25 and the mid-1830s.

The memory of these financial reverses had only just begun to fade by 1844 when Josiah Hitchens, one of Cornwall's leading mining experts, made his way to London to find support for his latest mining venture. Hitchens was much sought after as a mining consultant, promoter and mine manager. One of his most profitable mines was Bedford United, on the Devon bank of the Tamar, near Tavistock. The concern was founded in 1840–41 with a paid-up capital of £9,500 to reopen several old workings. It quickly became Devon's third largest copper producer. Between 1844 and 1856, 21,000 tons of copper ore worth £138,846 were produced, generating dividends totalling £36,000.[18] The mine stood on land owned by Francis, seventh Duke of Bedford, and its success led Hitchens to request permission to begin prospecting in Blanchdown Woods, also on the Devon bank of the Tamar, just north of the area leased by Bedford United. For many years, local miners had suspected the existence of rich deposits of copper ore in the district. However, the Duke, one of the biggest landowners in south Devon, fearing that his pheasant coverts would be ruined, was very reluctant to agree to allow mining operations on his land. He insisted on substantial royalties on ores and compensation clauses, and several proposals were rejected because the applicants lacked sufficient capital. Hitchens' impressive reputation, however, ensured a more favourable reception, and he was offered a salary of 100 guineas a year to promote the new venture on the Duke's behalf. He was firmly instructed to secure the backing of London financial interests rather than local adventurers, who were dismissed as mere dabblers only interested in immediate returns.[19]

Later in the century, Hitchens would have found many City stock-brokers with a specialist interest in mining company finance. The choice in 1844 was far more limited, and his enquiries soon led him to the door of P.W. Thomas & Sons. The Thomases were by no means pioneers in the field, but they were certainly early participants. The firm and its associates, like the Morris brothers, were seasoned risk-takers, and they were actively seeking first class mining opportunities. The Thomases were very favourably impressed by Hitchens and his plans, and William Morris Sr was brought into the negotiations at an early stage. Morris in turn brought in his brother Thomas and partner Richard Gard. Without delay, the consortium decided to invest heavily in the venture. A lease was agreed with the Duke of Bedford's land agent on 26 July 1844, and work began on 10 August. Initially, the new mine was known as Wheal Maria after the Duke of Bedford's wife. The first shaft dug was named Gard's Shaft. Here rich deposits were found in November, just 18 fathoms below ground. The lode, which was 40 feet or more in width, was traced eastwards for over two miles, and a succession of other mines were opened up, including Wheal Fanny, Wheal Anna Maria, Wheal Josiah, and Wheal Emma (1848), named after Emma Shelton Morris.[20]

The Devonshire Great Consolidated Copper Mining Co., or Devon Great Consols, as it was usually called, was registered as a joint stock company on 25 March 1845 under the 1844 Joint Stock Companies Act, with an authorised capital of £10,240 in 1,024 £10 shares. The subscribers were listed as: Richard Sommers Gard, Discount Broker, London, 288 shares; Josiah Hugo Hitchens, Mine Agent, Tavistock, 144 shares; William Morris, Discount Broker, London, 272 shares; Thomas Morris, Coal Merchant, Surrey, 32 shares; William Alexander Thomas, Stockbroker, Essex, 144 shares; John Thomas, Stockbroker, Essex, 144 shares. William Thomas (chairman), Richard Gard and Thomas Morris were appointed directors of the company; William Morris became trustee and auditor. In May 1846, at the first Annual General Meeting, William Morris and John Thomas were added to the board. It was agreed that the directors should receive 100 guineas per annum for their services. Hitchens was not elected to the board, but his expertise and local knowledge was very valuable – after all, the London subscribers lacked any practical experience of copper mining – and he was duly appointed consulting engineer to the company. Local banking facilities were provided by the Tavistock firm of Gill & Rundle, one of whose partners, Reginald Gill, married William Morris's sister Alice in 1864. Once it was apparent that the mine would be long-lived and profitable, Thomas Morris moved from London to Tavistock, serving the company as resident director until his retirement in 1879.[21]

The Morris family, it can be seen, had a substantial stake in Devon Great Consols from its inception, holding 304 out of 1,024 shares, nearly 30 per cent of the issued capital. Although Thomas Morris took up only 32 shares, his position as resident director made him responsible for the day-to-day management of the company. William Morris Sr's 272 shares committed him to the investment, if required, of £2,720 – a sizeable sum to risk in such a speculative venture, even for a wealthy man. As it turned out, however, he was not obliged to pay out the full £10 per share. There was an initial call of £1 per share, but profits flowed freely from the start and were more than sufficient to meet development costs. The shareholders in the original company were never troubled by requests for additonal funds.[22]

The new concern was astonishingly successful. In the first full year of operation, 13,292 tons of ore were sold for £116,068. After all operating costs had been met, £72,704 (£71 per share) was available for distribution to the shareholders. Not surprisingly, there was enormous interest in Devon Great Consols in mining and financial circles. Stockbrokers quoted bid prices of up to £850 in an attempt to acquire the £1 paid shares, but the prospects of the mines were so good that none of the subscribers was tempted to sell.

However, expenditure soon began to mount, and the initial rate of return could not be maintained. As the lode was followed eastwards it plunged to greater depths, requiring the company to invest heavily in pumping equipment. The softness of the ground called for extensive timbering, and, as the scale of operations increased, expensive surface works – buildings, roads, water-wheels, and so on – were needed. Total expenditure almost doubled between 1846–47 and 1847–48, from £30,000 to more than £57,000. Dividends were cut to £25 and then £15 per share. These figures led many observers to conclude that Devon Great Consols was an ephemeron, like so many brilliant prospects in the history of mining. This was quite wrong. The decision to spend heavily on development work rather than distributing a large part of the profits was undoubtedly correct. In the long run the company's shareholders

Figure 2.1

Devon Great Consols: Output and Dividends, 1845–80

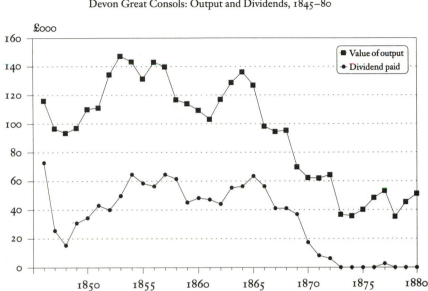

Sources: *Mining Journal*; PRO,BT31 142/445, 8645/63035, 1613/63035; Companies House, Cardiff, 211T.

were to reap the benefits of the work carried out in the late 1840s. The end of the decade saw an upturn in Devon Great Consols' fortunes which reached a peak in 1856, when 29,425 tons of ore were sold for £143,045. Annual dividends were regular and substantial, ranging from £43 to £62 per share between 1851 and 1865.[23]

The purchase of a large stake in Devon Great Consols proved both fortunate and timely for the Morris family. The year 1847 was marked by unforeseen tragedy. On 8 September, William Morris Sr died suddenly at the age of 50. Seven days later Sanderson & Co. suspended business with total liabilities amounting to £2,606,569. Shock waves reverberated throughout the City. Morris's death was not the sole cause of the crisis at Sandersons, although his death may well have 'accelerated the suspension of the House'.[24] Sandersons was one of the victims of the British commercial crisis of 1847–48. The origins of the crisis have often been attributed, both by contemporaries and banking historians, to the policies of the Bank of England.[25] Following the passing of the Bank Act of 1844, the Bank began to lend and discount freely at low rates of interest, competing for business against the discount houses. But in April 1847, alarmed by falling reserves, it suddenly reversed its policy, making it 'almost impossible to discount in Lombard Street or to borrow money even on good security'.[26] As a result, the speculative boom in railway investment of 1844–47 was brought sharply to a halt. The discount houses subsequently came under pressure, as creditors began to doubt the worth of bills held by them. Matters were made worse for Sandersons because they held large numbers of corn bills which, in consequence of a threatened fall in corn prices, were suspected of being 'bad'.[27] This loss of confidence led depositors to demand the repayment of money held at call, and, to meet its commitments, the firm had to raise cash by rediscounting sound bills at disadvantageous rates. As the liquidity crisis deepened, Sandersons' assets diminished rapidly, and the sudden death of its managing partner – which may well have been due to the stress and worry caused by the crisis – was a serious blow. Creditors were informed that:

It is with extreme pain that we have to announce to you that our house is under the necessity of suspending its business, an event which was wholly unforeseen and unexpected by us. The retirement, some time ago, of our late partner, Mr Gard and recently the sudden and lamented death of Mr Sanderson's remaining partner, Mr Morris, threw upon Mr Sanderson alone the responsibility of the concern, the details of which had been chiefly under the management of his late partners; and this, with the pressure of the times, has left him no alternative but to proceed to wind up the affairs of the house.[28]

As things turned out the financial situation of the firm was healthier than originally had been feared. Sandersons' creditors included many leading London bankers, and they expressed confidence in the solvency of the firm. There was no evidence either of misconduct or poor management. Bills totalling £1,725,000 had been rediscounted before the suspension to meet depositors' demands for repayment, and consequently deposits, which in normal times exceeded £2 million, had fallen to £790,989. Of this, £622,569 was covered by securities lodged with creditors, leaving £168,420 unsecured. To cover this liability, and any unsound bills which it had endorsed, the partnership had assets valued at £259,000, while the private property of the partners was worth a further £188,000.[29] *The Times* remarked that 'a large proportion of the bills on which the house is liable are of the most unquestionable description, while at the same time the amount of those which are bad is less than has been generally supposed. Under these circumstances, there can be little doubt of an early resumption'.[30] All creditors received 20 shillings in the pound, and the firm recommenced trading as Sanderson, Sandeman & Co., with a new partner, T. Fraser Sandeman, who had stockbroking and banking interests. It survived until the crisis of 1857, when it was again forced to suspend business on 11 November. On this occasion, its liabilities exceeded £5 million, and, although much of this was backed by sound securities, the firm was wound up.[31]

The collapse and reconstruction of Sandersons was a severe financial blow for the Morris family. Emma Morris not only lost her husband's regular income, but she also lost his share of the partnership capital, which in the normal course of events she might have withdrawn and reinvested in gilt-edged securities. Moreover, it seems likely that she had to liquidate some personal assets in order to pay off Sandersons' creditors, though this cannot be stated with any degree of certainty; Morris Sr died intestate, and detailed information about his estate is unavailable. When his wife applied for Letters of Administration, which were duly granted in October 1847, his estate was valued at about £60,000.[32] The 272 shares in Devon Great Consols accounted for much of this, even though their market value had fallen to a low point of £150 as a result of reduced dividends in 1846–47. Assuming that William Morris's holdings were assessed at this price, their market value would have been £40,800, or roughly two-thirds of his estate.

The Morrises had to give up Woodford Hall. In the autumn of 1848 they moved to a smaller and more manageable home, Water House in Walthamstow. The family was now heavily dependent upon the fortunes of Devon Great Consols, and, when the share price began to recover, Emma sold some shares in order to invest in less profitable but safer securities. Twenty-two shares were sold by her in 1850 and 50 in the following year, realising just over £20,000. In the 1850s, the annual income from the remaining shares in Devon Great Consols was more than sufficient to maintain Emma Shelton Morris and her children in considerable comfort, but the sale of the shares was justified when in later years dividends declined and eventually ceased altogether.

Emma Morris was advised in financial matters by her brothers-in-law, Thomas and Francis Morris. The success of Devon Great Consols was magnetic for the Morris brothers, and they took an increasingly keen interest in West Country mining. Francis bought 20 Devon Great Consols shares from Emma in 1849 and he replaced his deceased brother on the board. Both Thomas and Francis had great faith in the capacity of the 'family business' to maintain its astonishing output and profitability. Emma was advised accordingly. The best way of safeguarding the future of her children, she was informed, would be to handover an equal number of shares to each as he or she reached maturity. It was decided that a total of 117 shares (13 for each of nine children) would be distributed in this way; giving each offspring a good start in life, while leaving Emma Morris with a substantial capital for her own use. A complex series of trust funds, managed by Emma, Thomas and Francis, was set up to implement the plan.[33]

In 1855 William Morris and his elder sister Henrietta became the first beneficiaries of their mother's munificence. Devon Great Consols was approaching the peak of its prosperity, and although Morris's income from this source never reached the 'something like £900 a year' cited by Mackail,[34] he did receive handsome dividends: £741 in 1855, and £715 in the following year, rising to a peak of £819 in 1857. This was a very large income when compared with those of his fellow-undergraduates. When Burne-Jones visited his friend at Walthamstow for the first time, he was astonished to discover how wealthy Morris and his family were. Wealth afforded him many pleasures denied to others. He hardly had to think twice before purchasing books like Ruskin's *Stones of Venice* at six guineas or *The Seven Lamps of Architecture* at a guinea. He could spend money on the works of Pre-Raphaelite painters he admired, and whom he was now beginning to meet. In 1856 he bought five Rossettis for around £200, Ford Madox Brown's 'Hayfield' for £40 and Arthur Hughes' much-admired 'April Love' for £30. Morris's cash also came in handy when Richard Dixon suggested to him that they, together with Burne-Jones, William Fulford, Charles Faulkner and Cormell Price, should produce a literary journal. Publication of the *Oxford and Cambridge Magazine* was only made possible by Morris's money. He was wholly responsible for financing the magazine, and, after putting together the first edition himself, he agreed to pay Fulford £100 per annum as editor. The total cost to Morris of the magazine was several hundred pounds.[35]

More important than the luxury of patronage, possession of a healthy unearned income gave the young William Morris the security to spend time searching for his true vocation. He could afford to experiment with architecture and painting before turning finally to a career in the decorative arts. Both the building of Red House in 1859–60 and the

Figure 2.2

William Morris's Income from Devon Great Consols, 1855–77

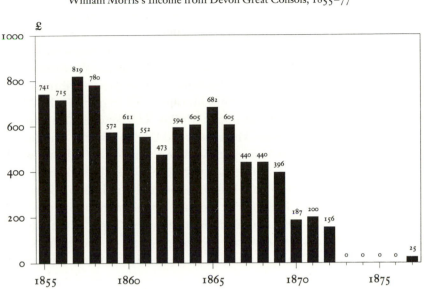

Sources: *Mining Journal*; PRO,BT31 142/445, 8645/63035, 1613/63035; Companies House, Cardiff, 211T.

launch of Morris, Marshall, Faulkner & Co. in 1861 depended upon access to a large capital. Indeed, Morris actually sold two Devon Great Consols shares between 1860 and 1862 to raise about £790. He later told Wilfred Scawen Blunt that 'my relations thought me both wicked and mad' to sell the precious shares on which the family income had depended, and, in order to prevent the shares from leaving the family's possession, Emma Shelton Morris supplied the money needed, transferring the shares to Stanley, her second son.[36]

For the Morris family, West Country mining had become more than just a matter of investment; its members, inspired by the triumph of Devon Great Consols, had a touchingly naive belief in the future prospects of the industry. Thomas and Francis Morris were forever on the lookout for another major strike, participating in the launch of at least 13 ventures between 1847 and 1874. They were never to hit lucky again, but the prospect of great wealth was enough to keep their nephew, William Morris's brother Stanley, involved in the industry until 1901. And Morris himself was not immune to the family's fascination with mineral wealth. He kept a stake in Devon Great Consols until 1877, by which time it had become obvious that the days of the company as a big earner were long since gone. Morris served as a director of the business between 1871 and 1875, and in 1865 he was also persuaded to join the board of British Mining & Smelting Ltd, a highly speculative concern which failed in 1874.[37] Between its formation in 1845 and its effective end as a dividend-paying proposition in 1872, Devon Great Consols yielded a net income of £317,927 for the Morris family as a whole. Of this, William Morris Sr, his wife, and children, received £270,624. William Morris earned £8,803. By the standards of the day, these were fabulous sums. When the source of this wealth began to run dry, Morris, together with other members of his family, received a severe financial jolt. His reaction to financial adversity was to put Morris, Marshall, Faulkner & Co. on a sounder and more profitable footing. In the early 1870s, under Morris's leadership, the firm diversified from stained glass towards the larger, more secure market for household goods. Morris emerged as a prolific designer and accomplished man of business.

NOTES

The authors are grateful to Mr Justin Brooke (Marazion, Cornwall), Dr Charles Munn (Chartered Institute of Bankers in Scotland), Dr Philip Ollerenshaw (University of the West of England, Bristol), Mr Richard Reed (National Westminster Bank PLC) and Mr Malcolm Thomas (Society of Friends Library) for their assistance in the preparation of this essay.

1. An earlier version of this chapter was published as 'The City and Mining Enterprise: The Origins of the Morris Family Fortune', *Journal of the William Morris Society*, Vol. IX No. 1 (1990), pp. 3–14.
2. William Morris Gallery, Walthamstow, J163, J.W. Mackail Notebooks.
3. It is better known as Overend, Gurney & Co., the title adopted following Richardson's death in 1827. W.T.C. King, *History of the London Discount Market* (1936), pp. 17–23.
4. L.S. Pressnell, *Country Banking in the Industrial Revolution* (Oxford, 1956), pp. 101–3; G.A. Fletcher, *The Discount Houses in London: Principles, Operations and Change* (1976), pp. 7–9.
5. King, *London Discount Market*, p. 119.
6. *Post Office London Directories*, 1812–37. Also see L.S. Pressnell and J. Orbell, *A Guide to the Historical Records of British Banking* (Aldershot, 1985), p. 102.
7. Pressnell and Orbell, *Guide to the Historical Records of British Banking*, pp. xiii–xix. Also see King, *London Discount Market*, p. xviii.

8. King, *London Discount Market*, p. 119; *idem*, 'The Extent of the London Discount Market in the Middle of the Nineteenth Century', *Economica* (Aug. 1935), p. 324.

9. N. Kelvin (ed.), *The Collected Letters of William Morris*, Vol. II (Princeton, NJ, 1987), p. 227, to Andreas Scheu, 15 Sept. 1883.

10. Society of Friends Library, Friends' House, London, Biographies of Members; R.S. Sayers, *Lloyds Bank and the History of English Banking* (Oxford, 1957), p. 181.

11. M. Daunton, 'Succession and Inheritance in the City of London in the Nineteenth Century', *Business History*, Vol. XXX (1988), pp. 269 *et seq.*

12. J.W. Mackail, *Life of William Morris* (1899), Vol. I, pp. 2–3; *London Gazette*, 18 Jan. 1824; 4 Feb. 1826.

13. Kelvin (ed.), *Letters*, Vol. II, p. 227, to Andreas Scheu, 15 Sept. 1883.

14. King, 'Extent of the London Discount Market', pp. 321–4.

15. D.P. O'Brien (ed.), *The Correspondence of Lord Overstone* (Cambridge, 1971), p. 363; *Economist*, 15 Sept. 1847, p. 1089.

16. Kelvin (ed.), *Letters*, Vol. II, p. 227, to Andreas Scheu, 15 Sept. 1883.

17. D.B. Barton, *History of Copper Mining in Cornwall and Devon* (Truro, 3rd edn., 1978), pp. 71–2. On the history of mining in the region also see C. Thomas, *Mining Fields of the West* (1871, reprinted Truro, 1967); J.H. Collins, *Observations on the West of England Mining Region* (1912).

18. J.H. Murchison, *British Mines Considered as an Investment* (1855), pp. 40–1; J.A. Phillips and J. Darlington, *Records of Mining and Metallurgy* (1857), p. 256; D.B. Barton, *A Historical Survey of the Mines and Mineral Railways of East Cornwall and West Devon* (Truro, 1964), pp. 96–7; F. Booker, *The Industrial Archaeology of the Tamar Valley* (Newton Abbot, 1971), p. 138; R. Burt, P. Waite and R. Burnley, *Devon and Somerset Mines: Metalliferous and Associated Minerals, 1845–1913* (Exeter, 1984), pp. 7–8.

19. Thomas, *Mining Fields of the West*, p. 79; Devon Record Office, Bedford Estate Papers, L1258/c bundle 52, John Benson to Christopher Haedy, 22 April 1843; ibid., bundle 54, 10 Jan. 1845.

20. Public Record Office (hereafter PRO), BT31 142/445, Grant of Settlement, 26 July 1844; Barton, *Historical Survey*, p. 71; Booker, *Tamar Valley*, p. 146; J.C. Goodridge, 'Devon Great Consols: A Study in Victorian Mining Enterprise', *Transactions of the Devonshire Association*, Vol. XCVI (1964), p. 229; M. Bawden, 'Mines and Mining in the Tavistock District', *Transactions of the Devonshire Association*, Vol. XLVI (1914), p. 258.

21. PRO, BT31 142/445, Deed of Settlement; Collins, *West of England Mining Region*, p. 265.

22. PRO, BT31 142/445, Balance Sheet and Auditor's Report, 7 May 1845.

23. Burt, Waite and Burnley, *Devon and Somerset Mines*, pp. 39–41; PRO, BT31 142/445, 8645/63035, 1613/63035; Companies House, Cardiff, 211T.

24. O'Brien, *Correspondence of Lord Overstone*, Vol. II, p. 763, W.G. Prescott to Lord Overstone, 4 Nov. 1857.

25. See, for example, D. Morier Evans, *The Commercial Crisis, 1847–48* (2nd edn. 1849), p. lviii; King, *London Discount Market*, pp. 136–42; W.M. Scammell, *The London Discount Market* (1968), p. 152.

26. Scammell, *London Discount Market*, p. 152.

27. Evans, *Commercial Crisis of 1847–48*, pp. 63–71; *idem, The Commercial Crisis of 1857–8, and the Stock Exchange Panic of 1859* (1859), p. 13; H.M. Boot, *The Commercial Crisis of 1847* (Hull, 1984), pp. 63, 81–2; National Westminster Bank Archives, 11523, Prescott & Co., Partners' Minute Book, 9 Sept. 1847; *The Times*, 15 Sept. 1847, p. 3; *Select (Secret) Committee on the Causes of the Recent Commercial Distress* (Parliamentary Papers, 1847–48, VIII Pt.I), Q.3892, Evidence of James Morris, Governor of the Bank of England.

28. Sanderson & Co. to Creditors, 15 Sept. 1847, reprinted in the *Economist*, 18 Sept. 1847, p. 1089.

29. National Westminster Bank Archives, 11523, Prescott & Co., Partners' Minute Book, 16 Sept. 1847; 23 Sept. 1847; *The Times*, 21 Sept. 1847, p. 3; *Economist*, 25 Sept. 1847, p. 1114. Evans, *Commercial Crisis of 1847–48*, pp. lviii–lix; King, *London Discount Market*, p. 142.

30. *The Times*, 21 Sept. 1847, p. 3. Also see National Westminster Bank Archives, 11450, Union Bank of London Ltd., Minute Book, 22 Sept. 1847.

31. National Westminster Bank Archives, 11524, Prescott & Co., Partners' Minute Book, 12 Nov. 1857; 10 Dec. 1857; 11456, Union Bank of London Ltd., Minute Book, 6 Jan. 1858; Evans, *The Commercial Crisis of 1857–58* (1859), pp. 35, 52.

32. PRO, PROB 6/223. This would place Morris Sr amongst the top 1 per cent of estates proven around mid-century: see W.D. Rubenstein, *Men of Property* (1981), p. 29.

33. PRO, BT31 142/445, Annual Returns; Companies House, Cardiff, 211T, Annual Returns.

34. Mackail, *Life*, Vol. I, p. 51.

35. *A Catalogue of Books of Various Branches of Literature* published by Smith, Elder & Co. (Feb. 1851); Mackail, *Life*, Vol. I, pp. 91, 108–9, 115; P. Henderson, *William Morris: His Life, Work and Friends* (1967), p. 37.

36. W.S. Blunt, *My Diaries, 1888–1914* (1932), p. 283, 31 May 1896; PRO, BT31 142/445, Annual Returns.

37. Guildhall Library, Stock Exchange Collection, British Mining & Smelting Ltd, Prospectus, 1865.

— 3 —

The Business Career of William Morris

WHEN BUSINESSMEN achieve fame, it usually does not prove enduring. Most educated people could name many notable Victorians; their lists would consist of politicians, writers, soldiers, social reformers, philosophers, scientists and the like, but few businessmen. William Morris was and is notable, and he was a business-man; but that is not what he is remembered for. He is remembered principally as an artist-designer, second as a socialist thinker, and third (by a long way) as a writer. In consequence, he has been investigated by historians of art, politics and literature, who cannot be blamed for neglecting an aspect of his life which, however important to Morris himself, does not greatly impinge on their particular fields, and may even be thought rather arid.

Yet Morris's business career does in fact reveal more about the essential man than any of his other achievements, simply because the more-or-less stylised output of writers and artists is controlled and self-conscious. It is in their more routine transactions in the ordinary world that people are at their most natural. The business of Morris & Co. would justify study for this reason alone. But there is one other principal justification, namely, that neglect of the subject has led to much mis-representation of Morris as businessman, from which one would hardly be able to infer the truth; that he was a practical, hard-working, hard-headed, imaginative and original man of affairs, and that the success of his firm owed little if anything to luck.

At an early age, William Morris was acquainted with the realities of business success and failure. His experiences were to colour and influence his actions and ideas for the rest of his life. But he also acquired during his childhood a profound love of art, architecture and literature, especially that of the medieval period. It was probably his taste for the medieval that drew him first to contemplate a career in the Church; he soon realised, however, that a love of artefacts is not the same as belief in God, and, while still at university, he decided that his true vocation lay in the world of art. At first, he considered a career as an architect, and in January 1856 he became articled to G.E. Street, one of the leading figures of the Gothic Revival. Then, at the instigation of the charismatic Dante Gabriel Rossetti, he tried his hand at painting before turning finally to a career in the decorative arts. Here he found his true metier.

The prestige of the decorative arts was growing rapidly at this time. Street himself insisted that a good architect should understand crafts like stained glass, metalwork and embroidery.[1] But the most influential advocate of the decorative arts was John Ruskin. In *The Two Paths*, published in 1859, he rejected the idea that decoration was an inferior or subsidiary art-form, and also pointed out that it could not be separated from its surroundings; that it was quite possible for a fine piece of craftsmanship to be in an inappropriate place; and that every aspect of a building should form 'a great and harmonious whole'.[2] One very important principle, which made a great impression on Morris, was that the artist or designer should be 'entirely familiar' with the processes and materials involved in the work.[3]

Morris's responsiveness to these ideas was not unusual; after all, the work of men like Street and Ruskin touched a remarkably wide cross-section of Victorian society. What made him unique was the immense effort he made during his lifetime to give their ideas practical expression – and indeed to develop them further. This process began with the building and decoration of Red House, Morris's home at Upton, Kent, which launched him on his career as a decorative artist, and led in turn to the formation of Morris, Marshall, Faulkner & Co. on 11 April 1861.

There were six other partners besides Morris in the firm: Dante Gabriel Rossetti and Ford Madox Brown, who were already well known; Edward Burne-Jones and Philip Webb, both at the start of careers in painting and architecture respectively; Charles Faulkner, a mathematics don; and Peter Paul Marshall, an amateur painter. With supreme self-confidence, these seven young men set out on a commercial venture whose ultimate purpose was to transform the British public's appreciation of the decorative arts. The task was harder than they expected. It was as though they had gone out to start a revolution, only to find that it had already begun. From the very beginning, the firm faced strong competition both in quality and price from firms like Lavers & Barraud, Clayton & Bell, and Heaton, Butler & Bayne in stained glass,

Plate 3.1 Queen Square, Bloomsbury, the location of Morris & Co.'s main workshop from 1865 until the move to Merton Abbey *William Morris Gallery*

Skidmores of Coventry and the Birmingham firm of Hardmans in ecclesiastical furnishings.

Clearly, the firm could only be successful by dint of much hard work; and the view later put about by Rossetti that Morris, Marshall, Faulkner & Co. was 'mere playing at business'[4] might well reflect his own attitude, but tells us little about the other members. Marshall, it is true, was a heavy drinker, and probably no great asset; but Morris, though blessed with a substantial private income, must have known that he could not rely on its continuing for ever, and had in any case a voracious appetite for work. Burne-Jones suffered all his life from anxieties about money, and may perhaps have been keener than anyone that the firm should be a paying proposition. He, like Webb and Faulkner, needed work and income, not membership of a pleasant, civilized, unremunerative club. Nor is it likely that the already established Madox Brown would have given much time to the sort of casual business concern so airily described by Rossetti.

There was nothing casual or lighthearted in the thinking which caused the partners to band together. Indeed, the records show that from the outset the firm's operations and finances were planned and worked out in strictest detail. Morris was made business manager, at a salary of £150 a year – according to Rossetti, 'because he was the only one of us who had money to spare'.[5] It is more likely that none of the other six was remotely interested in taking the job. Next, they devised a system of sharing out commissions according to the actual contributions made by individual members, which would inevitably vary as demand dictated. This did not merely apply to the quantity of work done: the greater skills of Rossetti, Burne-Jones and Madox Brown as painters and cartoonists would be rewarded with higher fees than were paid to Morris and Marshall. Faulkner (the mathematician) was to be responsible for keeping detailed accounts, and presenting quarterly financial reports.[6]

The idea which led to the setting up of the firm did not come from nowhere. Morris and his circle were quite familiar with the concept of an association of artists. The Pre-Raphaelites provided an artistic precedent, as did the Hogarth Club, founded towards the end of 1858 by Madox Brown and his friends.[7] A more influential and more commercially orientated model was the 'Art Manufactures' group led by Henry Cole, which was certainly known to Morris and his friends. Since the 1840s, Cole and his group had been, along with Pugin, the foremost critics of the severe shortcomings of much industrial design. Cole was particularly significant in that he encouraged the idea of an association of artists and designers which would provide designs for commercial producers.[8] But Morris, Marshall, Faulkner & Co., rather than rest content with a loose association between designers and manufacturers, determined to involve itself in the production and marketing of its designs. They were well aware of the advantages which this type of association could confer: a group of artists working together could offer a much more complete service than they could possibly do as individuals – a point which was explicitly made in the firm's prospectus.

The establishment and development of the firm were also soundly based upon the partners' appreciation of a rapidly growing market for ecclesiastical products. The expansion of this market was largely caused by the unprecedented growth of the population as a whole during the nineteenth century. Moreover, as urbanisation proceeded apace, the established church came to fear that its hold on the population was threatened by the lack of churches in the towns and cities. The result was a constant demand for new churches, and the early decades of Victoria's reign saw an upsurge of church building on a scale unknown since the thirteenth century.[9] Between 1840 and 1876, the Church of

England built 1,727 new churches in England and Wales, and rebuilt or extensively restored a further 7,144, at a total cost in excess of £25 million. Between 1861 and 1866 alone, 397 new parishes were created by the Ecclesiastical Commissioners.[10] As the years passed, the favoured styles became more elaborate, decoration more lavish and costly. All kinds of furnishings were in demand, and stained glass for windows was particularly favoured.[11]

Splendid opportunities existed for those who could harmonise their thinking on interior design with that of leading architects. Plainly, this is something that Morris and his friends could do. Members of the firm made effective use of personal contacts in securing commissions, and efforts of this type were crucial to establishing the reputation of Morris, Marshall, Faulkner & Co. Morris and Webb got work from Street, Bodley and other architects of their acquaintance. Rossetti, with his wide social circle and ready charm, also managed to win numerous contracts for the firm.

Within a few years of its formation, however, the firm ran into trouble. Events were to show that it had become too dependent upon stained glass, and the market for this declined sharply in the general depression of the late 1860s; in the building industry, gross domestic fixed capital formation in housebuilding maintained a steady upward trend, but expenditure on ecclesiastical and public works fell sharply between 1865 and 1869 (see Figure 3.1). Another problem was that by the late 1860s most Morris windows were being designed by Burne-Jones, and the distinctive qualities of the firm's stained glass became for a time an actual disadvantage, with several customers abandoning Morris, Marshall, Faulkner & Co. for other firms which provided more straightforward Gothic Revival work.[12]

Meanwhile, the firm had also undertaken some large secular projects in the mid-1860s, notably the redecoration of St James's Palace and the creation of the Green Dining Room at the South Kensington Museum in 1866–67. The St James's Palace commission was one of Rossetti's greatest coups: he persuaded William Cowper, First Commissioner of Public Works, to engage Morris, Marshall, Faulkner & Co. to carry out the work in preference to the then fashionable firm of Crace & Co. of Wigmore Street, which had previously been responsible for decorative work at the Palace.[13] The Green Dining Room was commissioned by Henry Cole, the first Director of the South Kensington Museum, and Francis Fowke, the architect of the museum buildings. Both these

Figure 3.1

Gross Domestic Fixed Capital Formation in Building at Constant Prices, 1856–99

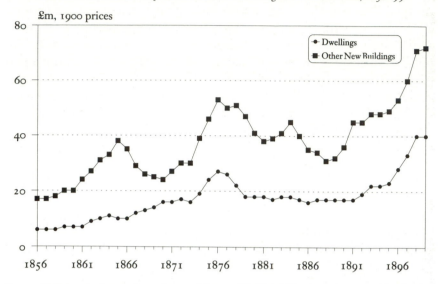

Source: C. Feinstein, *Income, Expenditure and Output of the United Kingdom, 1865–1955* (Cambridge, 1972), Table 40.

prestige projects were very profitable, and helped to establish the firm's reputation, but opportunities such as these were inherently unpredictable in a market so small and so subject to chance as scarcely to qualify for the name. There were no more major secular commissions until 1870–71.

It was clear that the business would never, in its existing form, provide large incomes for the partners in the firm. For some of them, this hardly mattered. Faulkner had returned to academic life, taking up a fellowship in mathematics at University College, Oxford, in 1864, while Marshall, who even at the height of his commitment had to be chased for designs,[14] had never given up his career in surveying. For Madox Brown and Rossetti, the firm was never more than a sideline, and they were earning substantial sums from their painting in these years. But Burne-Jones and Webb were not so well placed. Both depended more heavily on their earnings from the firm, and were hard hit by the slump in church sales. In 1867 Burne-Jones actually ended the year with a deficit of £91 on his partnership account, having drawn far more than he had earned in commission.[15] In May of the same year,

Plate 3.2 The Armoury at St James's Palace *National Monuments Record*

Webb, who had always worked for Morris, Marshall, Faulkner & Co. at low rates of pay and who was now seen to be experiencing hard times, was offered £80 per annum 'as consulting manager of the firm to commence from December last'.[16]

It was William Morris, however, who was most affected by the changing fortunes of the firm. As the other partners attended to their own careers, Morris was becoming more and more dependent upon Morris, Marshall, Faulkner & Co. for a living, and was having to think seriously about the firm's future. These deliberations took on a certain urgency as Morris's income from his inherited shareholding in Devon Great Consols began to shrink. The company had been generating enormous profits for upwards of two decades, but falling output and the collapse of world copper prices brought an end to this period of prosperity. Morris's dividends fell progressively from £682 in 1865 to £396 in 1869 and just £187 in 1870. Through necessity, he became a committed man of business, intent on expanding trade and acquiring an income that would safeguard his financial future.

The principal lesson Morris learnt during his early years in business was that if Morris, Marshall, Faulkner & Co. was to prosper, it would have to move beyond the artistic circle which had hitherto generated much of its commission work, and establish its reputation with the general public. It would also have to create a much wider range of products if it were to provide a complete interior decorating service. All this, of course, was easier said than done. A distinctive and complete decorating service called for a whole range of products of good quality and design. In the years immediately following, Morris had to work very hard, producing new designs for wallpapers and chintzes, and spent a good deal of time getting suppliers to meet his needs. He was often disappointed with the results, but still managed to impart a characteristic style to his interiors.[17] The wealthy responded with some enthusiasm. Once again, Morris was well served by his social connections. Rossetti and Burne-Jones had their homes decorated by the firm. Webb, as architect, introduced important clients, like the fashionable George and Rosalind Howard.[18] And friends like the Ionides family, wealthy members of the Greek merchant community, gave their social blessing to the Morris venture, informally spreading the word that Morris, Marshall, Faulkner & Co. was the only truly artistic design firm in London.[19]

Fame and financial success brought new problems in their wake. The firm remained a partnership, and each partner was legally entitled to an equal share of the profits, but almost all the hard work which generated them was being done by Morris and one or two key employees. Now that Morris desperately needed to increase his income, and had set the firm on a course which offered the prospect of sustained growth, he was no longer prepared to provide an income for sleeping partners. Accordingly, in August 1874, he announced his desire to wind up the firm and reconstitute it under his sole ownership.

The result was a prolonged and acrimonious argument. Madox Brown, Rossetti and Marshall demanded a share of the firm's assets, and Madox Brown was particularly incensed, insisting that he was not 'inclined to go at Morris's dictation'. Morris considered that their demands were unreasonable, and most of his biographers have been equally critical. In this they follow Mackail, who believed it quite wicked that 'each of the partners, who had confessedly contributed nothing beyond a trifling sum towards the capital, and who had been paid at the time for any assistance they gave towards the conduct of the business, was entitled to an equal share of the value of the business which had been built up by the energy, the labour, and the money of Morris alone'.[20]

This last comment rather overstates the case, as Morris did not, and would not have been able to, build up the business on his own. Rossetti had been an invaluable source of commissions in the early years, and both he and Madox Brown had unique talents which had been amongst the firm's greatest assets. The same was not exactly true of the inebriate Marshall, though it has to be said that he, like the others, had as a partner remained liable for the firm's debts for the past 14 years. As risk-sharers, Rossetti, Madox Brown and Marshall felt entitled to an equal share of the profits and assets of the firm, just as they accepted 'joint and several' liability for its debts. They had a point, and it is quite possible that a court would have upheld their claims to substantial compensation.

Yet, even if one accepts the logic of their argument, it is hard to resist the conclusion that Morris's disaffected colleagues, in differing degrees, got more out of the firm than they had put into it. Morris made the mistake of not acting sooner, before the furnishing and decorating business had really taken off and profits were flowing in. Even so, the balance of sympathy must lie with him, for while the other partners had been building their own careers, he had devoted much of his time to reviving the fortunes of Morris, Marshall, Faulkner & Co., and now had to look to it for his livelihood. In the end, however, fearing the damage an all-out legal battle might cause, Morris agreed to pay each partner £1,000, although Burne-Jones, Faulkner and Webb decided not to take their share. On 31 March 1875 it was announced that the partnership had been dissolved, and that thenceforth the business would be carried on under Morris's sole ownership and control, trading as Morris & Co.[21]

The years which followed were the most creative of Morris's career in business. Within a decade, his designs and products were widely admired throughout the Western world. The strenuous efforts which Morris made in these years to master new techniques in dyeing, weaving, tapestry making and the like are celebrated in the literature on Morris and the firm. Nor, given the work of historians like Linda Parry, Paul Thompson and Ray Watkinson,[22] is it necessary to emphasise the high standards of manufacture achieved by the firm and its subcontractors. But the reasons underlying Morris's incredible productivity in the decade or so following the breakup of the partnership deserve investigation.

In the first place, Morris was powerfully motivated by the need to safeguard his financial future, and guarantee his own 'freedom of work, which [was] a dear delight' to him.[23] The desire to ensure the well-being of his family was also an important factor. He remembered the financial stress his mother faced after his father's sudden death; besides which, his daughter Jenny, diagnosed as severely epileptic in 1876, would require constant nursing and general care for the rest of her life.

Secondly, Morris's appetite for work was fundamental to his character. This creative impulse was so strong in him that, as Burne-Jones observed, Morris mainly derived his pleasure from the anticipation of reaching a goal, and that once a thing was done, it was quickly set aside in favour of the next challenge.[24] However, Morris's appetite for new projects did not make him hasty in his approach to work. His dedication to perfection prevented that. Only after the most meticulous research into the principles and practices that underpinned fine art-work would he move on to the creative process. The thoroughness of his approach ultimately made for a higher level of personal efficiency. This is not to say that Morris mechanistically worked through a series of stages, for we know that he was capable of carrying out many tasks in parallel, and that he was meticulous in all his works.

The need for commercial success became even more important with the move to Merton Abbey in 1881. Though an essential step if Morris was to take full advantage of his years of experimentation, and develop the product range as he desired, this was an expensive undertaking for a relatively small firm like Morris & Co. Precisely how much it cost to convert and renovate the Merton Abbey works is not known, but the investment must have been substantial compared to the existing capital employed by the business. The old buildings had to be thoroughly overhauled and modified, and new tools and equipment acquired. Many months were to pass before the works were fully operational; block printing, for example, did not begin in earnest until late in 1882.[25]

Of course, the commercial success of Morris & Co. did not depend solely upon the energy of its owner, any more than it was solely dependent upon the high quality of its designs and products. From an early stage in his career, Morris had been aware of the importance of marketing, and now he did not intend to leave anything to chance. If Merton was to become a paying proposition, then a big effort had to be made to win favour with the public and to stimulate demand. The firm therefore published advertising brochures emphasising the beautiful design and colouring, and the uniqueness of Morris & Co. products, and asserting that, though expensive, they were good value for money,

Plate 3.3 Morris & Co.'s workshops at Merton Abbey *William Morris Gallery*

since their quality and durability was assured by first-rate materials and high standards of manufacture. The emphasis on 'the luxury of taste' rather than 'the luxury of costliness', first set out in the firm's prospectus of 1861, remained a characteristic theme of its publicity in the 1880s and 1890s.[26]

Another feature of the firm's marketing strategy in this period was the expansion of its range to include goods of varying grades and prices. Handmade Hammersmith carpets were extremely costly (£113 for a 16ft. x 13ft. example), but by the late 1870s Morris designs were available in all the principal types of Victorian carpet – Wilton, Axminster, Brussels and Kidderminster – and at a range of prices.[27] This placed more and more of the firm's products within the reach of the middle classes. Most customers had relatively modest incomes and bought wallpapers, fabrics and carpets for inclusion in their own decorative schemes. Likewise, throughout the 1880s and 1890s, Morris & Co. made and sold a limited number of large, high quality pieces of embroidery at high prices; but small items such as cushion covers, work bags, firescreens and the like were increasingly important, most being sold for £0.75–£1.50. Embroidery was a popular and respectable occupation for middle-class women at that time, and, in addition to selling finished work, Morris & Co. met this demand by offering embroidery kits; most of the firm's designs were available with the pattern ready-traced on silk, or as transfers.[28]

In 1877, Morris & Co. opened an elegant showroom at 264 Oxford Street (later renumbered 449), in a new block of buildings on the corner of North Audley Street. The firm's full range of goods could now be displayed in a fashionable location in the heart of the West End. This end of the business was handled by two brothers who had recently been taken on, Frank and Robert Smith, who were later to become junior partners in the firm.[29] After the establishment of the Merton workshops, the showroom extended to provide more display space, and Morris took steps to reach a wider clientèle beyond the metropolitan élite and wealthy provincials who regularly travelled to London. In 1882, he decided to open a showroom in Manchester, a wealthy city, with a reputation for patronage of the applied arts. The firm showed its wares at the Manchester Fine Art and Industrial Exhibition of 1882, to critical acclaim, and a shop was rented at 34 John Dalton Street, in the prosperous central shopping and commercial district around Albert Square. In January 1883 Morris & Co. opened for business as 'cabinet makers, upholsterers and general house furnishers'. Additional premises were rented shortly afterwards in nearby Brazenose Street for cabinet making and upholstery, and in 1884 the retail side of the business was transferred to Albert Square where the firm traded as 'Art Decorators, Art Furnishers, Manufacturers and Designers'.[30]

The appointment of reliable agents was seen as the best way of making sales in the rich markets of the United States and continental Europe. Morris was exasperated by the generally high level of import duties, often complaining of 'almost prohibitory' tariffs;[31] but he was not put off, recognising that wealthy Germans and Americans were willing to pay premium prices for goods of the highest quality and originality. As early as 1878 he had appointed Cowtan & Tout as his main agent in the United States. By 1883 this function had passed to Elliot & Bulkley of New York, who in turn dealt with specialist retailers in the nation's richest cities.[32]

Though William Morris may have looked to past ages for technology and artistic models which he could develop, the commercial side of his business was very much of the present. Morris knew his markets, and he knew how to arrest the attention of those who could afford to purchase his goods. The shop in Oxford Street, not the factory at Merton, was the strategic hub of his operations, where his creations were displayed in a

Plate 3.4 Morris & Co.'s shop, 449 Oxford Street *William Morris Gallery*

tastefully fashionable setting. The business was managed in a prudent and professional manner, and costs such as subcontractors' fees were carefully controlled. Although Morris had the reputation of being a good employer who paid somewhat above the market rate, the firm was

always careful to ensure that wage bills did not drive the price of its
goods up to unsaleable levels. This was important, for while its leadership of the market may have allowed Morris & Co. some flexibility in
setting prices, it could not completely ignore those of its rivals. All the
firm's products faced competition of one sort or another from the many
firms seeking the approval of fashionable society.

Morris & Co. demonstrated considerable shrewdness in combatting
such competition. This was manifested in the effective exploitation of
the reputations of its principal designers, Burne-Jones and Morris.
Originally, when the main task had been to establish the identity of the
firm, the partners had agreed to keep secret the names of individual
designers. This policy was later reversed. In the 1880s and early 1890s,
Burne-Jones' reputation was at its peak, and his work commanded high
prices. He was lionised by fashionable society, and much in demand
as a portrait painter. It was thus with some pride that Morris & Co.
announced in 1882 that 'Mr Burne Jones entrusts us alone with the
execution of his cartoons for stained glass'.[33] Even more important to
Morris & Co. than the reputation of Burne-Jones was that of Morris
himself. He was by now a famous figure, and his very name drew
fashionable people to take an interest in his art, whether or not they
agreed with his political ideas. His conversion to socialism appears to
have done little to deter customers. Nor did his lofty attitude and
forthright opinions. Rossetti was surely correct in observing that
Morris's 'very eccentricities and independent attitude towards his
patrons seems to have drawn [them] around him'.[34] The firm was not
slow to exploit the celebrity of its owner. Morris was always available to
advise wealthy customers on big decorative schemes and expensive
purchases. In a brochure of the early 1880s, it was announced that
thenceforth interior design would 'be under the special supervision of
Mr WILLIAM MORRIS, who will personally advise Customers as to
the best method and style of Decoration to be used in each case'.[35] By
the late 1880s, as Morris's personal reputation soared, he felt obliged to
ration his time by charging fees for personal visits to the homes of
clients – 5 guineas (£5.25) in London, and £20 elsewhere. He made it
clear to his managers, however, that the charges did not apply to 'well
known and useful customers, ... but only to stop fools and impertinents'.[36]

Morris also realised that the firm's methods of design and manufacturing could themselves be used to strengthen its position. From the
first the Merton Abbey works attracted a steady stream of visitors, and

these personal tours, directly or indirectly, helped make the reputation of the firm in the 1880s and 1890s. But while many of his admirers believed that he had managed to combine high principles and standards with an impressive degree of business success, Morris himself was becoming more and more critical of his achievement. His disillusionment was summed up in his oft-quoted assertion that 'art cannot have real life and growth under the present system of commercialism and profit-mongering',[37] and found practical expression in his commitment to socialist action in 1883 and the years that followed.

This commitment to socialism, deep and passionate though it was, did not release Morris from the need to earn his living. The work of the firm continued to occupy much of his time. He continued to visit Merton two or three times a week to ensure that there was no falling off in standards, and his enthusiasm for the work continued unabated.[38] Yet, given the extent of his political commitments, it was necessarily a role different in kind and less intensive than that played when he was building up the business. This he recognised by delegating responsibility for day-to-day management to others. Throughout his business career, Morris had the knack of getting the best out of his senior colleagues and workpeople. He appointed managers who combined enthusiasm, shrewdness and integrity, and allowed them considerable freedom to carry out their designated tasks. The role of George Wardle, the general manager from 1870 to 1890, who took overall control of operations at Merton, is considered further in other chapters. J.H. Dearle, Morris's pupil as a designer, and the Smith brothers, with whom he entered into a partnership in 1890, also made important contributions to the Morris firm.

The reorganisation of the firm left Morris free to concentrate upon the crowning achievement of his life: the establishment of the Kelmscott Press. Morris's various skills all played a part in the success of the Press. As decorative artist, he was responsible for the design of elegant founts, page layouts, borders, title pages and special lettering. As scholar and man of letters, Morris was the author of 23 of the 66 Kelmscott volumes, the editor of one, and the translator of another four. It was he, moreover, who determined what books the Press should produce. Indeed, his personality so dominated the enterprise that his executors decided that it should close on completion of the work in hand when he died.

In celebrating the literary and artistic achievements of the Kelmscott Press, however, we should not lose sight of the fact that its success was

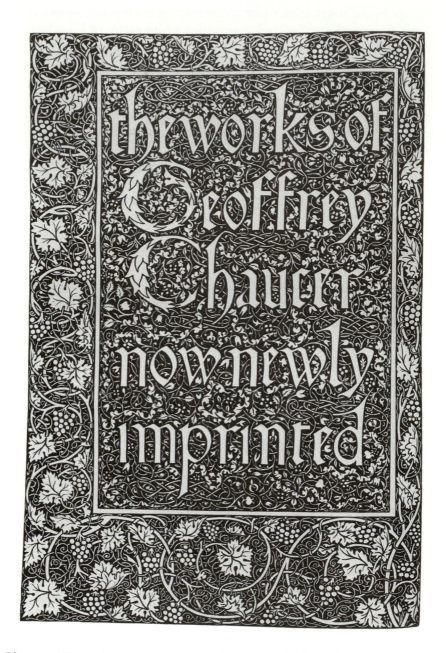

Plate 3.5 The *Kelmscott Chaucer* – opening pages of the Prologue

William Morris Gallery

HERE BEGINNETH THE TALES OF CANTER
BURY AND FIRST THE PROLOGUE THEREOF

WHAN THAT Aprille with his shoures soote
The droghte of March hath perced to the roote,
And bathed every veyne in swich licour,
Of which vertu engendred is the flour;
Whan Zephirus eek with his swete breeth
Inspired hath in every holt and heeth

The tendre croppes, and the yonge sonne
Hath in the Ram his halfe cours yronne,
And smale foweles maken melodye,
That slepen al the nyght with open eye,
So priketh hem nature in hir corages;
Thanne longen folk to goon on pilgrimages,
And palmeres for to seken straunge strondes,
To ferne halwes, kowthe in sondry londes;
And specially, from every shires ende
Of Engelond, to Caunterbury they wende,
The hooly blisful martir for to seke,
That hem hath holpen whan that they were
seeke.

BIFIL that in that seson on a day,
In Southwerk at the Tabard as
I lay,
Redy to wenden on my pilgrym-
age
To Caunterbury with ful devout
corage,
At nyght were come into that hostelrye
Wel nyne and twenty in a compaignye,
Of sondry folk, by aventure yfalle
In felaweshipe, and pilgrimes were they alle,
That toward Caunterbury wolden ryde.

also dependent upon Morris's experience as a man of business. It is clear that Morris applied the same perfectionist approach to his final venture as he had to his earlier projects, including a lengthy period of preliminary research and a further period spent mastering all the necessary techniques. The production, too, was directed at a similar, or more refined, market. But, just as Morris & Co. offered goods at a range of prices and qualities, from high works of art down to simple domestic articles, so too the Kelmscott Press produced books of differing size, lavishness of illustration, and consequently price. The average price of a paper volume was £2.19; but around this there was considerable variation, so that 36 titles went on sale at £1.50 or less. Only 11 volumes on paper cost more than £5, with the *Chaucer* in a league of its own at £20. A vellum edition of a work cost between five and six times its paper counterpart, and these were very much the preserve of the wealthy collectors.

In his book on the history of the Press, Sparling devoted some space to the proposition that Morris never intended the Kelmscott Press to make money, stating, for example, that 'he had never contemplated the sale of any book whatever at any price, until *forced* to do so by finding that there was a real and widespread demand for his books'.[39] The idea that the Kelmscott Press was in essence non-profit-making has been reiterated by later writers, most notably by William Peterson, whose *Bibliography of the Kelmscott Press* contains a wealth of detail on all aspects of the books produced by Morris. Peterson writes that the Press 'was in effect an amusing diversion for Morris' which he fully expected would cost him money.[40] Its commercial success accordingly is seen as an incidental consequence of artistic genius rather than something for which Morris may have striven for as a matter of course. There is indeed some evidence to support this interpretation. Morris himself rejected any suggestion that the high prices charged by him meant that Kelmscott books made large profits, stating that 'if the people who go about talking of my profits could see my balance sheet, they would speak quite differently'. In the case of the *Chaucer*, the 'cost will hardly be covered by the subscriptions', and with the *Beowulf* the effect of several sheets getting spoiled in the printing was to convert a profit into a loss so that 'the book is sold at less than what it cost me to produce it'.[41]

The Kelmscott Press, it is quite clear, was no ordinary commercial venture. Morris's primary objectives were artistic, not financial. But, this said, it is hard to believe that Morris, with all his experience over the years of marketing high-quality products, would have set up this complex and costly enterprise oblivious of the notion that the end product would attract buyers. All Morris's creative endeavours gave him pleasure, but this did not make them merely amusing diversions. His was a serious purpose, and that purpose demanded that he stay in business. To do this he had to trade at a profit. To trade at a profit he had to keep down costs, stimulate demand, and fix his prices at a remunerative level. The Kelmscott Press was a remarkable creative adventure; but it was also a commercial concern with orthodox financial aspirations.[42]

All the signs are that the Press conducted its affairs on sound financial lines. This is not to suggest that the business was completely free from risk. Morris invariably used one achievement as a platform for new and higher things; and, in this case, his artistic ambition was channelled towards the production of an edition of Chaucer that would rank amongst the finest books of all time. After two financially successful years, in 1892 and 1893, a large part of the resources of the Kelmscott Press was turned over to the project. Morris, as ever, was prepared to invest heavily in things about which he cared deeply. No expense was spared. The direct cost of producing 425 paper copies and 13 vellum copies was a staggering £7,217, expended over a period of three years. The gross value of the books was £10,128, but if this sum is trimmed by 25 per cent to allow for costs of distribution, making £7,596, it can be seen that Morris was not exaggerating when in 1895 he claimed that the *Chaucer* would yield little or no profit. The reason for this is almost certainly that Morris announced his prices and took orders at too early a stage, before the full costs of the project were known. Its instant success indicates that a lot more could have been charged for a book which from the first was eagerly sought after by dealers.

By and large, however, most Kelmscott books were a financial success. The surviving data provide detailed information of only half the Press's titles, but this does permit us to calculate the ratio of gross income to operating costs for 33 Kelmscott books, both individually and collectively. The weighted average ratio for all 33 titles is 1.94 to 1. In other words, gross income from sales was almost double the sum needed to meet costs of production. Even when overheads and distribution expenses, including trade discounts, were taken into account, there was still a fair margin for profit. Of course, there was considerable variation between titles. At the upper end of the profit range were some of Morris's own works. *The Life and Death of Jason* and *The Earthly Paradise* had gross income-to-cost ratios of 3.47 to 1 and 3.46 to 1 respectively, compared to 1.4 to 1 for the *Chaucer* and 1.46 to 1 for *Beowulf*. The highest income to cost differential, with a ratio of 12.79 to 1, was that of the 26-page *Syr Isambrace*; the lowest ratio, at 1.31 to 1, was that of the three-volume *Poetical Works of Percy Bysshe Shelley*, which cost £832 to produce.[43]

The overall picture is that of a financially healthy business with considerable scope to charge premium prices for its products. And this picture is confirmed by the only surviving financial statement for the Kelmscott Press, a balance sheet drawn up at 31 December 1895. It shows a firm in a very solid financial position, with plant and machinery written down to a low figure, and sufficient liquid assets to cover its debts many times over.[44] For Morris, the success of the Kelmscott Press may have been the most satisfying aspect of his whole career – and it was an achievement which depended as much on his own business experience as it did on his artistic expertise.

One of the purposes of this chapter has been to provide a refutation of the views of those who, like Martin Wiener,[45] have associated Morris's ideas and influence with Britain's relative economic decline. These people are in part the victims of their own prejudices. But Morris himself contributed to their misjudgements through some of his own pronouncements and writings. After all, he constantly declares his detestation of the modern age, and, with equal vehemence, asserts the primacy of medieval art, architecture and methods of production. On this basis, it might be reasonable to see Morris as a nostalgic idealist.

The truth is rather more complex. For Morris appears (like many of us) to have formed compartments in his mind. His idealism, his revolutionary socialism, his zeal for the past, live in one compartment; his commitment to the world of business lies in another. There is no moral inconsistency here: even idealists have to provide for themselves and their families. At the intellectual level Morris may well have hated the age he lived in. At the practical level, he accommodated it quite well, and at this level he was no crank. He was happy to use modern methods and machinery in production if they were consistent with his artistic purposes.

There were many original and unorthodox aspects to his firm, which is unsurprising, in the light of Morris's own character. The principal unorthodoxies were the products themselves, and the methods of production; but there was nothing impractical then, any more than there is now, about originality – it was, in fact, the firm's greatest asset. Nor was there anything impractical about its strategy with regard to marketing, pricing, and employees' pay and conditions. Morris was, like many others of his time, by no means an unscrupulous employer, but he was not an excessively generous one, either. He operated in a highly competitive environment, and succeeded because he understood it very well.

NOTES

1. G.E. Street, 'On the Future of Art in England', *Ecclesiologist*, Vol. XIX (1858), pp. 232–40.
2. J. Ruskin, *The Two Paths* (1859), in E.T. Cook and A. Wedderburn (eds), *The Complete Works of John Ruskin* (39 vols., 1903–12), Vol. 16, p. 320.
3. Ibid., p. 319.
4. *Athenaeum*, 10 Oct. 1896. This view has been repeated in more recent works. See, *inter alia*, P. Henderson, *William Morris: His Life, Work and Friends* (1967), p. 63.
5. Ibid.
6. Hammersmith and Fulham Archives Department (hereafter HFAD), DD/235/1, Morris, Marshall, Faulkner & Co., Minute Book, 1861–74, 10 Dec. 1862, 28 Jan. 1863, 1 April 1863. The account books of Webb, Madox Brown and Burne-Jones have survived, and are respectively in the City of Birmingham Museum and Art Gallery, the Lady Lever Art Gallery, Port Sunlight, and the Fitzwilliam Museum, Cambridge.
7. J. Mordaunt Crook, *William Burges and the High Victorian Dream* (1981), p. 75; A. Vallance, *Life and Work of William Morris* (1897), pp. 25–6; R. Watkinson, *Pre-Raphaelite Art and Design* (1970), pp. 143–4.
8. See Sir H. Cole, *Fifty Years of Public Work* (1884), Vol. II, pp. 179–80.
9. K.S. Inglis, *Churches and the Working Class in England* (1963), pp. 23–4; O. Chadwick, *The Victorian Church*, Vol. I (1966), pp. 363–9; F.W. Cornish, *The English Church in the Nineteenth Century* (1910), Vol. I, pp. 110–17; B.F.L. Clarke, *Church Builders of the Nineteenth Century: A Study of the Gothic Revival in England* (1938, reprinted Newton Abbot, 1969), *passim*.
10. *Return showing the Number of Churches (including Cathedrals) in every Diocese in England, which had been built or restored at a cost exceeding £500 since the year 1840*, Parliamentary Papers, 1876 LVIII, pp. 553–658; G. Kitson Clark, *The Making of Victorian England* (1962), p. 169.
11. Clarke, *Church Builders of the Nineteenth Century*, pp. 24–30; M. Harrison, *Victorian Stained Glass* (1980), pp. 20–1; P.F. Anson, *Fashions in Church Furnishings, 1840–1940* (1960), especially pp. 206–17.
12. Harrison, *Victorian Stained Glass*, pp. 43, 47.
13. C. Mitchell, 'William Morris at St. James's Palace', *Architectural Review* (Jan.

1947), p. 38; J.Y. LeBourgeois, 'William Morris at St. James's Palace: A Sequel', *Journal of the William Morris Society*, Vol. III (1974), pp. 7–9; J.C. Troxell, *Three Rossettis: Unpublished Letters to and from Dante Gabriel, Christina, William* (Cambridge, MA, 1937), p. 54.

14. HFAD, DD235/1, Morris, Marshall, Faulkner & Co., Minutes, 5 May 1863.

15. In this year, Burne-Jones leased a large house in Fulham known as the Grange, which he largely furnished with articles from Morris, Marshall, Faulkner & Co. See Fitzwilliam Museum, Account Book of Sir Edward Burne-Jones.

16. HFAD, DD235/1, Morris, Marshall, Faulkner & Co., Minutes, 16 May 1867.

17. See G. Wardle, 'Memorials of William Morris', British Library, Add. Mss. 45350, ff. 6, 10.

18. The Howards' London house, 1 Palace Green, was built by Webb between 1868 and 1872, and was decorated by the firm between 1872 and 1882. Their other homes, Naworth Castle and Castle Howard, also included carpets, tapestries and textiles by Morris & Co. George Howard became ninth Earl of Carlisle in 1889. William Morris Gallery (hereafter WMG), Files 15a, 15b.

19. The Ionides family's patronage of the Morris firm is discussed further in Chapter 7.

20. J.W. Mackail, *Life of William Morris* (2 vols., 1899), Vol. I, p. 307.

21. Ibid.

22. L. Parry, *William Morris Textiles* (1983); P. Thompson, *The Work of William Morris* (1967, 3rd edn. Oxford, 1991) ; R. Watkinson, *William Morris as Designer* (1967).

23. N. Kelvin (ed.), *The Collected Letters of William Morris*, Vol. I (Princeton, NJ, 1984), p. 178, to Aglaia Coronio, 11 Feb. 1873.

24. M. Lago (ed.), *Burne-Jones Talking: His Conversations 1895–1898 Preserved by his Studio Assistant Thomas Rooke* (1982), pp. 64, 109. A similar point was made by George Wardle: in his 'Memorials of William Morris', he remarked that Morris was 'capable of trampling on his dead self more resolutely than any man I have known'. British Library, Add. Mss. 45350, f. 11.

25. Kelvin (ed.), *Letters*, Vol. II (Princeton, NJ, 1987), p. 143, to Jenny Morris, 19 Dec. 1882.

26. See, for example, Victoria & Albert Museum (hereafter V & A), Box I.276.A, Morris & Co., brochure, 1882.

27. V & A, Box I.276.A; O. Fairclough and E. Leary, *Textiles by William Morris and Morris & Company, 1861–1940* (1981), p. 49; Parry, *William Morris Textiles*, pp. 59–60.

28. V & A, 86.cc.31, Morris & Co., Record of Embroidery Work, Nov. 1892–Nov. 1896. Also see Parry, *William Morris Textiles*, p. 29; B. Morris, *Victorian Embroidery* (1962), pp. 91, 110.

29. Kelvin (ed.), *Letters*, Vol. I, p. 385, to Lucy Faulkner Orrinsmith, 20 July 1877.

30. C. Harvey and J. Press, 'Morris & Co. in Manchester', *Journal of the William Morris Society*, Vol. IX No. 3 (1991), pp. 4–8; *Slater's Manchester and Salford Directory* (Manchester, 1883–86); *Kelly's Directory of Manchester and Suburbs* (1887); Kelvin (ed.), *Letters*, Vol. II, p. 149, to Jenny Morris, 9 Jan. 1883; *Cabinet Maker and Art Furnisher*, Vol. 3 (1883), pp. 83–4, 99, 160.

31. Kelvin (ed.), *Letters*, Vol. II, p. 134, to Catherine Holiday, 9 Nov. 1882.

32. G. Wardle, *The Morris Exhibit at the Foreign Fair, Boston 1883* (Boston, MA, 1883).

33. V & A, Box I 276.A. Also see P. Fitzgerald, *Edward Burne-Jones: A Biography* (1975), p. 182; M. Harrison and B. Walters, *Burne-Jones* (1973), pp. 126, 148; Arts Council, *Burne-Jones: The Paintings, Graphic and Decorative Work of Sir Edward Burne-Jones, 1833–98* (1975), pp. 7–9.

34. Theodore Watts-Dunton's recollections in the *English Review* (Jan. 1909), quoted in E.P. Thompson, *Romantic to Revolutionary* (2nd edn, 1977), p. 109.

35. WMG, File a, Morris & Co., circular, n.d., c.1881.

36. Kelvin (ed.), *Letters*, Vol. II, p. 622, to Frank or Robert Smith, 24 Feb. 1887.

37. William Morris to Andreas Scheu, 5 Sept. 1883, reprinted in A. Briggs (ed.), *William Morris: Selected Works and Designs* (1962, reprinted 1980), p. 30.

38. See, for example, H.H. Sparling, *The Kelmscott Press and William Morris, Master Craftsman* (1924), p. 32; Wardle, 'Memorials', ff. 22–3.

39. Sparling, *Kelmscott Press*, pp. 75–8.

40. W.S. Peterson, *A Bibliography of the Kelmscott Press* (Oxford, 1982), p. xi.

41. Ibid., p. 111.

42. See, for example, P. Faulkner (ed.), *Jane Morris to Wilfrid Scawen Blunt: The Letters of Jane Morris to Wilfrid Scawen Blunt together with Extracts from Blunt's Diaries* (Exeter, 1986), p. 53.

43. S.C. Cockerell, 'An Annotated List of All the Books Printed at the Kelmscott Press in the Order in which they were Issued', in Sparling, *Kelmscott Press*, pp. 148–74; Peterson, *Bibliography of the Kelmscott Press, passim*.

44. PRO, IR59/173.

45. M.J. Wiener, *English Culture and the Decline of the Industrial Spirit* (Cambridge, 1981).

— 4 —

William Morris and the Experience of Iceland[1]

$\mathbf{M}$ ORRIS'S FIRST encounter with Iceland was literary, and a consequence of the enormous expansion of antiquarian studies which began towards the end of the eighteenth century. At that time, an awakened interest in England's ancient Germanic past was bringing it out of the shadow of classical Greek and Latin literature, under which it had lain in obscurity for many centuries. To some extent, these developments were part of a wider movement in European culture, as a result of which, through the advancement of science, most old fields of study were being carefully re-examined, and many new ones developed. It was in all a remarkable period of intellectual enquiry. Nordic and Germanic studies appealed – in Germany and Scandinavia too – to a kind of nationalistic sentiment, which sought not merely to investigate old matters out of curiosity, but also to assert their enduring value as cultural monuments, speaking, as was often thought, with quintessential purity from the very heart and origin of the modern nation.[2] Unfortunately, very little purely Germanic literature had survived from the Anglo-Saxon era, and even less of an overtly pagan nature. It was left to scholars to make what inferences they could about the pagan past from such sources as the unique Old English epic *Beowulf*, some short poems and fragments of longer ones, and one or two pagan charms.

In Iceland, however, though the country had been nominally Christian since the year 1,000 AD, medieval piety did not wipe out the memory of the pagan religion, and scholars therefore turned to Iceland to supply what was missing from the native record. This was in some ways a dubious venture, since it is a reasonable assumption that the Icelandic represents a later and more sophisticated version of the paganism which was familiar to a sixth- or seventh-century Englishman. Nevertheless, the Norse accounts of mythology clearly had their uses, apart from their intrinsic interest. They consist principally of two great collections. One is the *Elder Edda*,[3] comprising short narrative poems, or lays, of which some tell of the Norse gods, and some of legendary matter, with historical origins in fifth-century Germany. The other is the *Younger*, or *Prose*, *Edda*, written in the thirteenth century by Snorri Sturluson (1178–1241), perhaps the greatest figure in all Icelandic literature.

These collections were first translated into English in the latter part of the eighteenth century, and were received with much enthusiasm by, among others, Thomas Gray, Walter Savage Landor, and Thomas Carlyle. The two *Eddas*, while entirely Scandinavian in tradition, call on ancient traditions of myth, legend and magic, which at one time were shared by the whole Germanic world. So indeed do some of the prose sagas, including *Völsunga Saga*. But the great family sagas, some of which were also being translated into English in the early part of the nineteenth century, were more firmly grounded, both historically and geographically, and it is they that provide the most distinctively Icelandic contribution to world literature.

What was the attraction of these 500-year-old voices? On the surface, Victorian England – industrialised, scientific, nominally Christian, sophisticated – had almost nothing in common with medieval Iceland. But what the enthusiasts nevertheless sensed was a kinship of spirit; a spirit which the Christian church had sought from the outset to suppress, but to which the Icelanders had given full, if qualified, expression. An illustration of this is a climactic episode from *Njál's Saga* (known to Morris through Sir George Dasent's translation).[4] Njál, a man in his sixties, and a Christian (the year is 1011), has sons who have killed, and an attempt at settlement by compensation has failed. He and his family have allowed themselves to be trapped in their house, to which the attackers have set fire. It is obvious that nobody can escape death unless the burners let them out; and Njál is described as going about the blazing building with words of comfort for the frantic household:

Be at ease about this and speak not of fear; for this will be but a passing storm, and it will be long before another such. Likewise trust that God is merciful, and will not let us burn in this world and the next.

A little later, the burners offer to allow Njál and his wife out of the fire, as they have no quarrel with them. Njál's response is to say: 'I will not go out, for I am an old man, and little fitted to avenge my sons; but I will not live in shame.' It is clear that the first of these sentences is purely

Christian, and the second purely pagan. One also feels that the pagan sentiment here expressed would find some kind of echo in the heart of any man at any time or in any place. The Christian sentiment, on the other hand, would be a complete mystery to the uninitiated. And this is the appeal of the Norse ethic: it is always real, always practical in its idealism, always of this world, without reference to any other.

Morris had acquired some knowledge of Icelandic literature in early adulthood, and had been fairly favourably impressed. It is a matter of record that he became an enthusiast in 1869. It is a matter of convention that he found in the northern stories a message which he could apply directly to his own marital unhappiness, and to his own sense of failure which Janey Morris's affair with Dante Gabriel Rossetti induced. It has also been suggested that reading the literature in the original language may have played a part in this striking change of direction.

These latter two propositions, while possibly containing some truth, are hardly adequate. In Mackail's *Life of William Morris*, we find that, in 1853, while Morris was still at university, 'Thorpe's "Northern Mythology", to which he was introduced by Burne-Jones, opened to Morris a new world, which in later life became, perhaps, his deepest love, that of the Scandinavian epic'.[5] Why 'in later life'? The reason seems to be that at 19 Morris still had rather a lot of growing to do. For Mackail tells us also that when Morris and Burne-Jones read together (which in practice meant that Morris read aloud to Burne-Jones), 'among the works thus read were Neale's "History of the Eastern Church", Milman's "Latin Christianity", great portions of the "Acta Sanctorum" ["Works of the Saints"], and of the "Tracts for the Times", Gibbon, Sismondi, and masses of mediaeval chronicles and ecclesiastical Latin poetry'.[6]

We must bear in mind that at this early stage Morris was intending to enter the Church, and these texts indicate an absorption with theology bordering on obsession. Furthermore, he was of a High Church, Romantic persuasion, and full of misty longing for the beauties of the Catholic Middle Ages. The charge that has been laid against Morris by certain highly practical men of more recent times[7] – that he was no more than a woolly minded idealist – may perhaps be considered valid regarding this particular period. The literature and mythology of Iceland, we conjecture, seemed valuable to him chiefly in that they were old: it was not until 'later life' that he became able to see in it the freshness and immediacy of something new. Morris himself, in a much-quoted passage, observed: 'the delightful freshness and independence of thought of [Icelandic writings], the air of freedom which breathes through them, their worship of courage (the great virtue of the human race), their utter unconventionality took my heart by storm'.[8]

These are perceptions derived from a more mature literary judgement, and only one of them (the matter of courage) can be made to have the slightest bearing on his personal problems, however acute they may have been. A contemporary critic, Henry Buxton Forman, wrote that:

Considered in the light of a poet and story-teller, [Morris] may be said to have started his career as an Anglo-Norman mediaevalist, drawing, however, considerable inspiration from with a widening area of knowledge and reading taking in at first hand influences from the sturdy literature of the Northmen who peopled Iceland.[9]

If this is wrong, it can only be wrong in that it does not go far enough, or rather over-simplifies a complex process, which has psychological aspects as well as cultural ones. We may unravel it by starting with what Morris himself wrote in the Introduction to the Saga Library: 'that the Icelandic historians and tale-tellers were cut off from the influence of the older literature, was ... a piece of good luck to them, rather than a misfortune'.[10]

The reason is that it left the Icelanders completely unrestricted by the stifling demands of classical pedantry and Christian piety. Morris found in the sagas and the Eddaic poetry qualities which in sum might be described as an antidote to the baneful effects of the twin foundations of conventional European culture: religion and the Classics. It was quite natural that he should find them imbued with the exhilarating spirit of freedom. There is indeed a sense of delight and discovery in Eiríkr Magnússon's words on Morris's reception of his translation of *Völsunga Saga*: 'I found him in a state of great excitement, pacing his study. He told me he had now finished reading my translation of "the grandest tale that ever was told".'[11] This is not the reaction of someone who has found something that merely points him back towards his own unhappiness, and tells him to face it like a man. It is the reaction of a highly educated yet open-minded man to a cultural revelation, and it wrought a remarkable transformation, which proved to be permanent, in Morris's literary aims.

Indeed, fired by a wish to become acquainted with the original Icelandic texts, Morris began almost at once the highly ambitious

project of translating the sagas into English from a language of which he
knew little or nothing. He had, of course, the help of Eiríkr Magnússon
in this venture, and the latter recalled, in a moving tribute after Morris's
death, how their method developed. They began by having Eiríkr read
a passage of the original, which Morris would attempt to imitate. Then
Morris became impatient and insisted on having the story 'as quickly as
possible', thus to some extent bypassing the Icelandic text. Perhaps to
compensate for this deficiency:

> The dialect of our translation was not the Queen's English, but it was helpful
> towards penetrating into the thought of the old language. Thus … leiðotogi, a
> guide, became load-tugger (load = way, in load-star, load-stone; togi from toga to
> tug (on), one who leads on with a rope); kvænask (= kvæna sik from kvan = queen,
> woman) to bequeen oneself = to take a wife, &c. That such a method of acquiring
> the language should be a constant source of merriment, goes without saying.[12]

It also goes without saying that the task presented many serious problems. 'Translation', wrote Professor Randolph Quirk, 'is one of the
most difficult tasks that a writer can take upon himself',[13] especially
when translating older literature – that is, the literature of a culture in
many ways radically different from one's own. Morris's method was in
general to use normal English words; but, largely due to the starting-
point of his technique of translating, he spiced these with flavours either
genuinely from the past, or which seem to the uninitiated to be from the
past. From time to time, he uses the convenient ploy – for the translator,
that is – of adopting the English cognate of an Icelandic word, whether
or not the sense of the English word is the same as that of the Icelandic.
Gordon for instance comments:

> His deliberate and frequent archaisms (often mere pseudo-archaisms) give an air of
> preciosity and affectation which is entirely out of harmony with the spirit of the
> sagas. It is hard to be patient with Morris's 'endlong' for 'along', 'ling-worm' or
> 'drake' for 'dragon', and the like.[14]

According to Quirk, on the other hand, Morris

wants to make us share the acute pleasure which the forms and arrangements of the
Icelandic have [sic] upon him. His readers must be made to share the magic
experience of a remote literature, dealing with a remote culture in a remote
language; they must read the sagas with just that extra concentration and care that
Morris had to use; they must find them couched in a language which would be as
intelligible to them as Icelandic was to him, but which would have the same areas of
unfamiliarity too.[15]

Quirk's statement is no doubt the more sophisticated of the two, although that does not in itself make it right. But the style which evolved so rapidly as a method of rendering the sagas into English became so natural to Morris that he retained it in later years for his own prose romances.

Anyone who has read the sagas is likely to find the idea of visiting Iceland alluring. There are the obvious facts of the spectacular scenery, and the romance of places described in the them. It is no surprise that less than two years after meeting Eiríkr Magnússon, Morris was actually with him in Iceland. The pair, together with Charles Faulkner and another friend, had set sail from Edinburgh on 8 July 1871, and after a short stay in the Faroe Islands reached Iceland on 13 July, putting into port at Reykjavík the following day. They left again for England on 1 September. The intervening period was later chronicled in great detail by Morris in his *Iceland Journals*.[16] There seems little doubt that he was troubled by something akin to depression, certainly at the outset. Nor is it clear from the journals what he hoped to gain from the voyage. His descriptions of the landscape – full of such adjectives as dreary, mournful, dreadful, terrible, barren, and the like – strongly suggest the kind of place a depressive would do well to avoid. Yet Morris knew what he was doing: as he later wrote, he had been drawn there by 'a true instinct for what I needed', and confessed in 1872 to knowing 'what a blessing & help last years journey was to me; [and] what horrors it saved me from'.[17]

But what did he need, and what were the horrors? If he had simply needed an antidote to an unhappy marriage, then Iceland would hardly have been a specific. Of course, the place had a fascination for him as the source of the sagas; but there was certainly more to it than this. Morris offers us something of a clue in a letter to Aglaia Coronio. The much-discussed paragraph starts:

When I said there was no cause for feeling low, I meant that my friends had not changed at all towards me in any way and that there had been no quarrelling: and indeed I am afraid it comes from some cowardice or unmanliness in me.

But a little later he writes:

Often in my better moods I wonder what it is in me that throws me into such rage and despair at other times: I suspect, do you know, that some such moods would have come upon me at times even without this failure of mine.[18]

It may well be thought that Morris's suspicion was fully justified: that Janey's affair with Rossetti, whilst undoubtedly a source of pain, served also to conceal deeper levels of dissatisfaction. For it seems highly likely that the demolition of his early idealism extended much further than to love and marriage. His attitude at this time to Rossetti, of whom he had been almost a disciple at the start of his artistic career, smacks more of irritation than of jealousy. In a curious way, the whole Pre-Raphaelite ethos, with its ethereal other-worldliness, and the languid melancholy of its literary expression in Morris's early work, utterly fails to accord with the practical, robust, positive approach to life which we associate with the image of the essential, mature man. It is as if he had been working for many years against the grain of his own personality – largely under the influence of Rossetti – and that this slowly began to dawn on him when he encountered Iceland. Practical, robust and positive are all fitting epithets for the spirit of the old saga writers.

From all this, there appeared to be good reasons for Morris to go to Iceland himself. Firstly, he could escape for a while from his domestic troubles; secondly, he could distract himself by means of a fairly exacting physical test, since the journey was certain to be relatively uncomfortable; and thirdly, perhaps most importantly, he could do some on-the-spot research into the geographical background of the sagas. Besides all this, the Icelandic landscape is not as grim and terrifying as selective excerpts from the *Journals* might lead one to believe. For instance, the entry for 22 July 1871, five days out from Reykjavík, begins with the unremarkable, even pleasant scenery around Hlíðarendi, scene of much of the early action of *Njál's Saga*, where the heroic Gunnar farmed, and which he found too beautiful to leave when sentenced to exile. It is not, however, to see unremarkable, but pleasant scenery that visitors go to Iceland. They want to see the spectacular, awesome crags, steep, black mountains, geysers, hot springs, sulphurous steam, volcanoes and glaciers. And all this – for the tourist, the very essence of the country – is what Morris confronted at first as though facing a mighty enemy, described in terms such as 'horrid', 'terrible', 'dismal', and the like.[19]

The entry for 22 July goes on to provide one of the first extended descriptions in the journal. It is a celebrated word-picture of a very wild area in the south-west of the country, the mountains and cliffs of Goðaland. At times the language employed to convey the horror of the place verges on the Gothic of lurid melodrama:

the cliffs were much higher … and most unimaginably strange: they overhung in some places more than seemed possible; they had caves in them just like the hell-mouths in 13th century manuscripts.

one could see [the glacier's] spiky white waves against the blue sky as we came up to it: but ugh! what a horrid sight it was when we were close, and on it … its great blocks cleft into dismal caves, half blocked up with the sand and dirt it had ground up.

More often the walls would be cleft, and you would see a horrible winding street with stupendous straight rocks for houses on either side.[20]

He added, 'surely it was what I "came out for to see", yet for the moment I felt cowed, and as if I should never get back again.'[21] He did not say this from fear of physical danger (about which he is quite unambiguous later on).[22] He seems, in fact, to have found something in this savage scenery that, in its dreadful correspondence with his own unhappy state of mind, served to confirm and reinforce his depression, without, as yet, allowing him to confront it.

This is not, however, the dominant tone of the journal, for the depression gradually eases. Indeed, anyone who reads the 1871 journal fairly quickly from beginning to end will be struck by a sense of the author's changing mood. It is possible that when Morris was actually making his rough daily notes which eventually became the *Journal*, he was himself unaware of a subtle process whereby his perception of Iceland was being transformed. Underlying this, there is an even more subtle transformation in his perception of his own life. About a week later, in Thorisdale, a region of west-central Iceland, we read again of 'jagged bare mountains', 'dreadful inaccessible ravines', 'toothed peaks and rent walls', and he declares this 'the most horrible sight of mountains I had the whole journey long'.[23] Yet the very next day, in much the same area, he describes with great relish an incident in which one of the pack-horses ran away and spilled one of the boxes on the ground:

and our candles and spare boots and a few other things strewed the soil of Iceland. It doesn't sound very funny to tell of, but it amused us very much at the time, to the extent of setting us into inextinguishable laughter; and in fact I remember still the odd incongruous look of the thing in the face of the horrible black mountains of the waste.[24]

From this time on, the landscape's power to horrify begins to diminish. Morris constantly emphasises the blackness of the mountains, the white of the glaciers, the green of the vegetation, and the barrenness of the wastes; but adjectives such as 'dreadful', 'awful', 'terrible', and the like become rarer, to the point of disappearing. Part of the entry for 10 August says: 'the mountains we look back on, toothed and jagged in an indescribable but well-remembered manner, are very noble and solemn'.[25] It is not that these mountains are in any meaningful way different from those in, say, Thorisdale. Their 'manner' could hardly be 'well-remembered' if they were. But Morris no longer finds them dreadful.

It is worth remembering that at this stage in the tour he had been in Iceland for approaching four weeks, and away from home for five weeks. Now Morris was a man who had hitherto lived all his life in highly comfortable circumstances. And here he was, having spent a rough week aboard a ship, and four weeks trekking over the wild terrain of Iceland, on horseback for much of the day, sleeping under canvas or in humble farm-dwellings. Morris not only cooked food for the party, but also hunted it, in the shape of small birds and fish. The contrast between his normal, civilised – one might almost say effete – lifestyle, and this simple existence could hardly have been greater. He is far from complaining about this; as quoted before, he writes of 'the pleasure of one's animal life'. He had, quite simply, taken more hard physical exercise over those few weeks than the entire sum of many preceding years. He was, by the standards of modern medical science, seriously overweight for most of his adult life. He may not have lost many pounds in Iceland, but must none the less have been physically fitter by far than when he arrived. It is not surprising that a combination of bodily well-being and the exhilarating vitality of primitive daily life helped to raise his spirits. And though these two things could no doubt have been provided in other locations, very few of them could provide a background such as Iceland, as an object to come to terms with. He returned from his voyage refreshed in mind and body, with the seeds beginning to germinate of a new outlook on both life and writing, and confirmed in his love of Iceland and its literature.

The consequences for Morris were of enormous significance, and spread beyond mere translations into much of his own literary output. Before going to Iceland, Morris had produced just two works on Nordic subjects. These are the poems contained in *The Earthly Paradise* called *The Fostering of Aslaug* and *The Lovers of Gudrun*, based on the latter part of *Laxdaela Saga*. About two years after his second visit, Morris had completed his version of the Volsung story, *Sigurd the Volsung*. There appears to be a consensus among critics that the last of these is far more successful than the first two, and that *Aslaug* is much inferior to *Gudrun*.

Without seeking to usurp the function of the literary critic, some reference to the qualities of these three works will serve to illuminate the changes which took place in Morris's outlook during this pivotal period of his life. The story of Aslaug, known to Morris from Thorpe's *Northern Mythology*, is, in Amanda Hodgson's words, a 'rather grim and cynical story' which Morris 'turns into a tender vindication of the power of true love'.[26] She adds that 'this is one of the few poems in which Morris's tendency towards romantic escapism leads him to distort completely the emphasis of his source'. It is noteworthy that *Aslaug*, the earliest and least successful of the three poems, was probably completed before Morris had begun his Icelandic studies with Eiríkr Magnússon. *The Lovers of Gudrun*, by contrast, was written when he was becoming increasingly familiar with Icelandic texts, and, to quote Hodgson:

closer contact with the sagas gave Morris an admiration for their stylistic reticence as well as the depths of emotion to be found in them. At this stage he was enjoying to the full his new freedom to present in art the real feelings of ordinary people. *Art and life were coming into contact again* [our italics] through the influence of the sagas.[27]

The saga literature was not altogether attractive to the spirit of the Pre-Raphaelites. Their medieval appetite fed more on fantasy than on realism, as their particular relish of Malory's *Morte D'Arthur* shows. The extraordinary world of knights errant, giants, enchanted castles, sorcerers, quests, magic swords, forest chapels, sinister guardians of well and grove, and that mystery of mysteries, the Holy Grail – all this, and a melancholy sense of a vanished and noble antiquity, was where their imagination flourished. The sagas, in complete contrast, take place in clearly designated time and space, and deal with real men and women, merchants, brigands, thieves, farmers and their wives, domestic squabbles, and rows with neighbours,[28] all of them characters with familiar motives, and all the events having clear causes.

Morris's move towards this literature represents, therefore, a significant step away from the artistic beliefs of his youth. But it still amounts more to a widening of their scope than to a complete rejection of them. Nor was the transition quick and straightforward. Although *Gudrun* is generally more highly regarded than *Aslaug*, and was at the time of publication perceived as having a greater degree of emotional depth than anything else in *The Earthly Paradise*, it is nevertheless marred compared to the original story by a lack of that very stylistic reticence that Morris so greatly admired. A notorious example of this is the long speech he puts in the mouth of Kjartan, lamenting for his lost love.[29] Now such laments are staple fare for the reader of romances; but they do not sit well in the grittier context of the saga, the writer of which simply observes: '[Kjartan] now heard about Gudrun's marriage and showed no sign of emotion at the news.'[30]

He felt, we are to suppose, a great deal. But he kept his feelings to himself, in the dignified way which the Icelanders thought proper, even in the most trying circumstances. Morris later showed himself to be fully aware of this essential quality of the sagas, saying that in all the stories of the north failure is never reckoned a disgrace, but it is reckoned a disgrace not to bear it with equanimity. From his own private point of view, the perceptive distinction – between failure and disgrace – must have provided much important consolation. The very word 'failure', in this context, may well be a kind of echo of the same word in the letter to Aglaia Coronio which he wrote years before. It is also possible that the lament which Morris composed for Kjartan had its origins in his own feelings about Rossetti and Janey. If so, it may be regarded as a piece of personal as well as literary self-indulgence; and illustrates an interesting coincidence whereby both life and literature, for different reasons, imposed on Morris the same demand for restraint.

It was a demand which, over the years following the journey to Iceland, he grew increasingly capable of meeting. The process culmi-nated in the publication of *Sigurd the Volsung* in November 1876. This immense poem (some 300 pages of long lines) equals or surpasses in sheer quantity the total lifetime output of a great many other poets, famous and not so famous. This apparently prodigious achievement was possible largely because the verses are not carefully crafted, in the manner of the great lyric poets; thus was it possible for Morris to produce this very long work in a matter of a few months, while still fully occupied with the affairs of his firm. It remains a remarkable achievement. His own view that *Sigurd* was his most significant poetic work is generally held to be justified.[31]

But the literary qualities of the poem are not of paramount importance to the biographer. Though critics have disagreed as to the merits of its structure, and the nature of its theme, very few will disagree with Hodgson's verdict on its significance with regard to Morris as *human being*: Morris finally and resoundingly rejects the feeling that as poet he is nothing but the 'idle singer of an empty day'. The day is empty no longer, and the singer has a specific and indispensable task to perform.

Morris never became a vicarious Northman. For though as a critic he responded with full sympathy to the sagas, and in his translations showed great insight into their spirit, he was unable or unwilling to follow their example in his own literary work. The late prose romances create imaginary worlds, containing, as all such worlds do, a commonplace, or realistic foundation which is overlaid with fantasy; and in this they are quite unlike the sagas.

Nevertheless, both the sagas and the Icelandic journeys served to provide both form and content to the romances. One short passage from *The Roots of the Mountains* will serve to illustrate both points:

And beyond these western slopes could men see a low peak spreading down to the plain, till it was like to a bossed shield, and the name of it was Shield-broad.[32]

Anyone who has read any of Morris's translations will recognise this kind of writing. It is the same language, with the same stylistic traits: the quaint syntax (could men see...), and archaisms ('till' for 'until', 'like to' for 'like', and 'the name of it' for 'its name'). Of course, this is English; and its origins may be found more readily in the monuments of late medieval and Renaissance prose, in particular Malory and the Bible, than in anything Icelandic. But, even so, it is a style which Morris originally devised as a suitable medium for conveying his understanding of the sagas. It evidently became so natural and congenial to him that he found a use for it in works entirely of his own imagination, where no questions of translation arose.

It has also been noted by critics from May Morris[33] onwards that many descriptions of scenery in the journals reappear in literary guise in the romances. The passage quoted above, for example, may be found in the *Iceland Journals* in the form:

As we ride on, we see ahead and to our left the wide spreading cone of Skialdbreið [Broad-shield] which is in fact just like a round shield with a boss.[34]

Jane Cooper[35] has found a great many examples of such correspondences – enough to make it quite clear that the Icelandic landscape made an impact on his imagination comparable to some extent with that of the sagas on his literary output.

Finally, it is well worth mentioning that Morris's Icelandic experiences went beyond the personal and the literary, and embraced the Icelanders themselves. The *Iceland Journals* say little explicitly about his feelings for them; but an implicit warmth indicates that he conceived an abiding affection for these cheerful people in their inhospitable environment. Though he made no third visit to the island, he worked very hard in the campaign to raise funds for the relief of a severe famine there in 1882;[36] and in his well-known quotation from 1883 about the baneful effect of class differences, there lies behind the obvious socialistic moral a strong sense of admiration for the Icelanders: 'I learned one lesson there, thoroughly I hope, that the most grinding poverty is a trifling evil compared with the inequality of classes.'[37]

Perhaps he also felt a debt of gratitude for this nation and its culture, which broke the surface of his life at its crucial half-way point, and proved a powerful ally in the painful retreat from sterile goals, and the creation of new, dynamic ones. He was not dissimilar to the Norseman of old, whom Morris himself described as 'a man who had his old religion taken from him and his new one hardly gained',[38] except, of course, that the Norseman's 'new one' was Christianity – which for Morris formed the basis of so much that he came to reject. It is clear that during the years from 1869 to 1871, Morris underwent something akin to a conversion. This was not to any specific creed or system of beliefs – that was to come later – but to something at once more vague and more substantial. It is impossible to put a name to the altered perspective or changed *Weltanschauung* that the Icelandic experience wrought in him; but the self-absorbed, pure artist of the early days of Morris, Marshall, Faulkner & Co. had gone for ever, to be replaced by a man increasingly eager to take part in the affairs of the everyday world, and to strive his utmost to set that world to rights.

NOTES

1. This essay originated in conversations between the authors and Martin Will. The authors have never had the pleasure of visiting Iceland, and were greatly stimulated by Mr Will's evident love of its landscape, history, language and literature. His journeys around Iceland have been somewhat less arduous that those of William Morris, but certainly had a similar effect! We are deeply indebted to him for sharing his knowledge with us, and for acting as a guide to Icelandic language and literature.
2. See, for instance, Morris's comment on what *Völsunga Saga* should mean to his

own age: 'This is the great story of the North, which should be to all our race what the tale of Troy was to the Greeks' (the concluding paragraph of the preface by William Morris and Eiríkr Magnússon to their translation of *Völsunga Saga*, 1870).

3. The meaning of the word has proved impossible to establish, and it remains an uncontroversial mystery.
4. G.W. Dasent, *The Story of Burnt Njal, or Life in Iceland at the End of the Tenth Century: From the Icelandic of the Njals Saga* (2 vols., Edinburgh, 1861).
5. J.W. Mackail, *The Life of William Morris* (1899), Vol. I, p. 39.
6. Ibid., Vol. I, pp. 37–8.
7. See, for example, M.J. Wiener, *English Culture and the Decline of the Industrial Spirit* (Cambridge, 1981).
8. N. Kelvin (ed.), *Collected Letters of William Morris*, Vol. II (Princeton, NJ, 1987), p. 229, William Morris to Andreas Scheu, 5 Sept. 1883.
9. Quoted in A. Vallance, *William Morris: His Art, Writings and Public Life* (London, 1897), p. 193. Buxton Forman's works included *Our Living Poets* (London, 1871) and *The Books of William Morris* (London, 1897).
10. W. Morris and E. Magnússon, 'Preface', *Saga Library*, Vol. I (1891).
11. Obituary of William Morris by Eiríkr Magnússon in the *Cambridge Review*, 26 Nov. 1896.
12. Ibid.
13. R. Quirk, 'Dasent, Morris, and Problems of Translation', *Saga-Book of the Viking Society for Northern Research*, Vol. XIV (1955), p. 64.
14. E. V. Gordon, *An Introduction to Old Norse* (Oxford, 2nd edn. 1957), p. lxxvi. This is not to give the impression that Gordon had a low opinion of Morris's Nordic work. Earlier on the same page he describes him as 'the greatest literary interpreter of the north that has been in England', and says of his translations that 'they have character, and in economy and strength of phrasing are not far behind the originals'.
15. Quirk, 'Dasent, Morris, and Problems of Translation', p. 76.
16. W. Morris, *A Journal of Travel in Iceland in 1871* and *A Diary of Travel in Iceland in 1873* (hereafter *Iceland Journals*), in M. Morris (ed.), *Collected Works of William Morris* (London, 1910–15) (hereafter *Collected Works*), Vol. VIII, *passim*. The original copies are in the British Museum. A fair copy of the 1871 journal written out for Georgiana Burne-Jones is in the Fitzwilliam Museum, Cambridge. Apart from the *Iceland Journals* and Morris's letters, his views on Iceland are most revealingly set out in his preface to the 1869 edition of *The Story of Grettir the Strong* and his 1887 lecture at Kelmscott House, 'The Literature of the North: Iceland'. On the *Iceland Journals*, see also J. Purkis, *The Icelandic Jaunt: A Study of the Expeditions made by Morris to Iceland in 1871 and 1873* (1962, reprinted 1991); H. Bushell, 'News from Iceland', *Journal of the William Morris Society*, Vol. 1 No. 1 (1961), pp. 7–12; F. Kirchhoff, 'Travel as Anti-Autobiography in William Morris's Icelandic Journals', in G. Landow (ed.), *Approaches to Victorian Autobiography* (Athens, OH, 1979); L.A. Baker, 'Iceland and Kelmscott', *Journal of the William Morris Society*, Vol. VI No. 2 (Winter 1984/85), pp. 4–9.

17. N. Kelvin (ed.), *Collected Letters of William Morris*, Vol. I (Princeton, NJ, 1984), p. 173, William Morris to Aglaia Coronio, 25 Nov. 1872.

18. Ibid., p. 172.

19. W. Morris, *Iceland Journals*, 22 July 1871, in *Collected Works*, Vol. VIII, pp. 50–3.

20. Ibid., p. 53.

21. Ibid., p. 54.

22. Ibid., pp. 133–4, 14 Aug. 1871.

23. Ibid., p. 77, 29 July 1871.

24. Ibid., p. 79, 30 July 1871.

25. Ibid., p. 119, 10 Aug. 1871.

26. A. Hodgson, *The Romances of William Morris* (Cambridge, 1987), p. 85.

27. Ibid., pp. 88–9.

28. There are supernatural elements in the sagas, but they seem to represent genuine folk beliefs, and in any case are rarely of any structural significance. An important exception is the fight with the undead Glam, a central episode of *Grettis Saga*.

29. W. Morris, 'The Lovers of Gudrun', *The Earthly Paradise*, in *Collected Works*, Vol. V, p. 320. Kjartan and Bolli are half-brothers, outstanding young men, but Kjartan is in every activity slightly superior. On the surface they are devoted to one another; but Bolli rather deviously gains the heroine, Gudrun, as his wife while Kjartan is away in Norway.

30. M. Magnusson and H. Palsson (trans.), *Laxdaela Saga* (Penguin edn, Harmonds-worth, Middlesex, 1975), p. 111.

31. On *Sigurd*, see J. Hollow (ed.), *The After-Summer Seed: Reconsiderations of William Morris's The Story of Sigurd the Volsung* (1978).

32. W. Morris, *The Roots of the Mountains*, in *Collected Works*, Vol. XV, p. 307.

33. There are numerous references to this topic in May Morris's introductions to the *Collected Works*; see, for example, Vol. XVII, p. xxi; Vol. XXI, p. xi.

34. *Iceland Journals*, 29 July 1871, in *Collected Works*, Vol. VIII, p. 76.

35. J. Cooper, 'The Iceland Journey and the Late Romances', *Journal of the William Morris Society*, Vol. 5 No. 4 (Winter 1983/84), pp. 40–59.

36. See Kelvin (ed.), *Collected Letters*, Vol. II, pp. 116–19, 129–33, 146; R.L. Harris, 'William Morris, and the Icelandic Relief Efforts of 1882', *Saga-Book*, Vol. 20 (1978/79), pp. 31–41; R.C. Ellison, 'The Alleged Famine in Iceland', *Saga-Book*, Vol. 22 (1988), pp. 165–79.

37. Kelvin (ed.), *Collected Letters*, Vol. II, p. 229, William Morris to Andreas Scheu, 5 Sept. 1883.

38. J.M.S. Tompkins, *William Morris: An Approach to the Poetry* (1988), p. 233. Tompkins is quoting from a letter from Morris to Charles Eliot Norton, 21 Dec. 1869. See Kelvin (ed.), *Collected Letters*, Vol. I, p. 99.

— 5 —

George Wardle's 'Memorials of William Morris'

I N 1897, WHEN J.W. Mackail was researching his two-volume *Life of William Morris*, he asked George Wardle to set down his recollections of Morris and the firm. Wardle, who had worked with Morris for 25 years until his retirement in 1890, responded promptly, sending Mackail 30 pages of manuscript. While Mackail's research notebooks were later presented by his wife Margaret to the William Morris Gallery at Walthamstow, the 'Memorials' came into the possession of May Morris, and formed part of the collection of family papers at Kelmscott Manor. After her death in 1938, they were presented to the British Library by her literary executor, Dr Robert Steele.[1] Though they were quoted at length by Mackail, and have frequently been used by more recent biographers, they have not been readily accessible to all those interested in the life and work of William Morris.[2] The 'Memorials' are one of the most significant items in the Morris Papers for the study of Morris & Co. and William Morris as businessman. They contain fascinating insights into Morris's work practices and the operation of the firm. We believe that they merit a wide readership.

Initial paragraphs describe the early years of the firm, with its emphasis on glass, tiles and wallpapers. Wardle notes the limits to the firm's capabilities in the early years. It had to rely upon outside suppliers for many products, and though Jeffrey & Co., which printed all Morris's wallpapers, produced satisfactory results, this was not true of other manufacturers. Wardle recalls the difficulties experienced with Kidderminster carpets, highlighting the gulf between the work practices of an established manufacturer and Morris's approach to design and production. In an oft-quoted paragraph, Wardle also relates what happened when Morris's design proved unexpectedly popular, and the manufacturer sold pirated versions to Maples.

Wardle goes on to describe the persistent attempts which were made during the 1870s to widen the product range – the origins of Morris's experiments with dyeing, and the move into carpets and woven textiles. Wardle recalls the role which Morris played in the management of the firm. He discusses the process of designing, painting and installing stained glass windows; emphasising that, though others might be responsible for preparing cartoons and the actual painting and firing of the glass, it was Morris's eye for colour and his oversight of the whole process which was largely responsible for the success of the firm's stained glass. Morris's role in designing for woven and printed fabrics is also discussed. Wardle provides a clue to Morris's extraordinary productivity during these years – his ability to work on many different projects in at the same time. Thus he could continue working on his poetry while at the same time designing for glass, wallpapers and textiles.

Wardle next describes the search for new premises, which led to the move to Merton Abbey in 1881. It was necessitated by the growth of the business, and Morris's growing determination to internalise dyeing, weaving and block printing. One immediate benefit was the development of tapestry weaving under John Henry Dearle. Wardle deals with the history and importance of the high warp loom, and the recruitment and training of the firm's apprentices. There is then a long section on Morris and the founding of the Society for the Protection of Ancient Buildings – with which Wardle was also involved. He collaborated with Morris and Webb in drawing up a programme setting forth the Society's views and aims, and regularly attended its meetings. In 1886, he was sent by the Society to Venice with Professor John Henry Middleton to examine the restoration work which was being undertaken at St Mark's. He subsequently became a Committee member, along with his brother-in-law, Sir Thomas Wardle. In this section, Wardle explains the kind of damage which could result to old stonework when new glass was inserted, and recalls the impact which the decision not to supply glass for the restoration of medieval buildings had upon the firm's business. This decision seemed a peculiar one to potential customers, who regarded Morris's work as intensely 'medieval', and thus ideally suited to restoration projects. In refuting the notion that Morris imitated any particular style, Wardle is able to provide a valuable assessment of Morris's approach to design.

As an afterthought, there is a discussion of Morris's socialism and its impact upon his work practices. The adoption of limited forms of profit-sharing is described, but it is emphasised that, for Morris, this could only be a partial and unsatisfactory answer to the problem – as Wardle put it, 'you cannot have socialism in a corner'. The location of this section as an addendum is not without significance. Wardle, as he once admitted to Sydney Cockerell, had little sympathy with Morris's socialism; his attention was focused on the running of the firm.[3] Nevertheless, he recognised the importance of Morris's socialism to an appreciation of the man as a whole.

For the most part, Wardle's 'Memorials' are fluently written and well organised. Marginal and other notes which he provides are given in curly brackets as close as possible to the relevant point in the main text. Deletions and alterations are also given in curly brackets where they add substantially to our understanding. A few explanatory notes are required. Brief additions are inserted in the text in square brackets; longer notes are given as endnotes.

CHRISTMAS 1897

I first saw Morris in '64 or '65 at Red Lion Square where I went to offer him copies of some drawings I had made of the pattern work etc. on the screens and roofs of churches in Suffolk. I showed him some drawings I had made in Southwold and Blythburgh.[4] He struck me as being a man overworked. Those were the early days of the Firm, business was unremunerative & perhaps a large share of the work had to be done by him. If he was writing also at the time he would have had more than his hands full and much anxiety added to the labour. The bad business seemed to have affected Faulkner.[5] He was then working at tile painting, I think. He had a harassed and forpined look which spoke of hard times. I saw also Warrington Taylor [sic],[6] and he already being seriously ill, helped to give me the impression of gloomy affairs which I carried away with me. Morris asked me soon after this to put on wood some drawings Burne-Jones was then making for illustration of the Cupid & Psyche.[7] {Marginal note: Sir Edward must excuse me for using the name by which I then knew him.} I was very glad to do so, & here began an experience often repeated when I came to know more of the ways of the Firm. It was practically impossible to get the drawings properly cut. Perhaps, if Mr. Morris could have given the price which a first rate cutter would have charged for doing the work *with his own hand*, they might have come out as they were drawn, but in the ordinary course of the trade it was impossible. I think also that [the] same 'course' would have prevented even the other arrangement, had there been no other difficulty. Mr. Morris asked me then if I would try to cut these blocks. This I did, & after a few experiments, he was well enough pleased to give me one & then another, but, after that, I got no more & wondered for a while, why? as I thought the second was certainly better than the first. The reason was a characteristic one. Mr. Morris became possessed by the idea of cutting the blocks himself. If I could do it, why not he? and he took them all in hand & carried them through, not without some lively scenes in Queen Square, for the Firm had now moved there.[8] He cut with great ardour and with much knowledge of the forms certainly, but the work did not always go to his mind. It was necessarily slow & he constitutionally quick. There were then quarrels between them. In the end, the idea of publishing was given up and 'Cupid & Psyche' appeared as one of the stories of the Earthly Paradise. The beautiful editions of later days were already in his mind, but indeed the time was too early.

It was in 1866 (?) when I joined The Firm in Queen Square as draughtsman and bookkeeper and utility man generally, poor Taylor being then about to retire.[9] I found Morris looking better and in good spirits. His literary work was well forward & the other part of his business was doing better, but there was not yet a profit, I think. There are accounts [which] will tell you precisely, if it is of importance. I can remember that after Taylor's retirement I had to dispute the claim of the Income Tax assessor & I showed that the business had paid tax during the three preceding years on a loss. That calculation however was probably made on the average of the three years & may not have been the last of them. Certainly things were improving & always went forward afterwards. It was high time for Mr. Morris had spent all or nearly all his private means.[10]

The business was then chiefly glass painting. Windows for churches – usually commemorative; 'grave stones' Morris called them. The cartoons for the figures, then almost wholly furnished by B-J [Burne-Jones] were much desired by certain Architects & their recommendation began to have [an] effect on a part of the public, so that a very respectable but necessarily small clientele was formed. Of course all the quality of what was called 'Morris glass' was due to the interpretation Morris gave to the designs he received & to the practical use of colour, which in his hands gave results no other glass painters could imitate, though some of them got now & then designs (cartoons) from Burne-Jones & the same raw materials were at the disposal of all of them. Morris often regretted he was not able to make the glass himself.[11] With a little more space & a little more money he might have done it & I have no doubt he would have succeeded as he afterwards did with other manufactures. If fortune had been kinder at first we should have had results in colour far surpassing in variety of the hues & in splendour of tone the best he was ever able to do with the rather commonplace material supplied by the makers. Not only the colouring of the windows, the design of it, taking it as a whole, was Mr. Morris's & usually also such details as were not human figures. For these he had the help of Mr. Burne Jones and Ford Madox Brown & there were certain cartoons which were invariably sent to Philip Webb, animals and certain ornaments. Since & even before the time when I began to have any knowledge of the working, Rossetti had ceased to design or take any part in the conduct of the business, Mr. Faulkner had gone to Oxford, & Marshall had returned to his practice as an engineer.

Besides glass painting there was still done a little tile painting; but since the practical retirement of Mr. Faulkner this was but little & mostly of pattern tiles for fireplaces.

Wallpapers were, next to glass painting, the most hopeful part of the business. It was not too difficult to get these fairly well done outside, & Mr. Morris therefore designed for them with pleasure. He never had a factory for printing wallpapers. They were done for us by Messrs. Jeffrey & Co. of Islington & were done so carefully & with such anxious desire to satisfy all Mr. Morris's requirements that there was no necessity to take them more completely into our own hands. Besides glasspainting & wallpapers the Firm had a reputation for its furniture. The partner to whom was due the success of this branch of the business was Mr. Philip Webb, & only when a piece of furniture had to be decorated did it pass into Mr. Morris's hands. In such a case he designed the gilded or painted pattern work, carving he did not attempt.

House decoration was, I think, begun as a business, after I joined, though the decoration of Mr. Morris's house at Upton[12] was probably the beginning of everything. This house, designed by Philip Webb was no doubt talked about, both for its architecture and the internal decorations, & after it the house in Queen Square, the upper part of which was occupied by Mr. Morris after selling the other.[13] The decoration of the drawing rooms in Queen Square in which both Mr. Morris and Webb had part was original & though extremely simple, very beautiful. No doubt this was talked about & a desire created to have the same methods of decoration applied elsewhere. Mr. Webb also, in his practice as an Architect was glad to have his house finished by Mr. Morris, when he could so far prevail with the client. There were also the houses of Burne-Jones & Rossetti; evidence of what might be done even in that most unlovely period, when clear ideas as to decorative design controlled the arrangement. I think the house of Mr. Thomas Wells, in Manchester Square, was the first Mr. Morris was called upon to decorate. This was done very simply but must have astonished those who had been accustomed only to the sombre platitudes of the ordinary 'decorator'. There had been however much more important work done before this at Cambridge, in the Chapel at Jesus College & at Queens' where the great chimney piece was covered with painted tiles. I do not know the dates of these works, they were both before my time.[14]

Such things, in which the handiwork of more or less cultivated artists could be directly employed, was all it was possible to do at that time. The furniture we were able to make, excellent in many ways but restricted absolutely within the limits of what could be planed or turned, was only made possible, even on that condition, by the admirably adapted designs Mr. Webb gave use. Wallpapers depended fortunately, once the blocks were cut, only on the fidelity of the colour mixer & this was secured by the loyal co-operation of Mr. Metford Warner, the acting partner of the Firm of Jeffrey & Co. We were not equally fortunate in another kind of printing, furniture chintzes, though the sagacity of Mr. Morris found a means of stopping at least for a time the want there was of decent design and colouring in this commonest article of domestic decoration. He found by inquiring of one of the old established firms of furniture printers, that the blocks of some of their earliest productions were still in existence & that the processes of printing the patterns were not yet forgotten, though long since superseded by modern 'styles'.[15] After a few trials the best of these patterns were reproduced in the original colourings & they took their places as novelties when exhibited in 'the shop'.

With these slender means: a few old fashioned chintzes, the wall-papers, an excellent pattern of rush bottomed chair, copied I believe from an old one found by Warrington Taylor in Sussex, the few but admirable pieces of furniture designed by Webb and Mr. Morris's eye for colour, we began our career as house decorators & furnishers. At first we had no carpets of our own and when a customer could not afford the cost of one of the fine India carpets which at that time were almost all that could be had of oriental manufacture, we could do nothing for him beyond recommending the quietest kind of Brussels or Kidder-minster. An excellent coarse serge, dyed to quiet but rather characterless colours, was supplied to us by a manufacturer in the north, J. Aldham Heaton, & we were able to make some use of it for curtains where chintzes were inapplicable; but this was only a makeshift and could scarcely be used without some additions of positive colours, only to be given by embroidery. {Marginal note: Mrs. Morris will tell you about the wall hangings made for his own house at [Upton] of this serge embroidered by her and others with figures of Helen, S. Catherine etc. etc. & also of the subsequent & later developments of the embroidery business. Also as regards the first part of the time Ph[ilip] Webb.} Amongst the furnishings most needed, then, were carpets & curtain stuffs. The history of our difficulties in producing the first Kidderminster carpet will be a good illustration of the general, invariable opposition, which Mr. Morris's efforts to improve existing methods, excited, not from ill will but from sheer ignorance and well intentioned desire to set him right.

You will think perhaps that we began in the wrong way & that Mr. Morris may have tried to reform too violently. Not so. What W.M. proposed to himself & the manufacturer was not that the latter should reform his styles or alter in any way his machinery, but that he should at the outset set out for our guidance whatever conditions were inherent to the manufacture itself & to these conditions the designs Mr. Morris might make were to be rigidly adapted. The endeavour, out of these conditions, to produce a better kind of design was to be made at our expense and with no risk to the manufacturer whatever. Under this arrangement it might be thought that the difficulties before us were only those inherent in the nature of the material & the limited capabilities of the loom, or in Mr. Morris's inexperience. By no means. The one & only difficulty was presented by the manufacturer himself by his narrow minded stupidity, by his incompetence & reticence. It was too funny when all was over & we discovered what was the true inwardness of all the objections raised from the moment he saw the design. But while it lasted, & it was certainly for six months at least, it was maddening & puzzling beyond words. The first objection however excepted, that was

easily understood and made us all shout with laughter. The manufacturer
gravely pointed out to us that the pattern Mr. Morris had designed
'would never do', – it would not sell – it was not in the style, & he
suggested that we should allow his designer to do something for us. It
was but a feeble reply to point out to him that the risk was ours; there
was nothing sordid in his intention, he wished to save our money for us
& also he had the very proper & natural disinclination to undertake
what he felt certain must be a failure. At that time the highest ambition
of a Kidderminster carpet was to represent, so far as it might, a Brussels,
& patterns were all of the kind known as 'Brussels'.[16] Mr. Morris
perceiving the real nature of the cloth and its peculiar attributes, had
designed an essentially Kidderminster pattern. It was this departure
from convention which had so disturbed the maker of Kidderminster.
He could not understand that Mr. Morris's object was to do something
characteristic, to get out of a given material & a given process the best
that was *natural* to both. His experience led him to suppose that ours
was only another case of the starting of a new firm & the preparation of
a set of patterns to be appropriated to it. Manufacturers' patterns,
differing in no respects from all his others but earmarked 'Morris' & to
be reserved for our special use. Well we got through all this, after
having elicited that there was no 'mechanical' reason why the pattern
Mr. Morris had made should not be produced as designed. The fight
began again over the actual production of the pattern. This was so far
proceeded with that a small trial piece of the carpet was submitted. It
was a horror, almost unrecognisable. One might have thought that the
designer, as they call in a carpet manufactory the man or boy who puts
patterns on to point paper, had determined to justify the first con-
temptuous opinion of his employer. Certainly, if so published the
carpet would never have sold to anyone. But no! all had been done in
pure & simple good faith. He intended no harm whatever, only, as he
could see no merit in the unpretentious design he was unable to
reproduce it fairly or make it other than he conceived it to be. Here
was a frightful stumbling block. We protested *that* was not what we
intended. We were told 'that was how it came out'. But why do you alter
the drawing? 'It is not altered, only it shows like that in the cloth.' But
surely it is not necessary to do so and so? 'He would see his designer
again and ask the question.' For it must be remarked that one of the
characteristics of the modern manufacturer is that he knows very little
about the manufacture he professes. He employs a 'manager' who sees

to the working of the machinery & executes orders and a 'designer' who makes what patterns are required. He himself is but a speculator, an employer of capital. Our manufacturer could therefore say very little in reply to our queries & helped us none at all. An interview was then arranged with the designer, who seemed to be the person to make our difficulties or remove them. I went down to Yorkshire for that purpose & in five minutes found out what was at the bottom of the whole matter – he could not draw! I brought back to London some point paper on which to transfer the design & in a week the pattern was correctly reproduced in Kidderminster cloth.[17] This pattern it is worth noting, as showing how thoroughly Mr. Morris thought out his work, is probably the best that has ever been produced for that kind of cloth. It is adapted perfectly to the nature of the material & and to the capabilities of the loom &, not less, to the low condition of the art of dyeing of those days. This last was not the least merit in a fabric which was essentially a cheap one made of coarse wool, incapable of much mingling of colours or of any great purity or brilliancy of dye & generally esteemed a low class article. By masterly use of the three or four colours permitted by the manufacture and by choosing only those which the coarse grey wool could not sully Mr. Morris gave us a carpet which was fit to go anywhere, which could maintain its proper place when used even with much richer material, & would form an admirable foil for more positive colour.

Mr. Morris had not then a dye house of his own & was dependent absolutely on others for the colours of woven stuffs. The dyes, colours, then in use were mostly fugitive as to their substance & shocking to the eye. The only resource for a colourist in those circumstances was to choose tones which were deep & rather neutral than crude. Being of deep full tone they would be able to give up something to light & air & still have something left for the purchaser. Mr. Morris showed his usual sagacity in adopting this system of colour so long as the production of the colours themselves was beyond his control. His skill as a colourist was shown in combining colours which, separately, were of but very mediocre character. This system of colour, which may be called provisional, marks very distinctly what may be called the first period of the history of the Firm: when Mr. Morris had not yet a dyehouse & when he was still in association, more nominal than real certainly with the original members. The peacock blues, rusty reds and olive greens of that period were not by any means Mr. Morris's ideal, but the best he

Plate 5.1 Design for *African Marigold* chintz, 1876 *William Morris Gallery*

could get done. As soon as he was able to set up his own dyehouse he turned at once to the frank full hues of the permanent dyestuffs – indigo blue, madder red, the yellow of weld etc. etc., & with these he produced the beautiful Hammersmith carpets and the Merton tapestry & chintzes.

An amusing story turns on the change from 'provisional' hues to the permanent dyes which he finally arrived at. Naturally a good many of our customers did not understand the reason of the change and there were some would-be customers who knew nothing of it. One such {marginal note: Mattey} asked for an interview, in Oxford Street, to discuss the carpeting of his new house. Mr. Morris laid before him the best specimens of the Hammersmith make. To these the customer gave a rather impatient attention & at last asked 'if there were others'. No said Mr. Morris unless you will accept a Kidderminster. These were out of the question & Mr. Morris never liked putting forward the Brussels or Wilton which we did not make ourselves. But, said the great man 'I thought your colours were always "subdued".' That irritated Morris intensely. He could not bear to be asked for those earlier productions when he had succeeded in obtaining what he himself so much preferred, & he told the customer that if he wanted *dirt* 'he could find that in the street'. Where I believe the man turned, & that was the beginning & and the end of the negotiation. Morris was capable of thus trampling on his dead self more resolutely than any man I have known. Another man & certainly a tradesman would have explained, but Morris's satisfaction with the new dyes was too great to allow him to think any discussion possible, & having himself cast the old makeshifts aside, once and for all, he could not bear any reference to them more.

A sequel to that story of the carpet-making is not less characteristic. Our manufacturer, who had feared that he would never be asked to deliver a single yard of the carpet, when he found orders coming in was at first very well pleased, then, becoming aware [that] there was some-thing in the design which 'took', thought he might make a little more profit out of it, &, without our consent or knowledge, he made and sold the carpet to a large furnishing house in Tottenham Court-road. The carpet Mr. Morris had designed, for which he had paid all initial expenses & a good price for the reproduction! In no case could it appear that the mere employer of machinery engaged in the production of a design had less claim to call the work his own. We had also his personal assurance that the pattern would be reserved exclusively for us. Never-theless, he sold this as his own, to another tradesman whom he may have supposed our rival! & we have reason to believe that he sold it at a lower price than that charged to us. When this came to our knowledge, Mr. Morris, thinking it useless to remonstrate with such a blackguard, decided to call on the London tradesman & and ask him if he was aware that the carpet was our private design & that the manufacturer had no right to sell it. He did so & the tradesman acknowledged at once that he was aware of the origin of the design. Then, said Mr. Morris, do you think it fair to treat me so? To which the man replied 'He thought it was fair that the sun should shine a little on him also.' (He was by the way one of the most successful tradesmen in London – Sir John Maple). I was with Morris at this interview & had to restrain myself from asking if he called stealing a pattern 'sunshine', but I left everything to Morris, who said not a word beyond 'good morning'. Whether he was flabber-gasted by the astounding impudence of this speech I do not know, but I supposed afterwards that he was struck by the truth at the bottom of the remark, – that the power of the design, as all other gifts of nature, is not created by the owner, & that his possessing such power did not make it his exclusive property. Of course it would be absurd to apply that principle under the present condition of things & Mr. Morris took care to insure himself against such accidents in the future, but Mr. Morris was then pondering those principles of socialism which he openly professed some years later & he gave loyal acceptance to a proposition he would have liked to see generally adopted. Shortly after, we were able to change the colouring of this pattern, using a dye the disloyal manufacturer knew nothing of & would not be likely to obtain, but the first success of that pattern clung to it & the new colouring, though most beautiful & in all respects finer, never displaced the first from favour.

The growth of the business prompted us about this time to take premises in Oxford Street {Marginal note: 1877} for showrooms & warehouse of the furnishing goods, but before that Mr. Morris had been obliged to give up the whole of the house in Queen Square to the business. {Marginal note: end of 1872} We used the old drawing room as showroom & the upper rooms as work rooms. In order to make room for us Mr. Morris moved to the little house on the Kew road, near Chiswick. {Marginal note: Horrington House. End of 1872.} He did not stay there very long. The house at Hammersmith became vacant & he took it. I cannot give the dates of these changes but they will be found in the books of the Firm.[18]

The conversion of the house in Queen Square into offices, workshop & showroom seemed almost a desecration, but I do not think Mr. Morris felt the change very much. He was rather elated by the prospect of getting out of it a little dye shop. This was established in the basement, in the old scullery and larder. Here he began at once to practise the ancient methods of dyeing with indigo, madder, weld, walnut juice & such other dyestuffs he found mentioned in the old books. Of such that is of which he could get specimens. He was much delighted by the present of a box of Kermes from Greece. This made the finest of the old red dyes – the deep vermilion we see in the tapestries of the 14th & 15th centuries. Quaritch and Ellis[19] will both be able to tell you of the enquiry he had been making before this for old books on the art of dyeing. The most helpful were those published in France in the 17th century. The reading of these & the mastery of the processes he soon acquired, working them all out in imagination, step by step, as the books described them, prepared him so well that he found himself at home when he had got a few vats and becks about him. This reading, moreover, excited him greatly so that he was impatient to begin and always more and more impatient of the poor results both in respect of colour & stability he was obliged to put up with until then. Mr. Morris did everything at first with his own hands or with the help of a boy (John Smith) who had been errand boy to the glass-painters. So well had Mr. Morris prepared himself for this experiment that I do not think a single dyeing went wrong nor was any appreciable quantity of yarn wasted. The yarns dyed were used for the pile carpets, for he began this business about the same time & in Queen Square. The first carpet looms were set up in the top storey of No. 26, & we got a carpet knotter (so called) from Glasgow to teach the girls the working.[20] She stayed with us a few weeks only. Afterwards, when Mr. Morris had removed to Kelmscott House he set up carpet looms of greater beam in the coach house there & so these carpets came to be called 'Hammersmith'.

About the same time we set up a silk loom in premises we hired in Great Ormond Yard, building an upper floor with proper lights for the purpose.[21] As Mr. Morris could not himself dye the fine silk required for damasks etc., that experiment was almost a failure until we got to Merton,[22] where having sufficient room for a properly furnished dye house, we engaged an old-style dyer whom we found in the East of London & with his help were able to do all the dyeing which needed Mr. Morris's immediate supervision.

Before bringing you to Merton it will be as well to say something of Mr. Morris's general supervision of the business & of the share he took in the work of the Firm.

As regards the glass painting and the designing pertaining to that, the ordinary course was this. The scheme or general plan of a window was settled by Mr. Morris & with the concurrence of the client, sometimes not without his extreme opposition. For some customers pushed by I know not what influence to employ us, resisted with fear & astonishment the proposals submitted to them & the discussion ended, if not by a refusal to go further, then sometimes in a compromise which impaired the originality and beauty of the first conception. Then, the window ordered, Mr. Morris distributed to the other members of the Firm the parts of the design for which they would make cartoons, reserving for himself usually the so-called 'ornamental' portions. But not always, for I found in the portfolio many cartoons for figures, Saints and Angels which had been made by Mr. Morris.[23] I am describing the later practice. In my time Morris was most pleased to undertake such designs as that of the great tree in the dais window at Peterhouse.[24] In after times, when other occupation left him little time for this work, he was able to hand it over to Mr. W.E. Pozzi, who became very skilful in the design of foliage. I mention his name as I shall those of other collaborateurs [sic] because as a founder of the Arts & Crafts Exhibition Society Mr. Morris established the principle of recognising all help he received in his work. When all the cartoons were completed then Mr. Morris 'coloured' the window – that is, he dictated to the foreman of the painters, G.F. Campfield,[25] what glass should be used for each part, in detail. This settled, the various parts were distributed to the painters, whose work as it went on Mr. Morris was able to watch, though he usually reserved any comments until the painter had done all he thought necessary. If then, or after the figure or picture had been burnt & leaded up, any alterations were needed, retouches were made or new glass was cut & the part began again. When all the parts were done came the final review of the window, a very difficult task in Queen Square, but here again Mr. Morris showed how quick was his perception and how tenacious the memory. In passing all the parts of a large window one by one before the light, he never lost sight of the general tone of the colour or of the relation of this part & that to each other. An important work he would see again after it was in its place. In designing for carpets everything of course depended upon him. He would first make a small drawing to a scale of, say, one-

Plate 5.2 Cartoon for stained glass: St Mary of Bethany, by William Morris
William Morris Gallery

eighth of the full size, which he would colour carefully. This drawing was enlarged by a draughtsman for the 'point paper', on which he made the final design, stitch by stitch. The 'point paper' on which all designs for woven stuff are made, is paper divided into minute squares each of which represents a thread of silk or a knot (tuft) of carpet. As already shown, the whole character of the work depends on the way the design is expressed by the 'points' or squares. For that reason it was impossible to leave this work to a subordinate, though, I must say that, after a while Mr. Morris had a most useful assistant in this part of the business in Mr. Robert West, who relieved him of the enormous labour of pointing large designs for silk, damasks, etc. containing many thousand points perhaps.[26] All the designs Mr. Morris made for woven stuffs were prepared in this way. After our first experience never again did we allow a professional 'designer' to interpret one of our patterns.

A word may be said about the designs for blockprinting, whether for wallpapers or for chintzes. These were in one respect simpler, for the drawing required no translation: mere transfer from paper to block. But even this had to be watched & the cutter's tracing on transfer paper was always submitted to Mr. Morris before he was allowed to rub it off. In preparing the design however all was not so simple – constant watch had to be kept for the effects produced by the necessary repetitions of the pattern on wall or curtain, & very curious experience we sometimes had when the repeats of a pattern came to be joined round the original unit. In order to see that all went well therefore, it was necessary to have at least parts of eight repeats of the design and sometimes entire repeats carefully drawn round the central 'model'. This precaution, which could not be neglected either in designs for woven fabrics, made the process of designing very laborious and costly also, but Mr. Morris never grudged pains or expense in the preparation of his designs.

While he was doing these things – designing for painted glass, for wallpapers & textiles & occasionally for wall decoration, superintending also the whole of the business; he was engaged also with his poems, more or less as opportunity served. His faculty for work was enormous & wonderfully versatile. He could turn his mind at once to the new matter brought before him & leave the poetry or the design without a murmur. How rapidly & accurately he wrote you know, almost without correction, page after page, but I may say that I always admired the easy way in which he turned from this ordinarily engrossing pursuit to attend to any other & resume his favourite work without apparently the loss of a single thread as calmly as a workman goes back to the bench after dinner. Of his dealings with the compositors you will hear from Ellis, but I think they were very easy, for his handwriting was most legible. There is, however, one fiend found in every printing office who is called 'reader'. Is that not so? I believe he was the occasion of frightful indignation on Morris' part for this man persisted in altering the punctuation of the MS. & Morris only got him to desist by threatening to kill him.

It was after the publication of the 'Earthly Paradise' & while he was writing shorter poems, 'Love is Enough' etc., that he began to put some of these into ornamental writing & to illuminate the pages.[27] This amused him greatly & was a refreshment after the strain of the longer work. In one way it had enduring effects for, having drilled himself to write formally & in beautiful characters, he established for himself a new cursive hand, which never left him. {Marginal note: His earlier writing had been at times difficult to read.} The MSS. written by him, not all of them his own poems, but many of them translations of Sagas, and illuminated partly by himself, partly by E. Burne-Jones and Fairfax Murray, have been exhibited at the Arts & Crafts.

With all this work & the increased business which Mr. Morris's activity in producing new designs and new fabrics brought with it, the premises in Queen Square, supplemented by the workshops in Ormond Yard, were insufficient & we looked round very anxiously for a suitable place out of Town, where we could have the necessary buildings & also good water for dyeing. Mr. Morris was inclined to take an old cloth mill in Gloucestershire of which he had heard. But that gave too little accommodation with too much inconvenience. We examined two sites near London and were delighted finally to hear that the old print works at Merton Abbey were to let. It was Mr. William De Morgan, himself casting about for a site for his kilns, who told us of this. It was almost ideally what we wanted; there were the requisite sheds for carpet weavers and block printers and dyehouse & others were easily adaptable for silk weavers & the glass painters. There was also Manager's House and Offices and caretaker's lodge. Moreover the Wandle, which ran through the premises is exactly the water we wanted for madder dyeing. There was an old fashioned garden too, long neglected and drooping, but under Mr. Morris's care it soon resumed its ancient gaiety. There were two large plots of kitchen garden & a croft. This last also useful to us for clearing the grounds of our calico prints after dyeing – a process called 'crofting'. Round this croft Mr. Morris immediately planted poplar trees. The kitchen garden he divided into plots & let to certain of the workmen. The transfer to Merton was made somewhat later than the opening of the showroom in Oxford St. {Marginal note: End of 1881.} We were obliged to keep open for a time the showroom in Queen Square. People had got to know it. I think some of our customers disliked the change to Oxford St.

The tapestry work was only fairly begun after we moved to Merton. Our first piece there was I think, a frieze for an old house {Crossed out note: Naworth?}.[28] Our next was the Three Kings for Exeter Coll. Chapel, from Mr. Burne-Jones's design.[29] The former piece, a greenery with birds, was designed by Mr. Morris. This art of tapestry was a revival by Mr. Morris of the ancient Arras. In beginning he had nothing to guide him, as to the mechanical part, but drawings of looms in old books & the practice at the Gobelins, where, though the art had been degraded to the servile purpose of reproducing oil pictures, the ancient loom is still in use. When Mr. Morris was first thinking about the possibility of making good tapestry he went to Windsor to see the looms established there. These he at once saw were useless to him, the only work to be done by them being of the most mechanical order. Now tapestry to be worth doing must be *picture making*, not the production of a picture & such kind of tapestry, in which the artist is free to think & combine & to act really as an artist, is only possible in the antique loom, the loom at which Penelope worked and Arachne[30] – by which stories are told at the will of the worker. This loom, equally fit for plain cloth & for picture work, is the original loom of the world, only superseded for the cheaper ordinary stuffs by the variously modified looms adapted each to some specific manufacture & like other specialists losing in the intensity of its production of one thing the power to produce any other. It is known in the old books as the 'high-warp' loom, de haute lisse (stamen, you know, & στήμων are the older names for the warp of a piece of cloth). The warp of the modern loom, whether for tapestry or plain cloths, is horizontal. The upright warp allows the weaver to see his work before him like a picture on the easel. Having decided that this was the only loom in which tapestry could be worthily made, Mr. Morris had such a loom constructed in his bedroom at Kelmscott House and there he worked at it, teaching himself, in the early hours of the summer days.[31] Very soon he had mastered all that belonged to knowledge of the process, the rest was practice, and then he had another loom built at

Queen Square when he taught what he knew to William Dearle [sic],[32] who was then a boy willing to adapt himself to anything which gave him a chance of employment. Dearle got on so well that very soon we took in two other boys, Sleath & Knight,[33] as his apprentices. When we moved to Merton therefore, we had already three 'hands' fairly competent in this art. The first piece Dearle accomplished was the 'Goose Girl' designed by Walter Crane, this was begun and finished I think at Queen Square. At Merton the boys who were still young lived in the house. We gave them board & lodging & a certain weekly stipend. It is worth while to note here that there was no sort of selection of these boys or of any others who were brought up by us to one or other branch of Mr. Morris's business. John Smith who is now the dyer at Merton[34] was taken into the dye shop because it was just being set up at the time he was getting too old to remain an errand boy. Dearle, equally, was put to the tapestry because that business then wanted an apprentice and so of the other two. They were put to the loom because at the time we were starting this, we were asked to do something for them. We took Sleath on that ground first of all & he introduced Knight. The same rule applied to all others, & its working justified Mr. Morris's contention that the universal modern system, which he called that of 'devil take the hindmost', is frightfully wasteful of human intelligence. In the ordinary operation of the system, bootblacking or running errands & from that to pot boy, perhaps is the fate of *lucky* youngsters who are thrown upon the world of London to shift for themselves. Under a proper system of organised education & employment we might get from our street arabs work which would make their lives happier and ours more beautiful. A few years later when we were able to set up a third tapestry loom, we found a lad with equal facility. Without selection of any kind, the nephew of the housekeeper at Merton, who made an excellent tapestry worker. She happened to tell me, at the time we were getting ready the new loom that her nephew had left school & was looking for something to do. It is however fair to add that in putting Dearle to the work in the first instance Mr. Morris was influenced by the evident intelligence & brightness of the boy. Dearle was the teacher of all who followed him & is now I think the Director of the Merton Works.

The making of tapestry, long thought of by Mr. Morris, was rendered possible & only possible by the possession of a dyehouse. It will easily be seen that when, as in mosaic & tapestry work the aim of [the] artist is the vivid presentment of a simple scene without such artifices of light &

Plate 5·3 High-warp tapestry weaving at Merton Abbey *William Morris Gallery*

Plate 5.4 *The Adoration of the Magi*, with figures by Edward Burne-Jones; ten versions were produced at Merton Abbey between 1890 and 1907 *Norwich Museums Service (Norwich Castle Museum)*

shade as the oil painter may use, the finer qualities of the work will depend upon the force & purity of a few colours and also that the preparation of the colours themselves is in that case of immense importance, more especially when that is limited by the number of available dyestuffs & by conditions of permanence. In such circum-stances a successful colouring can only be got by one who knows all the conditions, those of the preparation of the colour as of the use of them. Morris the tapestry weaver therefore had a great advantage on this side, over Morris the glass painter, for he was at once colour maker and colourist.

Of the work at Merton there seems nothing to say except that it was altogether delightful. We had a spacious ground floor, well lighted, for the carpet looms &, over it, a 'shop' for the block printers. This was another advantage gained by the change: we now began to print chintzes. We had a dyehouse appropriated to them & other necessary 'ageing' rooms etc., etc.; we had also a dyehouse for silk and wool and blue vats for silk, wool & cotton. There was an abundance of pure water, light & air. The glass painters had also their studio and Mr. Morris his own. Mr. Morris occasionally slept there, but not latterly. I found it necessary to be more constantly on the premises & then he seldom stayed the night, though a room was kept for him. He came down twice or thrice a week in those days. It is noticeable perhaps in remembering his nervous temperament, that, though he disliked the journey by rail intensely – underground to Farringdon Street and thence from Ludgate to Merton Abbey {Marginal note: 2 hours travelling} he showed no irritation on arriving. The latter part of the journey perhaps, through the fields, was soothing – then there was the short passage from the station through the garden of the Abbey & the prospect of being soon at work, which together may have restored the equilibrium but there remained a certain *impetus* in his manner as if he would still go at 20 miles an hour & rather expected everything to keep pace with him. This was I think the effect of the railway journey. I had noticed it in Queen Square if he arrived from a journey. His first business on arriving at Merton was to discuss any new matter, then he visited the workshops & after seeing that all was in tune he settled to his own easel. There was always a design in progress & often more than one, for it was necessary to break off now and then to have parts repeated, if it was a repeating pattern, & while these repetitions were being made he took up another. He drew as quickly & as accurately as he wrote.

It was at Merton that the Exeter College tapestry was begun & after that came the commissions from D'Arcy for the Holy Grail series. These last were part of the decorations of Stanstead House at [blank left here].[35] I never saw this house.

Of the house decorating in my time the most successful was for Wickham Flower[36] at Swan House, Chelsea and for Lord Revelstoke (E. Baring, Esq, then) at Coombe Cottage & (somewhere near Plymouth).[37] Both these gentlemen had the good sense to adopt Mr. Morris's recommendations in all ways. The decorations of the Hall and Combination Room at Peterhouse was certainly a very important work, but here a good deal had been done by the architect, Mr. George Gilbert Scott (not Sir Gilbert). Mr. Morris filled in the windows with painted glass & painted the walls of the Hall. This work by the way (and the glass at Salisbury and Ch. Ch. [Christ Church] Oxford) was done before the foundation of the Society for Protecting Ancient Buildings and the contemporary declaration from Mr. Morris that he would no longer undertake to paint glass for ancient buildings. {Marginal note: There were also the windows in Jesus Coll. Cambridge & the nave & transept roofs there (painted).} As this circular which he sent in reply to all enquiries for painted windows in ancient buildings was much discussed, it may be as well to recall the precise terms of it – (copies will I have no doubt be found at Merton).[38] Though so plainly written its object was ill understood & so little liked moreover, that we found it necessary to repeat orally & with asseverations our firm intention to abide by it and, at the back of this, to get it believed that we had not given up glass painting altogether. For a year or two certainly our business suffered from the rumour, not wanting in echoes, that Mr. Morris had given up glass painting & we had to make many advertisements to the contrary. These appeared in the *Athenaeum, Pall Mall Gazette & Saturday Review*. In the minds of most people who took any interest at all in Mr. Morris's work the raison d'être of 'Morris glass' was its so-called mediaevalism & it was supposed nothing could be more suitable for an ancient building. The profound misconception which this opinion implied & the other hopeless mistake which assumed that Mr. Morris's work was *purposely* 'mediaeval', made it impossible that the circular could be understood.

The grounds of Mr. Morris's protest were two. The first lay open to all who cared to know, it was the obvious material damage ancient buildings suffer by the process of removing existing glass from the windows & by the insertion of the new. The second was sentimental & belonged to his feelings as an Artist. In regard to the first I may say we had ourselves several frightful experiences, though we used every precaution in our power. How much damage has been done where no such care was taken & where it was not even suspected that the original tracery and framing of a window was of any peculiar value! It was not uncommon, when a painted window was offered to an old church that, as part of the 'improvement', new tracery & mullions were also decided on. Even when it was intended to preserve the old stonework it was almost inevitable that some part of it would fall when the support of the ancient glass with its saddlebars and stanchions was removed, and new stonework would *have* then to be prepared hastily. Even if all went well, which would be a large concession, for there was always the cutting into the old stonework for the new saddlebars, the hammering & the vibration, most dangerous to old masonry, there was the final blotting out of the entire window by the wire guards, which modern taste does not find incompatible with a process of beautifying. These guards are almost equivalent to the abolition of the windows as part of the architecture of the building, since they hide much of the thickness of the masonry & all the refinements of the mouldings & tracery. What horrors!, but I need not expand on this part of the subject. It was not so easily shown that the modern art introduced into the ancient framework is incongruous, destructive equally of the sentiment of antiquity & of the repose & dignity of our mediaeval buildings. The removal of some ancient feature of a building is a demonstrable loss, though people may not regret it, but a building which only suffers from loss still preserves the antiquity of what remains. We can still admire a ruin. A modernised building loses its ancient character for ever, the modern work being always apparent, & *predominant*. Never, let people say what they will about the suitability of Mr. Morris' glass to mediaeval buildings, *never* do the old and the new rightly harmonise. This last opinion very few were able to adopt, for so few recognised the real originality & modernness of his art. It was supposed to be mediaeval. In popular estimation design necessarily takes one of several recognised forms which are called 'styles' and as Mr. Morris's design had many of the characters of mediaeval work he was supposed to be intentionally imitating that style. On the contrary, Mr. Morris was too unaffected & in the broadest sense natural in his art to allow himself to imitate, and, as he did not intentionally make his work mediaeval he did not pretend it could be suitable for a mediaeval building. But beyond & apart from that he felt that the industrial arts of today, tinged & impressed as they are by the vices of modern methods of production, could never, under any disguise of 'style', be worthy to be placed side by side with the untrammelled productions of the great artistic epochs. His self-denying ordinance had reference then to other works than his own &, in abstaining himself, he may have hoped to persuade some others to refrain also. As regards the character of Mr. Morris's design, it may be described in one word: natural. Not in the vulgar sense, as when it is said that a laborious copy of a hawthorn spray on table cover or gas bracket is 'naturalistic', but in the fuller and truer sense, in that the artist submits in his designing to all the natural conditions of his task. The nature of the material he works in & of all the mechanism by which the work is produced, the nature of the thing proposed for decoration or invention have all to be carefully considered & their several demands respected. To all the conditions inherent in material or use the artist has to submit faithfully & fully before proposing to himself the decorative forms he will develop out of them &, being guided by all these, he will guide them in turn & the recreation becomes itself a part of nature, as truly as the form of a tree is to, given the nature of the soil, the climate & its own organising force. Of this kind was Mr. Morris's art; and if leaves & flowers & birds adapted by him to the conditions of block printing or weaving took forms which resembled those which older designers had recognised as proper to them in such service, that is because these forms are essentially right & appropriate. Such art is not necessarily mediaeval nor Greek, but natural. Its *diversities* only will be Greek or mediaeval or modern & that of Mr. Morris was infused, as it could not fail to be, with his own predominant force & sweetness of character. It is never by any chance feeble or aimless; it is always easy, graceful, unaffected. It could not fail to be original, being always appropriate to its object, suggested & directed by it. Never did Mr. Morris take a design he had made for a chintz, say, & clap it onto a wallpaper, or weave it into a curtain stuff. Others have done such things with his designs, but in his own practice, each material & each process of manufacture had the design natural to it.[39]

The names of glass painters & others who have worked for Mr. Morris will be found in the wages books. Among them the two Goodwins (water colour painters) and Napier Henry, Weigand, etc. etc. Campfield was the first assistant he got. He was a student in the evening drawing class of the 'Working Man's College'.[40] He became foreman of the glass painters & remained so until the last I presume. If now alive he would give you information about the earliest days.

APPENDIX 1

Since I sent the former MS. I bethought myself that I had omitted a rather important matter, viz. the relations between Mr. Morris & his workmen & how he adapted the ordinary conditions of service to his own ideals as a socialist. This must be a very interesting subject to many who would care at all about his doings, because, as both a Socialist & employer of labour, he had the opportunity of carrying out, as most people would think, his views regarding the fair share of labour in the profits of industry.

What were Mr. Morris's views on the distribution of profit is well known. At least there are speeches & writings of his on the subject. He would have had one purse & one table & one workshop, one interest only for workman & foreman. This as part of a universal system of communistic life. Why then, some people ask, without much reflection, why did he not, when the Merton works were set on foot, at once organise them on that basis? and so form a little communistic society there for production according to his ideal. {Marginal note: A member of the League did actually put this proposal into print, in the very evident desire for his own advantage.} The answer to this, though very simple, needs apparently to be given. It is that *you cannot have socialism in a corner*.

The idea of socialism is the regeneration or reorganisation of the human family on the basis of equal rights & opportunities for all. In any given quarter of the world, or in a single country, you can have only a modified socialism because of the impossibility of isolating completely any nation or people from the rest of the world. A Cistercian monastery, for example, may exist as a separate community so long as it is able to provide itself with all it needs & to consume all it produces, but when it has tanned all the hides of slaughtered cattle or made the skins into parchment & there is no need for such store of leather & the books accumulated beyond the needs of the house & the scriptorium can no longer convert all the parchment into books it must go beyond its own bounds to dispose of the parchment & the books, & if it needs medicines or pigments or machinery which the land of the convent cannot produce, it must either accept a lower degree of civilisation than the outside world or trade with it & then it is drawn irresistibly into the economic system of the world. The monastic houses of the XIc. say, which began on the simplest basis of social existence were forced by their very success to become more complex and general. Their separate existence ceased when they could not be distinguished from other merchants or producers. They sold their wool or their iron or whatever, in the same markets with other people & were practically merchants, manufacturers or country gentlemen long before the dissolution came. From the same causes, acting more swiftly in these days, the little communistic societies established in America (chiefly) have been broken up. They could not exist according to their ideal except by complete isolation & independence of the outside world, a condition rarely if ever possible, & obviously quite impossible in such a business as Morris's which existed only to supply the demands of an unsocialistic society {Marginal note: This was its economic reason, not its primary one – that was of course to afford Mr. Morris opportunity for exercising his powers as a designer}, & was also compelled to draw all its material from the same. Since, then, buying & selling were both controlled by external conditions, production also was bound to follow them. Mr. Morris would gladly have had it otherwise but the problem for him was not how to defeat the invincible but how to make the best use of adverse conditions Just as, to take a parallel case, hugely as he would have liked to abolish the smoke nuisance, he was quite unable to make an atmosphere to himself in this great workshop which we call London. Perforce he must need & breathe the same air as his fellows unless he could persuade them to come round to his opinion of the injurious nature of the atmosphere of coal dust & sulphurous acid.. He was, at Merton as at London, precisely in this position with regard to his social theory. He regarded the modern conditions of labour as unjust to the workman & also pernicious in their influence on his temper & intelligence. He knew, as an Artist and student of history, that no art had ever flourished or could prosper, where the workers were not free & happy. Never mind what form that freedom took, if only it gave the workman liberty to follow the bent of his inclination, to exercise his inventive power to follow the leanings of his art into new developments. {Marginal note: All the times of decay in the arts have been those in wh. [which] the master was *all*, the workman nothing. Compare the woodcarver with the unintelligent rigidity of the (sweated) industrial arts of today. They witness clearly to the degradation of the worker, to his subordination to a type – a standard fixed by his employer.} Where such liberty existed Art grew strong and pushed out innumerable branches: where the workman had no such liberty it shrank & withered. It was in the contentedness & co-operation of his workmen that Mr. Morris looked for any success he might have. His object then was to secure this, while acknowledging the economic conditions which surrounded all modern industries. These conditions forbade absolutely the equality he would have liked to introduce. They did not prevent him from raising the standard of wages to the highest which each particular product would afford. He substituted piece work founded on the advanced rates for wages for time work wherever the occupation permitted it, thus giving the workman a greater liberty as to the disposal of his time. Wage workers were necessarily obliged to be on the premises at a fixed hour in the morning & to work a given number of hours. Piece workers were not under that obligation. {Marginal note: They could thus occasionally knock off for an hour's work in the garden – the garden having been allotted in sections to the piece workers.} Contracts for piece work were made according to a scale first agreed between master & workmen & every contract was absolutely a free one. Any objection or claim made by a workman was listened to as if it came from an equal & decided according to the equity of the case, as fairly as might be. The clerks & those whom I may perhaps call the officials of the establishment were dealt with on the same principle. The lower clerks received fixed salaries for so many hours work a day. The upper clerks & foremen of the various departments had salaries computed at the end of each year & bearing a certain proportion to the profit for the year. These last were practically partners with Mr. Morris, though without any articles of partnership, & were consulted by him singly or collectively. Once a year at least there was a meeting to discuss the balance sheet & the state of the business. In this way, though the formal communism of convent or phalanstère was not observed, there was practical communism: an identity of interest & solidarity. Mr. Morris's share of the profits was the greatest, the principle of graduated remunerations & a sort of hierarchy being unavoidably mixed with the communistic theory. For a long time Mr. Morris's savings were absorbed almost as fast as they were made by new experiments, but latterly these experiments having reached a limit, he appears to have spent his surplus in books, so much as he was able to withdraw from the business, which naturally required each year, as it grew, a greater capital.

It was in [date omitted] (before going to Merton) that Mr. Morris asked me to draw up a plan by which a certain number of the employees might receive a share of the profits, & the plan I proposed he accepted. It will be found probably at Merton, but I think when it was adopted Mr. Morris wrote a letter to us, as a memorandum, which you will find printed in the letterbook from his MS.[41]

No-one having worked for Mr. Morris could willingly have joined any other workshop or, having passed through any other, would have given up Mr. Morris's for that. Egan & Fletcher (I don't know if that firm still exists) were glass painters before they came to us. They could tell you what was the great difference between working in Mr. Morris's shop & another.

NOTES

1. R. Flower, 'The William Morris Manuscripts', *British Museum Quarterly*, Vol. XIV (1939–40), pp. 8–12. They now form Volume XIII of the Morris Papers, Add. Mss. 45350. We are grateful to the Society of Antiquaries for permission to reproduce them in full.
2. They have recently been printed in a pamphlet on George Wardle and his wife, but this version unfortunately contains numerous transcription errors and some omissions. Y. Kapp, *In Search of Mr and Mrs Wardle: Footnote to a Murder Trial, together with George Wardle's Memorials of William Morris, Some of his Drawings for his Letters to Messrs. Morris, Marshall, Faulkner & Co., and Other Documents* (Oxford, 1994), pp. 45–62.
3. M. Morris, *William Morris: Artist, Writer, Socialist* (Oxford, 1936), p. 605, George Wardle to Sydney Cockerell, 24 Aug. 1898.
4. Many of Wardle's drawings are now in the Print Room of the Victoria & Albert Museum.
5. Charles James Faulkner, partner in Morris, Marshall, Faulkner & Co. and later a mathematics don at University College, Oxford.
6. George Warington Taylor was the first manager of Morris, Marshall, Faulkner & Co. On his role, see J.W. Mackail, *Life of William Morris* (1899), Vol. 1, p. 175; S. Cockerell, 'Notes on Warington Taylor and Philip Webb', *Journal of the William Morris Society*, Vol. 1 No. 2 (1962), pp. 6–10; and, as a corrective, C. Harvey and J. Press, 'William Morris, Warington Taylor and the Firm, 1861–1875', *Journal of the William Morris Society*, Vol. VII (1986), pp. 41–4.
7. This story was part of *The Earthly Paradise*, which occupied Morris from 1865 to 1870. It was originally to be a single volume with 500 woodcuts. Burne-Jones prepared more than 100 designs, including around 70 for the story of

Cupid and Psyche, and Morris eventually cut over 50 of them, but the project was finally abandoned due to printing difficulties. F. MacCarthy, *William Morris: A Life for Our Time* (1994), pp. 201–3. *The Earthly Paradise* was published without the illustrations by F.S. Ellis in 1870.

8. Morris, Marshall, Faulkner & Co. moved from 8 Red Lion Square to 26 Queen Square, Bloomsbury, in November 1865.

9. Though the exact date is not known, Wardle appears to have joined in late 1865 or early 1866. George Warington Taylor suffered from consumption, and went to live in Hastings. He died in 1870.

10. Morris's income from his shares in copper mining declined sharply in the later 1860s. After reaching a peak of £682 in 1865, it fell to £605 in 1866, £440 in 1867–68, £396 in 1869 and £187 in 1870. See above, Chapter 2.

11. Morris, Marshall, Faulkner & Co.'s white and coloured glass came from the Whitefriars firm of Powell & Sons. Powells worked with Charles Winston, whose research into medieval glass had resulted in the publication of his influential *Inquiry into the Difference of Style Observable in Ancient Glass Painting* in 1847. Rossetti, Madox Brown and Burne-Jones designed a number of windows for Powells before the establishment of Morris, Marshall, Faulkner & Co. On Powells, see also J. Gordon-Christian, 'The Archives of the White-friars Studios, London', *Artifex*, Vol. I (1968), p. 36; M. Morris, *William Morris: Artist, Writer, Socialist* (Oxford, 1936), Vol. I, p. 15; R. Watkinson, *William Morris as Designer* (1968), p. 41.

12. Red House, designed for Morris by Philip Webb. Morris lived there from the summer of 1860 until 1865.

13. The Morris family shared 26 Queen Square with the firm from the autumn of 1865 until late 1872.

14. The fireplace at Queen's dates from 1862–64. The nave roof at Jesus College Chapel was begun in 1866 and completed at Easter 1867. Other painted decoration in the Chapel was undertaken by the firm later in the decade, and the stained glass which the firm provided dates from 1872–76. D. Robinson and S. Wildman, *Morris & Co. in Cambridge* (Cambridge, 1980), pp. 37–8; A.C. Sewter, *The Stained Glass of William Morris and His Circle*, Vol. II (New Haven, CT, 1975), pp. 42–4.

15. The firm was Thomas Clarkson's Bannister Hall Print Works, near Preston. At least three Bannister Hall printed cottons from the 1830s were copied around 1868 by Morris, who called them *Small Stem*, *Large Stem* and *Coiling Trail*. L. Parry, *William Morris Textiles* (1983), p. 147.

16. In a Brussels carpet, raised loops are left in the warp, forming a looped pile. (If the loops are cut, leaving a free pile, the result is a Wilton.) Kidderminsters – also called double or triple cloths – are in effect composed of two or three separate woven fabrics on top of each other, each of a different colour, with its own weft and warp. The different colours might be brought to the surface wherever the design demands, thus linking the cloths together. Multiple cloth carpets were less durable than pile carpets, but were cheap, and can be very attractive, if the pattern is bold enough to exploit the limited range of colours available – though, as Wardle notes, most contemporary designers sought to

emulate pile carpets rather than exploit the opportunities which the technique offered. Two- and three-ply Kidderminsters were made for Morris & Co. in Yorkshire by the Heckmondwike Manufacturing Co. See Parry, *William Morris Textiles*, pp. 59, 77; O. Fairclough and E. Leary, *Textiles by William Morris and Morris & Co., 1861–1940* (1981), p. 49; Tattersall and Reed, *History of British Carpets*, p. 148. Also see J.N Bartlett, *Carpeting the Millions: The Growth of Britain's Carpet Industry* (Edinburgh, 1978); L.D. Smith, *Carpet Weavers and Carpet Masters: The Hand Loom Carpet Weavers of Kidderminster, 1780–1850* (Kidderminster, 1986).

17. Wardle describes the process of pointing later in his 'Memorials'.

18. As Wardle notes in the margin, the Morrises moved to Horrington House towards the end of 1872. Morris always felt it a temporary expedient, as it was too small. The family remained there until 1878, when Morris leased The Retreat, Hammersmith, renaming it Kelmscott House.

19. Bernard Quaritch was a well-known bookseller from whom Morris bought antiquarian books and manuscripts, and the publisher of some of the earlier Kelmscott Press books. Frederick Startridge Ellis was Morris's publisher from 1868 until his retirement in 1885, he shared the tenancy of Kelmscott Manor with Morris from 1874 to 1884. He was one of Morris's executors and trustees.

20. In 1877.

21. A Jacquard loom was set up in 1887, and a Lyons silk weaver named Bazin was recruited via Thomas Wardle to operate it, with the assistance of an old Spitalfields weaver. P. Henderson, *William Morris: His Life, Work and Friends* (1967, Pelican edn, 1973), p. 230; Kelvin (ed.), *Letters*, Vol. I, pp. 409–11, to Thomas Wardle, 14 Nov. 1877.

22. The workshops were moved to Merton Abbey, Surrey, towards the end of 1881.

23. Sewter records around 150 designs for stained glass by Morris, mostly dating from 1861–68. Sewter, *Stained Glass*, Vol. I (New Haven, CT, 1974), pp. 60–1.

24. The restoration of the College Hall and Combination Room at Peterhouse College, Cambridge, was begun by the firm in 1868 and completed in 1874. Kelvin (ed.), *Letters*, Vol. I, p. 164; Sewter, *Stained Glass*, Vol. II, pp. 44–6.

25. George Campfield joined the firm in the early 1860s. He had previously worked as a glass painter for Heaton, Butler & Bayne. He soon took charge of the stained glass department, and was still its foreman at the time of Morris's death. MacCarthy notes that Morris 'was dependent upon Campfield's professional skill and knowledge in establishing the Firm's early reputation'. MacCarthy, *William Morris: A Life for Our Time*, p. 176.

26. In recognition of his value, Morris paid him the substantial sum of £400 in 1884. Kelvin (ed.), *Letters*, Vol. II, p. 283, to Georgiana Burne-Jones, 1 June 1884.

27. Notably 'A Book of Verse', completed in August 1870 and given to Georgiana Burne-Jones; a translation of the Eyrbyggja Saga (completed April 1871); and two copies of the Rubáiyát of Omar Khayyám (1872). Wardle also contributed to 'A Book of Verse'; in an inscription at the end of the book, Morris recorded that 'George Wardle drew in all the ornaments in the first ten pages, and

I coloured it; he also did all the coloured letters both big and little'. A. Vallance, *William Morris: His Art, His Writings and Public Life* (1897), p. 381.

28. Naworth Castle was one of the homes of George Howard, later Lord Carlisle, who was an important patron of Morris & Co. Wardle notes below that it was predated by *The Goose Girl*, to a design by Walter Crane, which he believed was completed before the move to Merton. Parry, however, states that *The Goose Girl* was not finished until March 1883. *William Morris Textiles*, p. 107.

29. Usually called *The Adoration of the Magi*, it was completed in 1890. Though not a gift, Morris and Burne-Jones' old college paid only £500, much less than the market price. One of the firm's most popular pieces, it was subsequently repeated for other customers at least ten times. H.C. Marillier, *History of the Merton Abbey Tapestry Works* (1927), p. 32; Fairclough and Leary, *Textiles by William Morris*, p. 61. For a full account of the firm's tapestry weaving, see Parry, *William Morris Textiles*, pp. 100–27.

30. In the *Odyssey*, when Odysseus did not return from the Trojan Wars, his wife Penelope was beset by suitors who hoped to marry her and take the throne. Penelope put them off by promising to decide between them when she had finished weaving a shroud for her father-in-law Laertes; but each night she unpicked what she had woven during the previous day. The story of Arachne, princess of Colophon in Lydia, is told in Ovid's *Metamorphoses*. She was renowned for her skill in weaving pictorial tapestries, and thus earned the wrath of Athene. Unable to find a fault in her work, Athene tore it up in a fit of rage. Terrified, Arachne hanged herself; whereupon the goddess turned her into a spider, to weave forever.

31. The result was Morris's first tapestry, *Acanthus and Vine*, which he jokingly called *Cabbage and Vine*. According to a notebook now in the Victoria & Albert Museum, it took him 516 hours to weave between 10 May and 17 September 1879.

32. Actually John Henry Dearle, who became Art Director of the firm after Morris's death. A number of biographers have repeated Wardle's rather surprising error.

33. William Sleath and William Knight. According to Parry, Knight was Morris & Co.'s most gifted weaver in the 1880s. *William Morris Textiles*, p. 111.

34. Smith had begun by helping Morris with his early experiments at Queen Square in 1872.

35. Wardle makes an error here. The *Quest for the San Graal* was commissioned in 1890 for the dining room of Stanmore Hall, Middlesex, by the Australian mining entrepreneur William Knox D'Arcy. The main panels were eight feet high, and the entire series took nearly four years to complete. A. Vallance, *William Morris: His Art, His Writings and Public Life* (1897), pp. 119–21; Parry, *William Morris Textiles*, p. 106.

36. Wickham Flower was a Fellow of the Society of Antiquaries and a member of the Society for the Protection of Ancient Buildings. Morris & Co. worked on Old Swan House, on the Chelsea Embankment, in 1881, and at his country home, Great Tangley Manor, Surrey, in 1890.

37. The banker Edward Charles Baring was raised to the peerage in 1885. Baring

bought Membland House, South Devon, in 1870. Morris & Co. was commissioned to work on the house in 1877, but few details are known and the house has not survived. See D. Hopkinson, 'A Passion for Building: The Barings at Membland', *Country Life*, 29 April 1982, pp. 1736–40.

38. The first meeting of the Society for the Protection of Ancient Buildings was held on 22 March 1877. Morris was a founder member, along with Thomas Carlyle, Holman Hunt, John Ruskin, Leslie Stephen, Coventry Patmore and Edward Burne-Jones, and wrote the Society's manifesto. The firm's circular announcing that it would no longer supply glass for medieval buildings which were undergoing restoration or improvement is dated 9 April 1877. William Morris Gallery, File 11a.

39. This principle was certainly of great importance to Morris. However, Parry has identified a few exceptions to the general rule. For example, Morris's *Larkspur*, registered 15 April 1875, and *Bird and Anemone*, registered 17 June 1882, were used both as wallpapers and as textiles. *William Morris Textiles*, pp. 148, 154.

40. The Working Men's College was in Great Ormond Street – where he first met Morris.

41. Morris described profit-sharing at Merton, and his objections to it, in letters to Georgiana Burne-Jones and the American poet Emma Lazarus. See Kelvin (ed.), *Letters*, Vol. II, pp. 275–7, to Emma Lazarus, 21 April 1884, reprinted in the *Spectator*, Vol. 32 (1886), p. 397; pp. 283–7, to Georgiana Burne-Jones, 1 June 1884.

Morris & Company at the Boston Foreign Fair of 1883

BY THE END of the 1870s, the reputation of Morris & Co. was beginning to spread beyond the British Isles. Its products were received with enthusiasm by overseas clients who were willing to pay premium prices for goods of the highest quality and originality. Like many British firms, it lacked the manpower and local expertise to set up retail outlets of its own, and the appointment of reliable agents was seen as the best way of making sales in the rich markets of Europe and the United States.[1] In Germany, Morris & Co. products were available in Berlin and Frankfurt am Main, and towards the end of the century Siegfried Bing sold Morris's fabrics from his influential Maison de l'Art Nouveau in Paris. Morris frequently remarked on the difficulties of the American market; a particular problem was the tariffs on imported goods, which he described as 'enormous' and 'almost prohibitive'.[2] Yet as the vogue for English designs and English products gathered pace during the late 1870s and early 1880s his designs were achieving such popularity amongst the well-to-do that United States manufacturers had begun to copy them, obliging him to publish the names of authorised agents, and warning that 'no others can supply the goods we make'.[3] In Boston, for instance, Morris & Co. supplied A.H. Davenport & Co. with wallpapers, cretonnes, damasks, dress-silks, embroidery silks and crewels, Joel Goldthwait & Co. with carpets, and J.F. Bumstead & Co. with wallpapers.[4] In New York, Cowtan & Tout of Madison Avenue was Morris & Co.'s general agent in the United States, though by 1883 this function passed to Elliot & Bulkley of 42 East 14th Street.[5]

Morris also made efforts to ensure that the American public understood what he was about. He sent his general manager, George Wardle, to America with letters of introduction to people whom Morris believed would be sympathetic to his ideas on design and the decorative arts. They included Charles Eliot Norton (1827–1908); the editor of the

North American Review and co-founder in 1865 of the *Nation*, he became Professor of the History of Art at Harvard in 1875.[6] In March 1880 Morris wrote to Norton to inform him that

Mr G.Y. Wardle, my manager, is travelling in America with the purpose of trying to disentangle people's ideas as to our business, & to show them what kind of things we are really making, and what our aims are: he would be very glad therefore to be introduced to anyone who is interested in these matters ... I may add that I believe you will find Mr. Wardle sympathetic in matters social, political & literary, as well as in matters artistic.[7]

Wardle arrived in America early in April 1880, and remained there until the end of May.[8]

Three years later, an opportunity to boost sales in the United States came with the organisation of a Foreign Fair at Boston, attended by buyers from all over the country as well as local citizens. Once again, Wardle went to America, where he was responsible for setting up a large stand, measuring some 45 feet by 30 feet. He also prepared a catalogue entitled *The Morris Exhibit at the Foreign Fair, Boston 1883*, which was published by Roberts Brothers of Boston. A copy may be found in the William Morris Gallery (reference K1598). It is a remarkable document, not just for its eloquence and persuasiveness, but because of the care taken to explain what Morris & Co. was trying to achieve and how it went about its work, and we are grateful to the Gallery for permission to reproduce it in full.

The catalogue reveals that the Morris & Co. stand was divided into six compartments, each featuring a particular class of products (see Figure 6.1). As Wardle notes in his introduction, the objective was to display the range of goods offered by the firm as effectively as possible, not to recreate 'typical' or 'real' rooms. Carpets, for example, had to be hung on walls rather than laid on the floor.

Many of the fabrics on display were relatively new designs, for in the late 1870s and early 1880s Morris was at his peak – and his most prolific – as a designer. His experiments into weaving and dyeing, which had occupied so much of his time during the 1870s, were now bearing fruit, and he was revelling in the new opportunities which were opened up by the establishment of the Merton Abbey workshops. Some of the designs, like *Bird* (1878) and *Dove and Rose* (1879), were already popular with clients. Others, such as *Violet and Columbine*, a woven wool and mohair fabric, were on show to the public for the first time. Other

Figure 6.1
Plan of Morris & Company's exhibit at the Boston Foreign Fair

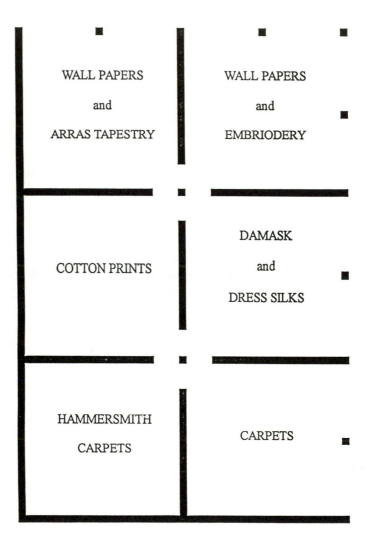

PLAN
OF
MORRIS & COMPANY'S SPACE,
Franklin Hall, Foreign Exhibition, Boston

WALL PAPERS and ARRAS TAPESTRY	WALL PAPERS and EMBRIODERY
COTTON PRINTS	DAMASK and DRESS SILKS
HAMMERSMITH CARPETS	CARPETS

recent additions included *Brother Rabbit* (1882) and *Strawberry Thief*, one of Morris's best-loved designs, which had only been registered in May 1883. Both of these depended upon the technically difficult indigo discharge process, only mastered by Morris after the move to Merton. The catalogue made frequent references to the dyeing processes which the firm used. It was explained how 'the dyeing is all done by ancient or well tried processes, and no expense has been spared to get from the East the dye-stuffs most suitable for each colour'. Likewise, attention was drawn to a rug with a red centre, said to be 'remarkable as being the first rug dyed with Kermes in Europe' in recent times, making its reds more beautiful and permanent than those made with wools dyed with cochineal. Many other fabrics, made from silk, wool, or a mixture of both, were suggested for a whole variety of uses, from wall-coverings to curtains and upholstery, and even ladies' dresses.

Wardle took particular pleasure in presenting Morris & Co.'s printed cottons and linens to the American public. He was aware that cotton prints had a 'reputation for vulgarity' in the United States and that there was 'much prejudice attached to a material selling for a few cents a yard'. But he considered the material 'in every way suitable for ordinary house-furnishing', provided due care was taken in matters of design and manufacture. With vegetable dyes instead of garish chemical substitutes, printing by traditional wooden blocks instead of steam-powered rollers, and good designs instead of bad ones, it was possible to get superb results. Wardle had no doubt that Morris & Co. had achieved these, describing Morris's *Honeysuckle* design as 'a peculiarly beautiful pattern, quite without parallel in the history of block-printing on cloth'. Equally successful, in his view, was a large framed example of the firm's embroidery, priced at $2,000: 'The workmanship is quite unrivalled. Notice the perfect gradations of shade and colour; how truly the lines radiate with the growth and play of the leafage, and how perfectly the lustre of the silk is preserved!'

Wardle's description of the firms' carpets drew largely on a brochure which Morris & Co. had circulated in the United Kingdom in 1882. Nearly the whole of the brochure was reprinted, in particular its insistence that the art of carpet weaving was in terminal decline in the East. Wardle added that 'the quality and style of carpet we call Hammersmith is a speciality of Morris and Company. There are no such carpets made elsewhere ... In all respects they have no rivals, except the few ancient carpets which may be found in the stores.' Similar claims were made for

Morris tapestries. After contrasting tapestry making with the high and low warp looms, it was asserted that 'the invention called the low-warp loom did a good deal to bring the art of tapestry weaving to its present state of degradation and deserved neglect. Our efforts to restore to it some of its earlier dignity naturally commenced by a restoration of the ancient method.' *The Goose Girl* tapestry, the first produced at Merton, was exhibited as an example of a magnificent and desirable art form, second only to mosaic as a durable wall decoration. Cartoons for tapestry by Burne-Jones were also exhibited.

Though pattern books were available to show the full range of Morris & Co.'s wallpapers, it was only possible to hang a few of them at the Exhibition. These included the large *St James* design which Morris had originally created for the Throne Room at St James's Palace in 1881, and *Sunflower*, an 1879 design. In contrast to fabrics, however, Morris made relatively few designs for wallpapers in the late 1870s and early 1880s, and the other designs on show were from earlier years. They included two of Morris's first designs, *Daisy* and *Trellis*. The former, designed in 1862, though not put into production until 1864, remained one of the firm's most popular patterns until the very end of the nineteenth century.

The catalogue concluded with a brief description of the stained glass windows and cartoons on display – all designs by Burne-Jones – and a list of Morris & Co.'s agents in the United States.

As well as providing a comprehensive guide to the goods on display, the catalogue provides a fascinating commentary on the design, colouring and manufacturing principles which set Morris & Co. apart from ordinary commercial manufacturers. In this, it echoes the publicity brochures which the firm prepared for the home market, and Morris's own lectures on the decorative arts, such as 'The Lesser Arts' (1877), 'Making the Best of It' (c.1879), and 'Some Hints on Pattern Designing' (1881).[9] The underlying message to potential customers was that buying Morris goods ensured quality and originality at prices which, though nominally high, represented good value for money. The impression created by the Boston catalogue, which must have been emphasised in the minds of those who actually visited the Foreign Fair, is of a unique enterprise, in touch with the past but aware of the needs of the present, preserving old methods and producing goods of exceptional beauty. For George Wardle, like his mentor William Morris, design was not simply a matter of embellishing an object according to the dictates of the latest fashion, as it was with many manufacturers; it was a matter of the utmost seriousness, requiring the study of classic examples of the art or craft concerned, so as to achieve the truest effect possible.

THE MORRIS EXHIBIT AT THE FOREIGN FAIR

The Morris exhibit is in the Franklin Hall, near the principal entrance. It covers a space forty-five feet by thirty feet, which is divided into six compartments, or rooms. This division is for convenience of exhibiting the various kinds of goods in groups; the rooms must not therefore be taken to represent the rooms of a dwelling, nor is the ordinary decoration of a house attempted. Morris and Company are exhibiting here as manufacturers only, and the arrangement of the goods is that which seemed best for showing them in the ways most accordant to their actual use. This is not, however, strictly the case with all. It was impossible to show the carpets, for instance, in the limits of the large space allotted to us, except by hanging them on the walls. As far as possible, however, the goods are shown as they would appear in one or other of their proper uses.

THE HEAVY CURTAIN STUFFS,

sometimes called Tapestries, though that is a misuse of the word, are hung on the outside of the booth, where the full effect of their folds and patterns can be fairly judged. These cloths are made of various kinds of wool – some fine, and closely woven, others rough, and open in texture, to suit all the purposes for which heavy or heavyish curtains are required. The material in every case is pure wool, prepared in various ways, to give the variety of effect which is observable. The dyeing is all done by ancient or well-tried processes, and no expense has been spared to get from the East the dye-stuffs most suitable for each colour. Some of the bold designs of these hangings are not strangers in America – the Peacock, more especially, having already won for itself a place; but others, like the Violet and Columbine, are quite new, and have not been shown anywhere before the opening of this exhibition. One use of these heavy cloths in England is the hanging of the walls of churches or large halls. The Peacock and the Bird pattern are very good for this use.

Mr Morris's own room is hung with the Bird pattern, from the skirting to within two feet of the ceiling. The cloth is hooked up to the top rail, and is but slightly plaited – only enough modulation of the surface being allowed to just break the pattern here and there. The beautiful effect of a long wall hung in this way is quite inconceivable, and we much regret we have not space for showing this use of the material. When so used these goods might more truly be called Tapestries than in their ordinary service as curtains and portières.

The first room we will enter is that marked

CARPETS

in the plan. It contains samples of real Axminster, Wilton, or Velvet-pile, Patent Axminster, and Kidderminster carpets. These are shown by large-sized squares on the floor, and three complete carpets are also shown on the walls. The carpet to the left as you enter is a real Axminster, so called to distinguish the make from various kinds of patent goods which have been invented since the method introduced from the East was first practised at Axminster in Devonshire. Some Patent Axminsters are very good for the price, but they differ essentially from the original fabric, and the palm still remains to it for durability and beauty of material, irrespective of pattern; though if pattern be also considered, the greater freedom of working gives the hand-made carpet an advantage quite beyond competition. The hand-made Axminster exhibited is a soft, close pile made in one piece. It is inferior to the Hammersmiths in weight, and variety of pattern and colour; but it is as much superior to Wiltons and Patent Axminsters in all the qualities desirable in a carpet. The size is sixteen feet by twelve feet. Wilton carpets must be classed as the best kind of machine-woven carpets. The patterns they bear are somewhat controlled as to size and colour by the capability of the machine; and they are necessarily made in strips, not more than twenty-seven inches wide, as a rule. A Wilton carpet is therefore sewn together, and the border is also sewn on. If well made the material is very durable, and by skilful treatment in the designing, the restrictions as to colour are not noticeable. In consequence of these restrictions a Wilton carpet is more embarrassing to a designer than are the happier products of the hand-loom; and good designs – that is, designs having form and character proper to the material, and good and beautiful in themselves –

are more rare in this cloth and in Brussels than in hand-woven fabrics. When Mr. Morris began to design for Wilton carpeting he aimed to produce pure and shapely forms with simple colouring, doing the best he could with the material, without straining its capacity for decoration. The large carpet facing the entrance to this room is a Wilton – the size, fifteen feet by twelve feet. The one to the right is also a Wilton, its size twelve feet by nine feet.

Among the patterns on the floor are three colourings of a bold design adapted to one of the best makes of Patent Axminster. This cloth may be easily distinguished from real Axminster by the uninitiated, if the backs of the two be compared. The Patent Axminster has a foundation of hemp; the real Axminster is all wool. As the Patent Axminster is also a coarser fabric, the designs for it are necessarily much bolder than for Wiltons and real Axminster. When a large pattern is wanted, therefore, and a Hammersmith carpet cannot be had, this patent cloth should be chosen.

The remaining carpets exhibited in the first room are varieties of Kidderminster. The heaviest sorts are three-plies – the lighter two-plies. These carpets are very solid, well-woven goods, and of great durability if properly laid. The colours are dyed in the same way as for the most expensive rugs, and the patterns are carefully adapted to the material. The samples shown are made up as rugs. They thus show the fringes with which we always border them in England. One of the best ways of using these carpets is to cover the floor entirely with China matting, and to lay the Kidderminster loose upon this. The China matting ought to be carefully made up, so as to cover the floor smoothly; and, to keep it in good condition, a pail of water should be used every week for cleaning it. By doing that, the rush of which the matting is made does not get too dry and brittle. The same matting may be used as a substratum for the better class of carpets, Wiltons and Axminsters, or it may be used for fitting the margin of floor around these carpets instead of parquet; but it is very much better, where the whole floor is not covered with parquet, to cover it wholly with China matting. The life of any carpet is much prolonged by having this kindly protection between it and the planking, and the decorative value of the matting is also an important item. Of course, if a parquet floor can be had, that is the best. It is unimportant whether the parquet be one inch thick or a quarter of an inch. The quarter-inch parquet, glued carefully on the existing floor-boards, is quite sufficient for all purposes, and can be easily applied to any floor. It may be suggested that only the simplest patterns should be chosen, and in timber of *one* kind. Oak is the best. Oak, however, when polished or oiled, has a very unpleasant yellow colour, quite unfit for combination with colours that are usually considered beautiful. To correct that yellowness, a little Prussian blue should be dissolved in the polish used for finishing. As much blue as will give a greenish tone to the polish in the bottle is sufficient.

It will be noticed that all the patterns of carpet exhibited have their appropriate borders.

Morris & Company also make one pattern in Brussels cloth. This is not shown at the Fair, but it may be seen in Messrs. Goldthwait's store, 169 Washington Street, Boston, or at our agents, in New York.

In going from this room to the next, two curtains will be noticed. The material is a fine wool, called challis; the patterns are printed. Though hung here they are not offered as suitable material for portières; they would be properly used for bed or window curtains. The material wears well, and may be repeatedly cleaned without serious loss of colour. Turning to the left you pass, between two heavier curtains of thick cotton-damask, into the room where the Hammersmith carpets are displayed. You will perhaps be more disposed to examine these curtains as you return, but we may at once note the weight and style, which are unusual qualities in this material. The cloth is reversible, the pattern showing equally, though with different effects, on each face. Curtains made of this cloth, which is really double, do not need lining. It may be used for portières in summer cottages, or for window-curtains.

THE HAMMERSMITH CARPETS

are named from the place where Mr Morris first began the manufacture. They are now made at Merton Abbey in Surrey, where we have recently established our factory. The carpeting, dyeing, weaving, printing, glass-painting, and other arts, being now collected there in work-rooms more convenient for our increasing operations. On some of the smaller rugs will be seen the Hammer and M., significant of the earlier place of manufacture. The later carpets have no trade-mark. The quality and style of carpet we have called Hammersmith is a specialty of Morris & Company. There are no such carpets made elsewhere, not even in the East, though the best India carpets may be compared with them in weight. In all other respects they have no rivals, except the few ancient carpets which may occasionally be found in the stores. This is what Mr Morris said about them in the circular announcing the beginning of this new manufacture in England:

We beg to call your attention to the beginning of an attempt, which we have set on foot, to make England independent of the East, for the supply of hand-made carpets which may be considered works of art.

We believe that the time has come for some one or other to make that attempt, unless the civilised world is prepared to do without the art of carpet-making at its best; for it is a lamentable fact that, just when we of the West are beginning to understand and admire the art of the East, that art is fading away; nor in any branch has the deterioration been more marked than in carpet-making.

All beauty of colour has now (and for long) disappeared from the manufactures of the Levant – the once harmonious and lovely Turkey carpets. The traditions of excellence of the Indian carpets are only kept up by a few tasteful and energetic providers in England, with infinite trouble and at a great expense; while the mass of the goods are already inferior in many respects to what can be turned out mechanically from the looms of Glasgow or Kidderminster.

As for Persia, the mother of this beautiful art, nothing could make the contrast between the past and the present clearer than the carpets, doubtless picked for excellence of manufacture, given to the South Kensington Museum by His Majesty the Schah, compared with the rough works of the tribes done within the last hundred years, which the directors of the Museum have judiciously hung near them.

In short, the art of carpet-making, in common with the other special arts of the East, is either dead or dying fast; and it is clear to everyone that, whatever future is in store for those countries where it once flourished, they will, in time to come, receive all influence from, rather than give any to, the West.

It seems to us, therefore, that, for the future, we people of the West must make our own hand-made carpets, if we are to have any worth the labour and money such things cost; and that these, while they should equal the Eastern ones as nearly as may be in materials and durability, should by no means imitate them in design, but show themselves obviously to be the outcome of modern and Western ideas, guided by those principles that underlie all architectural art in common.

Such a manufacture we have (in default of other people) attempted to set on foot, and we hope, for the above-stated reasons, that you will think our attempt worthy of your support.

We should mention that we are prepared to give estimates and execute carpets of any reasonable size, in design, colouring, and quality similar to the goods exhibited.

The largest carpet on the room is the one called Illyssus; it measures seventeen feet ten inches by nine feet six inches. Opposite to it is a smaller carpet, of very deep, rich colouring, the size, twelve feet by eight feet. These, and some of the smaller rugs, were bought soon after the opening of the Fair. The carpet with the light blue border measures about fifteen feet by ten feet six inches. It will not leave Boston, nor will the one opposite, called the Orchard – perhaps the most remarkable carpet of all for design and colour. It has this inscription in the border:–

ꝺurum et ꝺurum non facit murum.

The size is sixteen feet by eight feet six inches.

Of the rugs on the floor, that with the red centre is remarkable as being the first rug dyed with Kermes in Europe, since cochineal was introduced and established in our dye-houses. Those who are acquainted with the cochineal shades on wool, will notice the greater beauty of the reds in this carpet; and we may also note, they are much more permanent – Kermes being the veritable grana from which ingrain-dyeing got its reputation. The floor of this room has, like the others, a centre-rug of three-ply Kidderminster. We ask you to note how well the cheaper but not necessarily vulgar material consorts with the more dignified Hammersmith. In the other rooms, you will see similar fringed rugs, which look neither cheap nor mean beside silk damasks, though their more appropriate place is certainly with wall-papers and chintzes.

We may go from the Hammersmith carpets to the next front room, where

DAMASKS AND DRESS-SILKS

are the chief display. Damask, for wall-hanging, is now a revived taste in Europe. Not that the use had ever quite died out; but just before the revival, damasks were seldom used except for palaces and the richest houses, and they were always silk damasks. One of those we exhibit is a mixture of silk and wool. We call the increased use of these wall-hangings a revival, because the covering of walls with stuffs, tapestries, or what-ever would *hang*, must have preceded the use of paper for walls; paper-hangings, by their name being evidently a substitute for something better, but more costly. The three walls of this room are covered with damask of different design. It is perhaps necessary to say that this is because we wished to exhibit as many varieties as there was space for.

The rooms must not be taken as consistent decorations, but simply as show-rooms. The large pattern in gold suffused with pink is a silk damask of the best quality – the name of the pattern, St James. It was first used, though not in these shades, for the Throne-Room at St James's Palace. The smaller pattern on the wall to the right, a Damascening of dark bronzy green, steely blue, copper and gold tints, is also a silk of the purest make. We call the pattern, Flower-garden. The colours suggest the beauties of inlaid metals. On the opposite wall is the silk and wool damask. This is very novel in effect, and an admirable wall-covering, even where pictures are hung. Though the pattern is large and full of variety, a tone of warm, broken grayness is the prevailing effect. It is quite warm enough to harmonise with the gold of picture-frames, and gray enough not to hurt the colour of a picture. The introduction of the fine wool through the pattern is the main cause of the subdued splendour.

It would be a real loss to give up such a pattern (and we have others equally valuable) from fear of the moth, which we know is much dreaded in America. The damage done by moths in woollen goods is a serious thought to a housewife; but it can only happen when goods are kept from the light and shut up generally. Stuffs exposed and stretched on walls are not likely places for the moth to choose when she lays her eggs, and the ordinary Spring cleaning should be an insurance against that; but in point of fact, this cloth is better guarded. A skin of silk covers the whole surface, visible in many places, and only hidden, where the other colours of the pattern come to the front, by single threads of wool. There is, therefore, nothing to attract the moth. The damask patterns shown on the walls of this room are but three out of many varieties of which the patterns are capable; many yards of wall-space would have been needed to display them all to any useful size. Our agents, Messrs Elliot & Bulkley, 42 East 14th Street, New York, or Mr Davenport, 96 Washington Street, Boston, will be happy to show other colourings and versions of these patterns. The Flower-garden, besides being woven all silk, is made with silk and wool, and so made is a most useful wall-covering or curtain. All these damasks, it must be kept in mind, are intended for curtain-use as well as for walls; and they are even more handsome so, the changeable hues being much more beautiful when the change is assisted by the folding of the drapery. We might have shown some of them as curtains in this room, but in doing that we should have lost the opportunity for showing the

UTRECHT VELVETS,

and we think these of too much importance in furnishing to be omitted. They make excellent curtains where rich, quiet colour, with but faint pattern, is required, and they make the very best covering, except silk, for chairs, &c. The various shades exhibited have all their proper numbers attached, and the prices are plainly marked. By quoting these numbers, the exact colours can at any time be had from the houses authorised to sell our goods.

In the centre of the room is a table on which are arranged a selection of the

DRESS-SILKS

we manufacture. It may be thought strange that Mr Morris should concern himself with the colours of ladies' dresses; but it is nevertheless a part of the purpose Mr Morris had before him when he undertook to give us the means of beautifying our homes. Had that even been otherwise, Mr Morris could scarcely have escaped the consequence of the reform he has worked in household decorations generally. In England the calls upon him to provide something that ladies might wear, in rooms he had helped to make lovely, were too many to be disregarded, and he offers these as his answer to the demand. The textures are of two kinds, damask and simple twill. The silk of which they are made is of the purest, and the dyes are also pure and good. The fabrics are designed to hang well, with sufficient body and richness; they are very pliable and substantial, without unnecessary weight. Two guarantees can be given – the silk will not cut with use, nor will it get greasy.

From the Silk room we will pass to the one behind, which is furnished entirely with cotton. This room is also used as an office for enquiries, &c., but it is open to the public as freely as all the others. In it we show six different patterns of

HAND-PRINTED COTTON CLOTH

as wall-hangings, and some others as curtains. These patterns are not a tithe of the great variety of furniture-prints we make on cotton, linen, and worsted. Two on worsted (Challis) you have already see at the entrance to one of the Carpet rooms; for the remainder, not exhibited, we can only refer you to our Agents in New York, or to Mr Davenport in Boston. The cost of most of our furniture-prints has lately been much reduced, and many new designs have been added to stock.

Those exhibited on the walls of this room are mostly new, and the method of making them is also new. Not absolutely, perhaps; but it is so long since rooms were generally hung with printed cloth, at least in England, that the proposal to make that use general is a novelty. We venture to do that partly on the ground of the moderate cost of the material, but more because of the beauty of tone and surface to be got by this means, much surpassing, in those respects, even very costly wall-papers. The hanging is exactly like that of the damasks in the other room. The cloth is fastened not to the walls, but to thin laths or batons first nailed to the margins of the wall – that is, above the dado, under the cornice or frieze, and round doors and windows. To these laths the cloth is tacked in folds (chintz should always be folded) and moderately strained – the edges of the cloth and the tacks being afterwards hidden by a suitable gimp or fringe. The fixing is very easy, and the cloth can be as easily taken down for cleaning, or to change from one room to another.

As regards the manufacture, we may say that great attention has been given to the permanence of the colours, more especially against light and soap; but we must caution you that some of the colours may not safely be sent to the ordinary wash. These can be pointed out by the salesman. There are none, however, that may not be *cleaned* with perfect safety and success. The cloth is a full yard in width, and is invariably finished without dressing or glaze. The curtains in this room exhibit four different kinds of printing. The Strawberry-thief is a many-coloured pattern on plain cotton, coloured by repeated processes both delicate and tedious, and all the colours being dyed, they are very fast. The red Brother-rabbit is also a colour produced by dyeing. It represents the cheapest and best of our single prints. Next it is a many-coloured pattern on linen, the Honeysuckle, a peculiarly beautiful pattern, quite without parallel in the history of block-printing on cloth. It represents a group of varieties, some on linen, others on cotton, for which there is not room in the stall. The colours of this pattern are printed directly on the linen. As one of them is indigo-blue, this may be worth noting. The fourth curtain is a sample of block-printing on cotton-velvet. These four are exhibited as curtains, but they are not all intended to be restricted to that use. The Honeysuckle makes a wonderfully beautiful wall-hanging, and being printed on a somewhat lustrous and better material than cotton, it bears hanging without folds. It may be stretched upon the wall exactly as silk. A room dressed with it should have the wood-work of very richly toned walnut or mahogany; or, if meaner wood be used, it should be painted a rich, deep green, and varnished. The Strawberry-thief would also make a very lovely wall-covering for a small room.

Some apology is perhaps necessary in America for presenting such a homely article as cotton for a decorative material. There is, in the first place, the prejudice attaching to a material usually selling for a few cents the yard, and covered with pattern at that; and there is the reputation for vulgarity which ordinary cotton-prints have acquired. We have ventured, notwithstanding, to offer our cotton-prints under no other name. They are simply cotton-prints, whether the material be the ordinary plain cloth, twilled cloth, or the heavier fabric called cretonne. We consider the material in every way suitable for ordinary house-furnishing. It is eternally washable; it is unmolested by moth; and it is the least costly of all the materials at our command. Disregarding, then, the discredit which the continued competition of manufacturers for success in the cheapest market has obtained for cotton prints; we have been engaged for some years in publishing a series of designs fuller and richer than this manufacture has heretofore seen – if we except the elaborate works of Javanese and Indian artists, never available, however, for the same purposes; and while aiming to present these patterns in tones available for decorative uses, we have sought first of all for durability in the colours employed. In doing this, we had to neglect all the processes employed in the production of cheap prints. Instead of the steam-cylinder, we use the primitive wooden block; and we dye our fastest colours with material long since discarded from the dye-shops of Alsace and Lancashire, because of the cost. We do this from no anti-quarian sentiment, but because there is no other way to produce permanent effects in colours an artist may use. This explanation will account to some extent for what may seem high prices, as compared with the ordinary cost of cotton-prints, and Americans will do us the justice to remember that the initial cost is aggravated here by an almost prohibitory tariff.

In the remaining rooms are shown wall-papers, curtain-damasks,

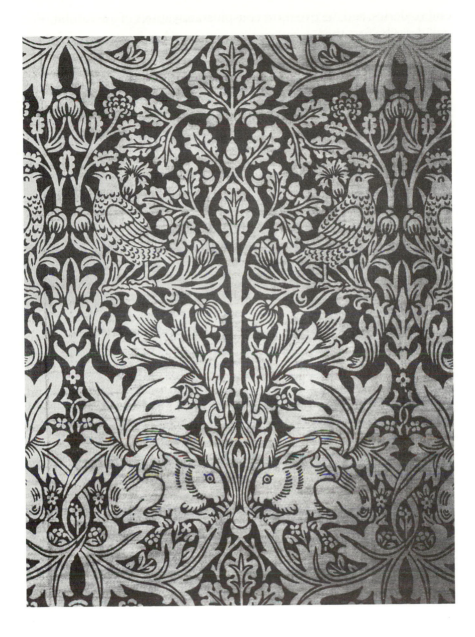

Plate 6.1 *Brother Rabbit* chintz, designed by Morris in 1882, and indigo discharge printed at Merton Abbey *William Morris Gallery*

embroideries, and the two most conspicuous features of our exhibit. We will describe first the

WALL-PAPERS,

as they are nearly connected with the wall-hangings we have been describing; and in speaking of them, something further may be said on the subject of wall-decoration.

In the Decorative Arts, nothing is finally successful which does not satisfy the mind as well as the eye. A pattern may have beautiful parts and be good in certain relations; but, unless it be suitable for the purpose assigned, it will not be a decoration. Unfitness is so far a want of naturalness; and with that defect, ornamentation can never satisfy the craving which is a part of nature. What we call decoration is in many cases but a device or way we have learned for making necessary things reasonable as well as pleasant to us. The pattern becomes a part of the thing we make, its exponent, or mode of expressing itself to us; and by it we often form our opinions, not only of the shape, but of the strength and uses of the thing. Now, since man became a wall-builder, three things have appeared necessary to him in the outward fashioning of every wall he has built – a base, or foot; the screen, or wall proper; and the cornice, or coping. The base must be big enough to give a sufficient footing for the super-structure; apparently, of course – the real footings being deep in the ground. The cornice, inside a building is for uniting the wall with the roof or ceiling. In a room the planes of wall and ceiling, by their different relations to the light, have quite different tints, though actually they may be of precisely the same colour white for instance. If the ceiling be dark the wall will be light, and vice versa. Now the artifice for uniting these opposing tints and planes is to fill the angle between them with a series of narrow fillets and alternating curved surfaces, by which the tints of wall and ceiling are interchanged and the transition is made. The cornice is completed by drawing a line somewhere below the moulded part, usually about as much below it as the depth of the moulding itself. This cuts off the cornice sharply and distinctly from the wall proper. Sometimes a piece of wall, just below the cornice, is cut off from the rest for greater dignity, or because the wall otherwise would look too high; this is not an essential, but it is often of great architectural value. Sometimes, in very refined work, the base of the wall is itself a wall of stouter and more solid appearance; it has then its own proper parts – base, superstructure, and cornice. This is the dado.

Only when a wall is very high, or the scale requires much detail, will dado, wall, and frieze, be all used. In our living-rooms, dado, wall, and cornice are generally sufficient; or, if there is no dado, only the skirting or merest base of the wall, a frieze may be worked in some way so as to diminish the apparent height of the room. There is no rule to fix the proportion absolutely; good sense and feeling must always decide; but the three essentials must in some way be exhibited. Then as to the social relations of the parts, the base, if skirting only, should be treated with great simplicity – either with suitable timber, or plainly painted, dark or light as the case may require, but without picking out of mouldings or other fidget. If a dado be part of the structure of the wall, it will probably have moulded panels and chair-rail; these will be quite sufficient decoration of its surface, and the painting will be as described for the skirting alone. If the dado be not panelled, do not make sham panelling; paint it of one colour, which must be that of the architraves of windows and doors. Never stoop to the ignominy of a paper dado; at a fancy fair, or some temporary thing, where effect without solidity may be excused, mere scene-painting is allowable – but scarcely at home. It must always be borne in mind that the essentials of a dado are those of the wall, base, superstructure, and cornice. The chair-rail is the representative of the cornice and cannot be omitted. If the wall obviously wants a dado, the effect may be at once got by fixing a rail of suitable section at the required height, and painting from rail to floor with one colour.

The cornice in our living-rooms is of somewhat uncertain relations; properly it belongs to the wall, of which it is the capping, or the broadened butt which gives support to the floors above it; but since our floors are concealed, and the plaster coverings are so unreasonably treated as to suggest, not a series of beams or arches resting on the wall, but one huge sheet of plaster suspended miraculously overhead – the cornice becomes by necessity the moulded edge of the ceiling, which, with this for a frame, gets that look of substance and strength so very desirable in a slab of plaster of that size. In ordinary cases, therefore, the cornice is part of the ceiling, and the two should be so decorated as to look *all one*. The readiest and often the best way of doing this is to distemper them both with one even clear tint, the lightest the tone of the room will permit. In England we find pure chalk-whitening, without mixture of blue or black (the usual correctives of its yellowness), is the best general tint; sometimes a little raw-sienna may be added to make it warmer – or green, to cool it and deepen it; but for most occasions positively no addition is the best. Not that the painting of ceilings should be discouraged; but the purposeless array of varied tints, the drawing of meaningless lines of colour, would be better discontinued. When a ceiling is patterned, the cornice of course shares in the decoration; and it is then possible to assimilate the tints with the colour of the ceiling, so far as to preserve homogeneity, and without losing the proper relation of the cornice to the wall. When a ceiling is well and properly moulded – panelled, that is, or coffered – it may be treated with more independence, and the cornice will then remain a true part of the wall.

In some cases it may be necessary to disregard the character of the ceiling entirely, and heighten the walls by painting the cornice like them. It may equally happen that a gawky room would be much improved by lessening its apparent height. All that is needed in that case is a string-moulding at the required depth below the cornice; the space above this string, or necking, is the frieze, and will be decorated or not decorated, according as the ceiling is plain or particoloured. If plain, tint the frieze with the same distemper you use for the ceiling and cornice. If the ceiling be decorated, the frieze should be as much, or perhaps a little more, decorated; but the difference should be in greater dignity, rather than elaboration. The decoration of a frieze, if it leave any pretension at all, should be done by hand; it requires more careful design than the wall itself, because nothing but absolute fitness will justify the separation of this part of the wall for special treatment.

It will be understood from this that Morris & Company do not print distinctive frieze patterns. One or other of the simplest yellow and white, or white-ground, wall-papers, is sometimes used for the frieze, when tone requires some faint patterning on the ceiling; but in this case the pattern is altogether subordinate to the tone, and its colour is the chief value. Ceiling-papers we seldom use; but for the occasions noted above, numbers 101, 18, 107, 11, 144, or the green tints of the sample patterns, are suitable. Those we should use for friezes in connection with them, are numbers 2, 5, 46, 120, 98, 99, 30, 63, 64, and such like. We now come to the wall proper – the space which our wall-papers, cotton-prints, and damasks are designed to cover. In choosing the pattern for this, there are some dangers to be avoided, to which all who are unaccustomed to the selection of decorative details are liable. In the first place it is difficult, when a pattern is presented on narrow strips, to know whether the shapes it will make on the wall are only those that appear, or if entirely new lines and shapes may not be developed by combination; it is also difficult to know whether the scale of the pattern is suitable. In the narrow breadth the pattern is apt to look much larger than it will on the wall; and from this cause, patterns miserably inadequate for the decorations of the space they are intended to fill are too often chosen. You cannot entirely guard against either danger by having two or three rolls displayed together; experience will still be wanting. Patterns which take the fancy when seen in the show-room will be disappointing on the wall, and you will almost certainly err on the side of smallness or feebleness in size and tone. This brings us to the great difficulty, the more serious because quite unsuspected; the risk there always is in choosing a pattern from simple *liking*, without consideration of the place the pattern has to fill. Pattern-choosing, like pattern-making, is an Architectural Art. A pattern is but a part of any scheme of decoration, and its value will be derived in great part from its surroundings. Personal liking, therefore, is not an infallible guide in the choice of wall-papers. There are conditions that must be respected if the liking is to last; and these depend entirely on the character of the room to be decorated, on the extent of wall-space to be covered, on the amount and kind of light in the room, on the colour of the timber if so-called 'natural woods' are used, and on many details which practised eyes only can properly estimate. We recommend, therefore, that the advice of someone accustomed to the work ought always to be had; but for ordinary cases the following simple rules may be laid down, which will perhaps answer most questions. If there is a reason for keeping the wall very quiet, choose a pattern that works all over without pronounced lines, such as the Diapers, Mallows, Venetians, Poppy, Scroll, Jasmine, &c., &c.

If you may venture on more decided patterning, and you ought always to go for more positive patterns when they may be had, choose the Daisy, Trellis, Vine, Chrysanthemum, Lily, Honeysuckle, Larkspur, Rose, Acanthus, or such. In deciding between those whose direction or set is horizontal, and those which have more obviously vertical or oblique lines, you must be guided entirely by the look of the room. Put very succinctly, architectural effect depends upon a nice balance of horizontal, vertical, and oblique. No rules can say how much of each; so

Plate 6.2 *Acanthus* wallpaper by William Morris *William Morris Gallery*

nothing can really take the place of feeling and good judgement. If you have no professional aid, you must decide for yourself whether the room most wants stability and repose, or if it is too stiff and formal. If repose be wanted, choose the pattern, other things also being duly considered, which has horizontal arrangement of its parts. If too great rigidity be the fault, choose a pattern with soft, easy lines, either boldly circular or oblique-wavy – say Scroll, Vine, Pimpernel, Fruit, &c. If the fault lie in the too great predominance of horizontal lines, without any marked stiffness in the parts, as when the walls are very low and long, choose one of the columnar patterns, as Larkspur, Spray, or Indian; or, better still, hang the walls with chintz, or other cloth, in folds. If the room has no marked defect, and you have the pleasure of choosing from a wider range of patterns, do not be afraid of choosing a large one, provided the tone of it be what you want. If the light in the room be bright and plentiful, choose from the fainter colourings. If the light is weak, choose patterns of strong relief.

As regards colour, you will be guided in the first place by the colour of the wood-work, if this be unpainted. The usual pitch-pine, ash, and hard woods, as they are varnished and finished for interior fittings, are so undecorative as to make the task of fitting wall-papers to them very difficult. If the wood be walnut or dark-stained oak, the papers with metallic grounds will be best, or the darkest many-coloured papers, like dark Trellis. If the colour of the timber be lighter and yellowish, you must choose from the olive or sage-green papers, and prefer the fullest and richest in pattern to the plainer ones. If the timber be nicely designed and finished, one of the stuffs already mentioned would be more suitable than wall-papers, unless the gold grounds be excepted; but these cases do not come under the ordinary class, and need special treatment.

Keeping then to rooms that may be described generally, we will notice next those which have painted doors, windows, and other fittings. In these rooms it is often allowable to determine the colour at pleasure; still, some things cannot be disregarded. Should the character of the wood-work be what is called *bold* – that is, coarsely, moulded, and neither nice in proportion nor style, you would do better to paint it of a dark shade than a light one; and that will influence the choice of wall-paper. Some patterns called light will go very well with paint decidedly dark – as for instance Daisy 75, or Venetian 74, with dark-green paint. Usually, if the paint be dark, the paper is chosen of nearly the same tone.

There is no great reason for this. Rooms with wood-work and walls of equal tone are sometimes very tame, and even dull. It is better to make the wood-work either darker or lighter than the walls.

In the choice of colour there is scarcely any help to be given except with the paint and brush. The best thing to say is that, when all is done, the result must be *colour*, not colours. If there are curtains or carpet or other finishings to be worked up to, you must consider which of them, if any, shall be the predominant colour of the room, and which the sub-ordinate or auxiliary colour. The walls and wood-work have generally the predominating colour, and the carpet the secondary. The curtains will then either blend with the walls, and help to surround the carpet with a frame of colour contrasting with it generally, but not necessarily with a strong contrast, or the curtains may be used to harmonize the carpet with the walls. The choice must depend upon the kind of room and the point of departure. Should you be quite untrammelled, you may prefer to select the carpet first, and then the wall-paper and colour of the wood-work; but having determined the predominant colour, the subservient colours must be so balanced as to soften it by variations or brighten it by contrast. Contrasting colour, if strong, must be kept within small quantities; if pale or gray, it may be more freely used. Chairs and sofas give great opportunities for introducing points of bright contrasting colour, and for those high lights and darkest shades which are essential in a complete scheme. Covers need not be uniform. They may be of two or three or four kinds, according to the size of the room and number of pieces.

If the chief colour be red, it will be desirable to have a large area of white for rest to the eye. Blues, gray, green, and lighter tints of red should be the variants. Contrast with it should be generally avoided; it wants rather quiet than excitement. Whenever white paint may be used for the wood-work, choose it in preference to any other. The use of positive colour is very difficult, and house-painters are peculiarly ignorant of it. Their incapacity may have led to the use of the dull, gray, or even dirty shades, which have become so general since house-decoration has begun to interest educated people. The revolt against crude, inharmonious colouring has pushed things to the opposite extreme, and instead of over-bright colours, we now have dirty no-colours. The aim was to get sobriety and tenderness, but the inherent difficulty was not less great than before. It is not more easy to paint grays that shall have colour, than to paint colour that shall be gray; and whichever it be, *colour* is still the essential. In this difficulty the use of white paint is the only way to safety. White is perfectly neutral; it is a perfect foil to most colours, and by judicious toning may be assimilated with any. It is, therefore, manageable without great art. When used in its highest tone, direct the painter to put no mixture of black or blue to the natural pigment, whether lead or zinc. If a little degradation be needed, use orange-chrome and green, either alone or together. Do not use black, and very rarely raw-umber.

Very few questions remain. If you ask whether the colour of the wood-work ought as a rule to be lighter or darker than that of the paper, the answer is, there is no rule. White or light-toned paints may be used if the wood-work is well designed and nicely finished – that is, if the shapes are agreeable and the surface pleasant. If the shapes be not bad, but the moulding be heavy and coarse, it is better to make the wood-work darker than the wall. If the shapes be bad – too many and too irregular – the ugliness will be reduced by painting pretty closely to the tone of the paper; and when this is necessary, choose for the wall the richest and most interesting design the room will bear – to avoid the fault of dullness, which might otherwise attend the use of a non-contrasting paint. When your room is already well designed and has nice detail, you can use much more liberty in the choice of wall-paper and paint.

How should the room be papered in which pictures are hung? That will chiefly depend upon the tone and colour of the pictures. Almost any of our wall-papers may be used as backgrounds for pictures, according to the sorts. There is no need to make a wall dull or strictly monotonous because pictures are hung against it. Most of the low-toned many-coloured patterns are as good for pictures as the self-colours. Those with a predominating warm olive-green have the advantage of assimilating with the shadow-colour of the gold frames, and so make the squares of frame and picture less spotty in the general effect. Deep-red papers are found good for some pictures. We would recommend such as the red-and-gold Sunflower, for the reason just given; or, if a plain red be preferred, we suggest one of the furniture-cottons – say Iris or Marigold – as a pleasanter surface than paper in conjunction with pictures; but if the pictures be light in tone, water-colours perhaps, some of the lighter floral patterns on white, or quiet green or blue grounds may be used.

For prints and photographs, sometimes the same, sometimes the simple yellow and white patterns. If the prints have narrow black frames and white mounts, these yellow papers make beautiful combinations.

Do we supply borders for our papers? From what we have said it will be seen that the natural architectural features of the room – the skirting or dado, the cornice or frieze, and the architraves of doors and windows – are the proper boundary-lines of the wall-paper. These parts in good building are always of different and better material than the mass of the wall – at least in outside effects, where architecture is perforce more natural. The wallpaper inside, like rough-cast or plaster outside, hides the coarser material of the body of the wall; it is a filling therefore, not a building-material, and should be used frankly for what it is. Panels formed by stripes or cuttings of wall-paper are futile decorations, as such, and they are ridiculous as architecture. Still more absurd is the practice of framing the whole wall with gilt mouldings, as if it were one huge piece of carpentry or a slab of stone. Our wall-papers therefore are simple fillings; they imitate no architectural features, neither dados, friezes, nor panellings.

We may say finally that the colours used in the printing are entirely free from arsenic. Of the one hundred and fifty or more wall-papers printed by Morris & Company it was possible to exhibit only a few. In the Embroidery room are two – the large St James pattern, first used for the banqueting-room at St James's Palace, and the red-and-gold Sunflower. In the tapestry room we have shown five of the ordinary pattern – the Fruit in its darkest colouring, the light Daisy, the Chrysanthemums, the coloured Larkspur, and the dark Jasmine. Other versions of these patterns will be found in the two books of patterns, which contain all the wall-paper we publish.

The portières and other draperies in these rooms must be taken, like all the rest, as simple exhibitions of the goods. The silk-and-wool and all-wool damasks make excellent wall-hangings and window-curtains, and all but the Dove-and-Rose pattern may be used for furniture-covers. The single chintz pattern shown in this room has been a favorite in England; it is called Tulip. There are many different colourings of this pattern. The printed cotton-velvet hanging, over the Chrysanthemum wall-paper, is a variation of the red pattern shown in the Chintz room. The names, widths and prices of all the goods are clearly marked.

We may now describe the specimen of hand-worked tapestry in the frame. This is one of the few things referred to beforehand, as necessarily exhibited in a somewhat unnatural way. Tapestry of this class is sometimes used for wall-hanging, and sometimes for portières. This specimen is framed and glazed as a picture, which in one sense it is; but the glazing was done only for the purpose of public exhibition, and is not consistent with the proper use of tapestry.

ARRAS TAPESTRY

is so called from the town in Flanders famous for the manufacture in the Middle Ages. Tapestry was made in many other towns, in England as well as on the Continent of Europe, but Arras was the general name for it. The art was not invented in Europe. It is older than the appearance of the European races. When the art of weaving attained the rudimentary condition of a few warp-threads fixed at one end to a weighted stick, and strained from the other by a bow, tapestry-weaving was invented. As a mechanical art it has made scarce any progress since. The artist has been able to increase the number of threads on which his pattern is woven, and so increase the size of his pictures; but this is all. The process remains exactly the same as when Penelope wove her web, and she was but practising an ancient art. To understand the process, you have but to imagine a coarse warp of twisted cotton or hemp placed *upright* before the worker. The colours are held on small bobbins, or quills, with long sharp points. Selecting the one he wants, he passes it through as many warp threads as the design requires, and brings it back, opening the shed, for those threads only, with the left hand. This is all the method. It can be readily understood how an artist, in such a way, may work any pattern or shape he will. Attempts have been made to improve this loom by making the warps horizontal, and laying on a table, under the warp, the cartoon or pattern for the weaver to follow. Time is saved, and cost, by so doing, but as the natural concomitant of time-saving in the arts, the art itself becomes less. Instead of an artist working freely with his model before him, you have a mechanical person peering through the warp-threads at a dimly-seen drawing, and imitating it in a purblind way. The invention called the Low-warp Loom did a good deal to bring the art of tapestry-weaving into its present state of degradation and deserved neglect. Our efforts to restore it to some of its earlier dignity naturally commenced by a restoration of the ancient method.

Of all kinds of wall-decoration, Arras tapestry is the most durable, except mosaic – and the most desirable, next to painting done by the hand of a good master.

The subject of this piece is the story of the Goose Girl. The cartoon was designed for us by Walter Crane. It is due to him we should say this, our figure-cartoons being done as a rule by Mr Burne Jones. Mr Crane has chosen the critical part of the girl's history for his picture; the accessories relate to the other passages. It may be for the convenience of many readers if we here give

THE STORY

Once upon a time lived an old queen, whose daughter was betrothed to a king's son, and when the time came that the princess should be sent to him, the queen dressed her in beautiful clothes, and gave her much treasure, and a maid to attend her, and sent them on the journey. But before they left, she called her daughter aside and gave her a talisman, which should protect her from all dangers by the way, and from all troubles. The princess placed the talisman in her bosom, and for a time thought much of what her mother had said. But one day, as she stooped to drink by a stream, the talisman fell out, and she did not perceive it; but the maid who waited on her did, and bad thoughts came into her mind; so that when the princess wished to continue the journey, she would not allow her to remount her own horse, Falada, but gave her the other horse, and took Falada to herself. She also made her take off her royal clothes, and swear by the 'open sky' that she would say nought of what had been done, to any one. And the princess, having lost her talisman, felt weak and helpless, and was forced to comply. But Falada noticed all that passed, and the tears stood in his eyes.

They soon arrived at the king's palace, where the servant was treated with great respect. The young prince lifted her from her horse, and led her to the chair of state while the princess was left standing in the court.

Just then the old king saw her, and remarked how delicate and beautiful she was, and he asked the bride who it was she had brought with her and left in the court below.

'Only a wench I picked up on the way; find her something to do.' And she was set to help the gooseherd.

Now the false princess was afraid that the affection of Falada for his mistress might cause her story to be doubted; so she complained to the prince that the horse had angered her on the journey, and she would not be content if it were allowed to live. Falada, therefore, was ordered to be killed; and when the princess heard of it, she fondled him for the last time, and with many tears begged the head might be given to her secretly. This she fixed over the gate of the yard where the geese were kept, and, as she passed under it in the morning with her flock, said sadly:

'Ah, my Falada, there thou hangest!' And was surprised at first to hear the reply:

'Ah, my princess, there thou gangest!' But this became their constant salutation.

Now the gooseherd, whose servant she was, noticed her beauty; and one day, when she had loosened her hair, which was of purest gold, he asked for a lock, and when she refused it, attempted to take one. Then the wind came to her help, and blew so strongly that the hair streamed in the sun like a flame; and the herdboy's hat was blown across the meadow, and the wind held it and kept it always from him until the princess had bound up her hair again; and when he came back she laughed at him, so that he was angry all day, and tended the geese in silence.

On the next day the same thing happened, and the boy was so befooled that he determined he would not herd geese with the witch-maiden again; and he made complaint to the king, telling him also of the horse's head that spake. The old king thought he would see this thing for himself; and he commanded the herdboy to go out one more day, and to try to get a lock of hair as before. And the king watched from behind a bush, and all happened as the herd had said. Then the king questioned the maiden, who told him of the oath, but was afraid to speak more. But the king found a way to surprise her story when she thought herself alone; and he had her dressed according to her rank, and presented to the prince, whose eyes were opened; and the wicked waiting-woman, seeing her treachery useless, confessed it all.

The piece of tapestry in which the central scene of this story is depicted is about 6 feet wide by 7¾ feet high, and is worth $1,500. If appropriately lined and fringed, it would make a very charming portière, or it might be framed as part of the design of a high mantle for a chimney; such a use of it might also be exceedingly effective.

Near by is a small framed drawing of Flora, a girlish figure in white drapery, with a background of scroll-foliage. This represents a piece of tapestry now in the loom, or about to go in. The size will be 10 feet by 7 feet. There is a companion figure of Pomona in the Damask-room, which we did not notice in speaking of the damasks. It is also a design for a piece not yet executed. The two figures, we estimate, will be worth $2,500 each, duty paid. The figures in these two designs are by Mr Burne Jones, the backgrounds by Mr Morris. We are now prepared to take commissions for wall-hangings in sets, for portières, altar-cloths, and other things for which this material is suitable.

There remains but the embroideries and the painted glass to complete the review of our exhibit. We will turn to the embroideries in the next room.

EMBROIDERY

must have been in its origin a much later art than tapestry, unless we suppose the dressed skins which preceded woven cloth were ornamented by stitches. If embroidery was originally an attempt to ornament plain pieces of woollen or silken cloth, the loom is presupposed for the making of the cloth; and the original loom, we have described, being as fit for pattern-weaving as for plain, the pattern or border would scarcely take longer than the unpatterned part. Decoration by means of the needle, after the weaving, therefore, implies such improved mechanism of the loom as would make the weaving of plain cloth a much quicker thing than pattern-weaving. It must, therefore, have followed the invention of the shuttle. The use of the shuttle at once quickened the process of weaving, but made all pattern-weaving, except the merest plaids, impossible for many years to come – until, in fact, the apparatus we now call a Jacquard was, not invented, but prototyped. The first embroideries were no doubt very simple affairs of borderings and powderings, and the weaver in course of time found means to imitate some of these; and since then has continually increased the size and richness of his patterning, but under conditions that limit him in many ways. He has succeeded in restricting the field of the embroiderer, but not in replacing him, and he will never do that. There will always be a limit to pattern-making by the loom, even by the tapestry-loom, the ablest of all; and outside that limit, embroidery is supreme. This unapproachable ground is therefore the proper field for the embroiderer; and his occupation of this ground – or of the lost country where the weaver, of whatever kind, is his superior in price and style – is a good test of the embroiderer's understanding of his art. We sometimes see a needle-worker trying to enrich a beautiful damask with cobble-stitch, or wasting much time in doing what the loom would do much better. Embroidery, to be worth the doing, should, in our opinion, achieve something that cannot be so well done in any other way. Its advantage lies in the perfect freedom of the worker, in the means it gives him to do what is quite unattainable by other means. When, therefore, we see embroidery getting daily coarser in a foolish competition with machine-work, and hear the boast that the machine can 'produce the effects of the best-class hand-work', it is not useless to show of what the art is capable. The large, framed piece is a work of pure embroidery. The surface is completely covered with stitching, so that the effect is wholly produced by the needle. The workmanship, we will venture to say, is quite unrivalled.

Notice the perfect gradations of shade and colour; how truly the lines radiate with the growth and play of the leafage, and how perfectly the lustre of the silk is preserved! The perfect beauty of the colouring is also due, in great part, to the sympathy and skill of the worker. How would it have been possible for any master, otherwise, to have directed the choice of so many shades, and to have obtained that blending of them which is part of the refinement of the work? Notice, also, how skilfully the ground has been used to modify the tint where gradations too subtle for the dyer were needed. This is truly a work *sui generis*. Oil painting would have had less depth and lustre; the Jacquard loom could not have given the immense variety, nor the tapestry loom the purity of gradation. It is emphatically embroidery, and we may say, without affectation, embroidery at its best. But what is it for? Well, it is permitted to some things to be simply beautiful, and no other service is asked of them. This is more beautiful than many useless things we buy and are proud to possess. If it should not be found worthy to join one of the collections of rare and beautiful things in America, it may perhaps find a place in the South Kensington Museum, as a model of excellence in this art. It was exhibited for a short time in our show-room in London before this Exhibition opened. Its value in the United States is $2,000. The size is 7 feet 9 inches by 5 feet 9 inches.

We are not exhibiting any other work quite so beautiful as this, but there are a few in the case only inferior to it. The most important is a coverlet worked after the same manner, but with filoselle upon cotton. It is about 6 feet 9 inches long by 4 feet 6 inches wide. There is a border of about 12 inches; inside this, the ground is covered with pale-gold, on which the design, freely flowing from the centre, is inlaid with yellow-green, blue, pink, purple, and dark-green. The border has a pink ground, with pale-blue, deep-blue, light-green, dark-green, purple, and yellow – the inner and outer lines of the border being blue. The subdued sheen of the filoselle makes this beautiful piece of work not too magnificent for its purpose. It is lined with silk and fringed.

As a sample of another kind of work is a table-cover of blue cloth, embroidered with silk twist. The work is necessarily of a firm, close kind; and the design is adapted to it, being somewhat more conventional in its forms and treatment. The stitch, we may say, is *not* chain-stitch, as so many visitors seem to think.

A quite different kind is represented by the embroidered cushion, which is intended to exhibit the full richness of floss. To get that, the silk is laid on the surface in long tresses, and bound to it by stitches which make a Diaper pattern. This kind of embroidery is of course only fit for shapes that can be treated flatly. The flowers, which give variety

Plate 6.3 *Flowerpot* embroidered cushion, 1880s; this version was embroidered by Morris's younger daughter May *William Morris Gallery*

and scale to the pattern, are worked with ordinary embroidery-stitch.

In the same case are many smaller things – chair-backs, five o'clock tea-cloths, &c. – worked mostly on linen, with washable silks; and there are some pieces of the simpler kind prepared for finishing.

The silks and wools we sell for embroidery are of our own dyeing, and are all washable. (Footnote: It may be a proper caution to say that for such washing only pure *toilet* soaps should be used, and that the object must not be soaped, but immersed in a warm lather made with the soap.)

To this explanation we are almost ashamed to add that none of the work is done by machinery. This announcement has already caused much surprise to visitors, who have asked if the work was really done by hand. It is equally surprising to us that there should be any belief the embroidery we are exhibiting could be done by means less delicate in operation, and less sensitive to the least change of the worker's intention. Our preliminary remarks will have shown that we consider the province of embroidery outside of all kinds of mechanical work. Machine-embroidery, lace-making, and weaving have all uses quite distinct from those of hand-embroidery.

STAINED GLASS

In the Damask room are two framed drawings of windows which we did not notice; they have their full descriptions appended, and we wished to reserve what we have to say on painted glass for this place. The stained glass we are exhibiting will be found by turning to the left as you step into the Hall out of the Tapestry room. It fills two of the windows of the hall. There are four single figures, about 5 feet high, and four small subjects. The figures represent St Cecily, Samuel the Prophet, St Mark, and Elijah. They are all of different scale, and are shown as examples of different treatments. The small subjects are in pairs: Eli and Samuel in the Temple, and Timothy with his Mother, in panels about 26 inches by 22; Christ in the Temple, and Christ Blessing Children, in panels about 23 inches by 19. They are all from cartoons by Mr Burne-Jones. It was thought better to show these portions of several windows, rather than one window completely. The framed drawings, and others in the portfolio, will give examples of more comprehensive designs. The larger Allerton window is a Paradise, that for Easthampstead a Doom, and the little Allerton window in the tapestry room is the Revelation to the Shepherds, *Gloria in excelsis Deo*. As regards the method of painting and the design, our glass differs so much from other kinds that we may be allowed a word in apology. Glass-painting differs from oil-painting and fresco, mostly in the translucency of the material and the strength, amounting to absolute blackness of the outlines. This blackness of outline is due to the use of lead frames, or settings, which are absolutely necessary for the support of the pieces of glass if various colours are used. It becomes therefore a condition and characteristic of glass-painting. Absolute blackness of outline and translucency of colour are then the differentia between glass-painting and panel or wall painting. They lead to treatment quite peculiar in its principles of light and shade and composition, and make glass-painting an art apart. In the first place, the drawing and composition have to be much more simple, and yet more carefully studied, than in paintings which have all the assistance of shadow and reflected lights to disguise faults and assist the grouping. In the next place, the light and shade must be so managed that the strong outlines shall not appear crude, nor the work within it thin; this implies a certain conventionalism of treatment and makes the details of a figure much more an affair of drawing than of painting; because by drawing – that is, by filling the outlines with other lines of proportionate strength – the force of the predominant lines is less unnatural. These, then, are the first conditions of good glass-painting as we perceive them – well-balanced and shapely figures, pure and simple drawing, and a minimum of light and shade. There is another reason for this last. Shading is a dulling of the glass; it is therefore inconsistent with the use of a material which was chosen for its brightness. After these we ask for beautiful colour. There may be more of it, or less; but it is only rational and becoming that the light we stain should not be changed to dirt or ugliness. Colour, pure and sweet, is the least you should ask for in a painted window.

Instructions for painted windows should be sent direct to Morris and Company, 449 Oxford St., London, England.

This closes our account of the things we are exhibiting at Boston. As a complement to the descriptions you have followed, we append a list of those tradesmen in Boston with whom our goods are placed. We sell only to them, and no others can supply the goods we make. This statement is the more necessary, as we know that unauthorized copies and various imitations are offered for sale, without explanation.

**Our Wall-Papers, Cretonnes, Damasks, Dress-Silks,
Embroidery-Silks, and Crewels**
Are to be had of A.H. DAVENPORT, 96 Washington Street

— — —

Our Wall-Papers,
From J.F. BUMSTEAD & CO., 148 Tremont Street

— — —

Our Carpets,
From JOEL GOLDTHWAIT & CO., 169 Washington Street

— — —

ELLIOT & BULKLEY, 42 EAST 14th STREET, NEW YORK,
Are our General Agents in America for the sale of any of the
above-mentioned goods.

NOTES

1. On the use of agencies see, *inter alia*, S. Nicholas, 'The Overseas Marketing Performance of British Industry, 1870–1914', *Economic History Review*, Vol. XXXVII No. 4 (1984); *idem*, 'Modelling the Growth Strategies of British Firms', *Business History*, Vol. XXIX No. 4 (1987); R.P.T. Davenport-Hines (ed.), *Markets and Bagmen* (1986), *passim*.
2. G. Wardle, *The Morris Exhibit at the Foreign Fair* (Boston, MA, 1883), p. 15; also see N. Kelvin (ed.), *The Collected Letters of William Morris*, Vol. II (Princeton, NJ, 1987), p. 134, to Catherine Holiday, 9 Nov. 1882.
3. Wardle, ibid., p. 30. In 1884, when a member of the Royal Commission on Technical Instruction asked Morris about the problem of piracy, he remarked that 'America is our friend in that respect chiefly'. See his evidence to the *Second Report of the Royal Commissioners on Technical Instruction* (Parliamentary Papers, c.3981, 1884 XXXI), Q.1588.
4. Bumstead's had sold Morris wallpapers in very limited quantities since at least July 1873, when *Scribner's Monthly* reported that the articles were very expensive and did not influence popular taste. C. Lynn, *Wallpaper in America* (New York, 1980), pp. 383–4. As well as selling imported wallpapers, Bumstead's was an important manufacturer in its own right. The firm had played a part in early attempts to mechanise the industry between the 1830s and 1850s, and by the

1870s and 1880s it was one of several firms which combined traditional block printing for its better-quality wares with the latest advances in mechanised printing for its cheaper products. See R.C. Nylander, 'Oceans Apart: Imports and the Beginning of American Manufacture', in L. Hoskins (ed.), *The Papered Wall* (1994), pp. 130–1.

5. See L. Parry, *William Morris Textiles* (1983), pp. 78, 136.
6. N. Kelvin (ed.), *The Collected Letters of William Morris*, Vol. I (Princeton, NJ, 1984), p. 66n.
7. Ibid., p. 563, to Charles Eliot Norton, 30 March 1880.
8. Ibid., p. 568, to Emma Shelton Morris, 23 May 1880.
9. Reprinted in M. Morris (ed.), *The Collected Works of William Morris* (24 vols, 1910–15), Vol. XXII.

— 7 —

Morris, the Ionides Family and
1 Holland Park[1]

IN THE MIDDLE decades of the nineteenth century, members of a
confident and dynamic middle class came to rival the aristocracy and
gentry as patrons of the arts, as they sought to furnish and adorn the
rooms of their substantial homes. Often, too, these new patrons began
to provide for municipal art galleries and museums, challenging
Matthew Arnold's belief that the emerging business élites of provincial
cities like Newcastle and Manchester represented 'the stout main body
of philistinism'.[2] Many of these patrons were captains of industry –
Middlesborough ironmasters like Henry Bolckow and Sir Isaac Lowthian
Bell, and James Leathart, the Newcastle lead manufacturer. Others
were members of the professional and commercial classes, such as
Thomas Plint, the Leeds stockbroker who was an admirer of Rossetti
and the Pre-Raphaelites. In London, members of the Greek merchant
community were intimately connected with cultural circles, and used
their considerable wealth to patronise artists, architects and interior
designers. Prominent amongst them were Alexander Constantine
Ionides and his son Alexander (Alecco). Between 1864 and the end of
the 1880s, they turned their house, 1 Holland Park, into a veritable
showcase of the decorative arts.

Holland Park was developed in the middle decades of the nineteenth
century by the owner of Holland House, Lady Holland. The houses,
built between 1860 and 1879, were designed by Francis Radford. No. 1,
which backed on to the park, and had splendid views of Holland House,
was bought by Alexander Constantine Ionides in 1864 for £4,500. He
owned the house until 1875, when he retired to Hastings and his
youngest son Alecco took it over.[3] The area quickly became popular
amongst artistic circles. Neighbours of the Ionides family included Sir
Frederic (later Lord) Leighton and Val Prinsep, who had houses built in
nearby Holland Park Road by George Aitchison and Philip Webb.[4]

Plate 7.1 1 Holland Park: the exterior from the front *Victoria & Albert Museum*

As was often the case with such developments, Lady Holland's agents closely supervised the work to ensure that the houses – large, detached villas – were of a suitably high standard of construction. Architecturally, however, they were not of outstanding merit. Walter Crane described 1 Holland Park as 'a builder's house of a not uncommon Bayswater type, though its detached situation ... gave it a certain character'. The architect Philip Webb who, among other changes, substituted a tiled roof for the original blue-slate one, was more critical: 'It was like a feather-bed – shapeless, and when you pushed it in one direction it stuck out in another.'[5]

Internally, however, the house was of great significance. Over the years numerous improvements were made. Philip Webb was responsible for the fabric of the building – one of his most important metropolitan commissions – and it featured work by leading figures in the decorative arts, including Jeckyll, Crane, and, especially, William Morris. Morris & Co.'s letters to A.A. Ionides are preserved in the Victoria & Albert Museum and elsewhere,[6] and provide the only surviving correspondence between the firm and one of its major customers. In describing the decorative work undertaken at 1 Holland Park, they tell us much about Morris & Co.'s business practices. The house was also the subject of several contemporary articles, and was photographed by the celebrated architectural photographer Harry Bedford Lemere. It provides invaluable evidence of the domestic environment preferred by two of the most cultured members of London's commercial élite.

Like many leading figures in the City of London, Alexander Constantine Ionides' financial fortunes fluctuated considerably. The Crimean War brought a severe setback, and he suffered further reverses in the financial crisis of 1866. The collapse of the Bank of London, of which Ionides was a director, lost the family more than £120,000.[7] But his income was always amply sufficient to entertain a wide circle of artistic friends, and he began the family tradition of patronising up-and-coming artists in his adopted country. In the mid-1830s, for example, he provided G.F. Watts with his first commission; a copy of his father's portrait by Lane, which was so successful that the copy was kept and the original given to Athens University. Watts was eventually to paint five generations of the family. In the years that followed, Alexander Constantine became famous for his hospitality amongst the artistic, literary and diplomatic communities of London. In 1853 he was nominated as Consul-General for Greece – a position he held from 1855 to 1866 – and in June 1855 he became a director of the Crystal Palace, and was responsible for setting up art exhibitions and organising concerts.[8]

Every Sunday the Ionides family held open house. Amongst its regular visitors was James McNeill Whistler (1834–1903), who had first met Alexander's sons Luke and Alecco around 1857 when they were students in Paris. Alexander commissioned a painting by Whistler of Battersea Bridge in 1859, and by the middle of the next decade many friends and family members had purchased examples of his work. Many other artists were introduced to the family circle. Fantin Latour, visiting London in 1861, was brought along by Whistler, and the Ionides family bought a number of his paintings. Dante Gabriel Rossetti came in 1862, and in turn he introduced the young Edward Burne-Jones. Burne-Jones soon became a close friend of the family, which provided a valuable outlet for his work. It was at Holland Park where he met Maria Zambaco, Alexander Constantine's niece, with whom he had a tempestuous affair. Other guests included G.F. Watts, Robert Browning, Edward Poynter and George du Maurier.[9]

All of Alexander Constantine's five children were eager and accomplished members of London's cultural élite. Of the girls, Chariclea Anthea Euterpe (1844–1923) married in 1871 the composer Edward Dannreuther who did much to popularise Wagner's music in Britain. Aglaia (1834–1906), who married Theodore Coronio in 1855, was a noted conversationalist, and developed close friendships with several leading artists and intellectuals. Among her correspondents were Alma Tadema, Holman Hunt, John Stuart Mill, Ford Madox Brown, Sir John Millais, Samuel Butler, Thomas Hood, Ellen Terry, Frederic Leighton, George Sand, William Wordsworth, Sir Edwin Landseer, John Ruskin, Beerbohm Tree and George du Maurier.[10] She is, however, best known to posterity as the close friend and confidante of William Morris. Mackail, Morris's first biographer, commented that 'the friendship between her and Morris was affectionate and unbroken through life'.[11] She flattered and rather embarrassed Morris but managed to break down his reserve. Aglaia was one of the very few people – Georgiana Burne-Jones was another – to whom Morris revealed his private thoughts and feelings.[12]

The eldest son, Constantine Alexander (1833–1900) is today best known for the magnificent collection of paintings, prints and drawings he bequeathed to the Victoria & Albert Museum.[13] Guided by the French realist painter and printmaker Alphonse Legros, Constantine Ionides bought widely in the 1870s and early 1880s. His purchases ranged from works by members of the Barbizon school, Jean-François Millet and Theodore Rousseau, and Degas' *Ballet Scene from Robert Il Diavole*, to old masters, most notably Botticelli's *Smeralda Bandinelli*. He also acquired an eclectic collection of drawings, and a large number of prints – including many fine etchings by Rembrandt. In the last 20 years of his life, he turned his attention to the acquisition of antique engraved gems and oriental porcelain. Constantine's taste may have most strongly reflected that of Legros, at least until the early 1880s, but he also had a wide circle of cultivated friends, including Walter Crane, Cobden Sanderson, Philip Webb, Rhoda Garrett, Edward Burne-Jones, Lord Leighton and Dante Gabriel Rossetti.[14]

Luke (1837–1924) joined his father's business in 1857 on returning from Heidelberg University. He later became an insurance and stock broker with offices in Threadneedle Street. He was not particularly successful in business. Like his father, his affairs were beset by periodic crises, and he was eventually declared bankrupt on 10 January 1900. He

did not systematically patronise artists and designers like his elder
brother, but he was nevertheless closely associated with artists and
designers like Whistler, Burne-Jones and Morris, about whom he wrote
a volume of *Memories* privately published in 1925.[15]

The youngest son, Alexander (Alecco) (1840–98) who was painted by
Watts and Legros, and appears as 'the Greek' in George du Maurier's
novel *Trilby*, was a Member of the London Stock Exchange like his two
brothers,[16] and was also a director of several private companies. In
contemporary directories he was described as a General Merchant, with
offices at 124/125 Old Broad Street. He followed in his father's footsteps
as Greek Consul-General in 1884. Alecco collected Tanagra figures
(early Hellenistic terracotta grave goods), and Persian embroideries
and antiques, including bronze and brassware, earthenware and tiles.[17]

It was Alecco who was largely responsible for the transformation of
1 Holland Park, although the work was begun in his father's time.
Already, in 1864, George du Maurier could describe 1 Holland Park as
'stunning'[18] – largely, one imagines, because of the vitality of the company at the Sunday gatherings, and the quality of the paintings, prints
and drawings which clothed the walls. It became even more splendid in
the years that followed. The first major embellishment came in 1870,
when a new wing was added by Thomas Jeckyll (1827–81). After beginning his career as an ecclesiastical architect, Jeckyll turned to domestic
work, and the new wing at 1 Holland Park was his first important
commission. He designed a billiard room, sitting room, bedroom and
servants' hall in the 'Anglo-Japanese' style, and was also responsible
for much of the furniture. His most impressive achievement was the
billiard room. The ceilings and walls were framed in oak, and the
cornice, dado and ceiling were panelled with red lacquered Japanese
trays. Lewis F. Day commented that 'hundreds of Japanese trays must
have been slaughtered to supply them'.[19] Japanese paintings on silk and
prints of flower and animal subjects in polished wood frames covered
the walls. The decorative scheme was completed by a high mantel of
oak and red lacquer, with tiles of red lustre framing the fire, yellowish-
brown leather settees for onlookers, and curtains in shades of light and
dark brown. Jeckyll also designed a suite of bedroom furniture for
Alecco at the time of his marriage, comprising a wardrobe, dressing
table and commode. The wardrobe in ebony and padouk, with Japanese
designs in the upper panels of the doors, was particularly splendid.[20]

Following his acquisition of the house in 1875, Alecco commissioned further rebuilding and redecorating work to provide a showcase for his collections. As noted earlier, Philip Webb had charge of the structural alterations, carried out between 1879 and 1888. He was responsible for the splendid main staircase, the hall, with its mosaic floor, and a remarkable smoking room in English marbles. In addition, he designed the wood panelling for a number of the principal rooms, and some important pieces of furniture, notably the dining-room sideboard and fireplace.[21]

Morris & Co., by then an established and influential concern with a number of large-scale projects to its credit, was commissioned to decorate and furnish the house. The earliest surviving documents relating to Holland Park date from March 1880, though the work probably began during the previous year. It was not completed until October 1888. The firm was responsible for carrying out paper-hanging, painting, wood panelling, supplying and fitting carpets, curtains and wall-hangings and stuffing and reupholstering chairs. The surviving bills and estimates reveal that great care was taken in the preparation of invoices, which listed every item and service, no matter how small. The total cost of the work recorded in the surviving invoices was £2,352 8s. 8d, though this is certainly an incomplete record. Notable omissions included the tapestries in the sitting room, which must surely have been amongst the most expensive items.[22]

Much of the decorative scheme was under Morris's personal control. This was the firm's normal practice with major commissions before the late 1880s, when an increasing amount of work was delegated to J.H. Dearle and others. In 1879–80, for example, Morris was advising Alecco on the decoration of the dining-room, drawing-room, antiquities room, staircase and principal bedroom, and superintending 'the execution of same including patterns and paint'. In this connection, a bill dated March 1880 included an item for £27 11s. 6d. 'to making 11 journeys to Holland Park'.[23] The work was completed in March 1880, when a bill for £559 10s. 10d. was submitted. Major work in the drawing-room and antiquities room was undertaken in May 1883. It was completed in May 1884 at a cost of £1,328 14s. 9d. Further decorations were carried out in 1888 in the morning-room. At the same time, the walls of the staircase, cloakroom and lobbies were covered in *Gold Poppy* paper; paintwork, panelling and stair treads were repaired; and an Axminster stair carpet was supplied at £51 including fitting. In all, the work undertaken in 1888 was costed at £464 7s. 1d.

The decoration of Holland Park was of great importance to Morris

& Co. Not only was it profitable, but also it helped to bring the firm to the attention of potential clients. Access to the fashionable homes of west London was an invaluable business asset, and it contributed to the very substantial upswing in the volume of business conducted by Morris & Co. in the 1880s and 1890s. Amongst those who were directly influenced by the firm's work for Alecco Ionides were the Beale family, who also had a London house in Holland Park. The Beales later commissioned Morris to decorate the house which Webb built for them at Standen.[24] As noted earlier, 1 Holland Park was also widely reported in contemporary journals, thus bringing the work of Webb, Morris and Crane to the attention of a wide and appreciative middle-class audience. In 1893, for example, Lewis F. Day wrote an account of a visit to 1 Holland Park for the *Art Journal*. Other articles appeared in the *Building News*, the *Studio* and the *Architectural Review*. Together with Lemere's photographs, and contemporary drawings, they allow us to reconstruct a vivid impression of the house in its late Victorian heyday.

Visitors entered the house through the new entrance hall, decorated with gilded ornamental ironwork and William De Morgan tiles. They proceeded up a staircase designed by Webb, 'where cleverly planned steps, beneath the hand-rail, afford a resting-place for bronzes'. Gleeson White, in his *Studio* article of 1898, recorded that every item of the pattern and decoration was 'selected to support a delicate scheme of colour wherein the pink and silver of the walls come as an important factor'. The Patent Axminster carpet, 'a pleasant harmony in pale greyish-green and cinnamon', was supplied by Morris & Co. It had a large-scale pattern with a centrally placed motif. As always, Morris's design was appropriate to the medium in which he was working. Patent Axminster was a relatively coarse fabric, and he believed that the design should consequently be much bolder than for Wiltons and real Axminster.[25] This was the second of Morris's two designs for the medium, and the firm evidently regarded Patent Axminsters as well suited to both stairs and large flat areas. At Holland Park, the same design was used on landings and in Jeckyll's billiard room, and a large quantity was also supplied for the dining-room at Clouds, the Wiltshire home of the Hon. Percy Wyndham. The hall and staircase ceiling was one of several in the house decorated with designs by Morris. It was completed in 1888 at a cost of £111 10s. Alecco's brother Luke stated that the design consisted of small arabesques, painted in gold and other colours upon a white ground.[26]

Plate 7.2 Holland Park: the main staircase by Philip Webb, with Patent Axminster carpet by William Morris, and an early picture of the Ionides family by G.F. Watts. *Victoria & Albert Museum*

Off the stairs was a marble smoking room designed by Webb. The principal architectural feature of the room was a recess on one side, supported on columns of Purbeck marble, with capitals of creamy-toned alabaster. This was fitted with a long, low, cushioned seat. The smoking-room was much praised by contemporaries. One reviewer described it thus:

the marble smoking-room ... is entered through a glazed door from a landing, off the almost equally fine staircase, both by Mr Webb. The marble in the smoking-room is of varying hues, used with restraint, and a real knowledge of the material. Picture a room, long and high in proportion to its width, lined to a height of eight or nine feet, white marble surrounding panels graduating from a creamy tint to a russet brown, forming a pleasant contrast to the slips of dark green marble that enclose the panels. On the right hand side of the room is a recess, across which runs a frieze, supported by columns of Purbeck marble resting on the floor, with bases of the same material, the caps being of alabaster enriched with simple foliage. Above the broad surfaced moulding forming a coping to the marble, and running round the room, is a range of small windows set in an effective treatment of wood, the far end pierced with a window of circular shape, through which the light falls on the translucent marble. Passing through the door again, and looking down the stair-case, is a large circular window at the farther end, following in parallel lines the segmental shaped plaster roof. The sides are panelled in wood and painted green, and from the cornice above springs the barrel ceiling.[27]

The antiquities room (referred to as the first drawing room in some contemporary accounts) had a painted ceiling and decorations by Morris & Co. Most of the work was carried out between 1883 and 1884. In May 1883, the firm quoted for fitting new panelling, cupboards and glass cases, installing a fireplace and grate, glazing the windows with leaded glass, and widening the opening into the drawing room. A Hammersmith carpet was supplied for £82. This was *Carbrook* – a design which had first been made for another client in 1879, and was rewoven for Holland Park. The Ionides version is now in the Victoria & Albert Museum.[28] The chief colours in the hangings were grey-greens and blues. According to the estimate, curtains of *St James* silk, lined and finished with tufted fringes, were to be provided for the bay window, the door opposite the bay and the opening into the drawing room, together with all necessary poles and fixings, at a cost of £245. To judge from photographs of the antiquities room, however, Morris's *Oak* woven silk damask appears to have been used instead. The chairs were upholstered by Morris & Co.

in grey-green Utrecht velvet, and *Flower Garden* silk and wool damask.

The walls of the antiquities room were covered in 'a gold lacquered paper rich in various colours, that at first sight suggests Japan, but proves to be a design of chrysanthemum (by Morris) embossed in silver, overlaid with washes of brilliant transparent lacquer'.[29] The cornice was also lacquered, and the ceiling painted with gold and silver upon an ivory ground. Metal foil and lacquer were widely used at 1 Holland Park to give the richness of effect which Alecco Ionides desired. There was quite a vogue during the 1880s for techniques which imitated expensive tooled and gilded Spanish-leather wall-hangings.[30] Lochnan notes that Morris & Co. responded to the fashion by producing a range of gilt and lacquered papers, including *Vine* and *Sunflower*, and cites an extra-ordinary version of *Vine* first produced in 1884: 'it was printed using green and black paint and dark-brown lacquer on gold foil which was subtly embossed using a roller to create a crinkled effect, resembling the grain of leather. This fragile surface was backed with thick, fibrous yellow paper.' These versions were expensive and only available by special order, but they remained popular for some time and were still listed in the firm's 1913 catalogue.[31]

The mantelpiece of the antiquities room was specially designed by Walter Crane to house Alecco Ionides' collection of Tanagra statuettes. The overmantel was of black marble with a central pediment, and all the sections were framed by red and yellow Siena marble columns – 'certainly a dramatic setting for the terracottas and one in accord with Ionides' rich and exotic taste'.[32]

Opening off the antiquities room was the drawing-room. Here again, the decoration of the ceiling was carried out by Morris & Co., at a cost of around £160. The walls were covered with *Flower Garden*, a jacquard handloom woven silk and wool damask designed by Morris in 1879, at a cost of £51 3s 6d. Given Alecco's liking for gilded and lacquered wall-hangings, it was an obvious choice. As Morris & Co.'s Boston catalogue noted, the colours were chosen 'to suggest the beauties of inlaid metal'.[33] It must have complemented the lacquered paper of the adjoining anti-quities room. Matching curtains and valances were supplied at a cost of £121 19s. 0d. When the opening between the drawing room and the antiquities room was widened by Morris & Co. in 1883–84, the firm charged £43 for a portière in the same fabric. William Morris proposed to embroider it, but as far as one can tell from contemporary illustrations this idea came to nought.

Plate 7.3 Holland Park: Crane's mantelpiece in the antiquities room, and
Alecco's collection of Tanagra figures *Victoria & Albert Museum*

Plate 7.4 Holland Park: view from the antiquities room into the drawing-room: *Carbrook* carpet, *Flower Garden* and *Oak* fabrics, Morris lacquered wallpaper and painted ceiling. *Victoria & Albert Museum*

The principal features of the drawing room were the grand piano and the Hammersmith carpet. Morris & Co. supplied pianos by John Broadwood to a number of its major clients. In March 1883, William Morris noted that he had 'spoken to Mr. A. Ionides about his piano & he will have one of the same make of [green] stained oak; I shall be glad to help as to the tint'.[34] The piano case was designed by Burne-Jones and W.A.S. Benson, and its simple lines were very different from most Victorian piano cases. It was, however, decorated in elaborate detail, with gold and silver gesso by Kate Faulkner. The sister of Morris's close friend and associate, Charles Faulkner, she was a successful commercial designer who produced wallpaper designs, painted tiles, pottery and gesso decoration for Morris & Co. and other manufacturers.

On the drawing-room floor was the *Holland Park* carpet, designed by

Morris in 1883 and handwoven at Merton Abbey. Gleeson White commented that it revealed 'the features which he has made his own – robust generous curves blossoming into flower-like patterns, and with a sense of space unlike the "tight" effect of most modern carpets'.[35] It was a large carpet, approximately 16' x 13', and cost Ionides the substantial sum of £113. According to Parry, it used 'Morris's most characteristic combination of a dark-blue indigo field with a madder-red border'; it was 'probably Morris's most original carpet design, and shows traces of all his greatest influences: mediaevalism, floral realism and eastern precision'. She adds that 'many of the motifs and separate elements used in the design can be traced to other techniques – wall-paintings, wallpapers and textiles in particular – and although the design is complex with a strong border design, field and subsidiary background patterns, Morris succeeded in controlling these to make a balanced composition.'[36] It was considered a great success at the time. At least four other versions were subsequently woven, each with variations to the background and border colours.

Striking though the antiquities room and drawing room undoubtedly were, they were nevertheless eclipsed by the dining room. The first stage in its decoration was the installation of the ornate sideboard and the fireplace. These features were the work of Philip Webb, as was the wood panelling. The fireplace was of Purbeck marble with antique Persian tiles of hunting scenes in slight relief, with lords and ladies out hawking on slender-limbed horses. Above the fireplace was a projecting and unusually elaborate cornice and shelf, carried by six brackets, with small flat arches between.[37] 'In admirable keeping with this combination' was the old Spanish leather with which the lower walls were covered, embossed with a pattern in gold, bronze-green, and a little dark red, on a sea-green ground. This formed 'a perfect background to a few fine pictures', including Whistler's self-portrait.[38]

Webb left the upper walls and ceiling of the dining room bare, and Walter Crane was called in to decorate them. Unlike the Gothic revivalists, who associated it with the classical tradition, Crane was an enthusiast for decorative plasterwork, and was largely responsible for its growing popularity with the Arts and Crafts movement in the 1890s. He was familiar with many High Renaissance examples, both English and Italian. With the assistance of Osmund Weeks, who collaborated with him on several projects, including 1 Holland Park, he spent a good deal of time investigating techniques, later contributing to discussions

Plate 7.5 Holland Park: the drawing-room. Piano case designed by Burne-Jones and W.A.S. Benson and decorated by Kate Faulkner, *Flower Garden* woven silk on the walls and *Holland Park* Hammersmith carpet on the floor

Victoria & Albert Museum

Plate 7.6 The *Holland Park* carpet, designed by William Morris in 1883. This version was woven in 1886 for Clouds, the Hon. Percy Wyndham's Wiltshire home *Sotheby's*

on the subject at the RIBA, and publishing his findings in 'Notes on Gesso', his first article in the *Studio* in May 1893.[39]

The ceiling was divided into coffered panels, which were decorated with the vine of life in conventional scroll patterns, in gold on a blue ground. Between the high dado and the cornice was a frieze with rectangular panels illustrating scenes from Aesop's fables, and above Webb's sideboard was a lunette of 'The Lion in Love'. The twelve main panels of the frieze were separated by small vertical panels, filled with trophies of fruit and arabesque ornament. Crane's designs featured in a series of articles in the *Building News* between December 1883 and March 1884. One of them is illustrated. The general view of the dining room by Bedford Lemere allows us to gauge the overall effect. A noteworthy feature was the attention paid to detail. Walter Crane designed a set of finger plates for the doors in lacquered gesso, together with bell pulls and light fittings. He later added low relief designs in gesso to Webb's wood panelling.[40]

Even this, however, was not sufficiently opulent for Alecco's taste. The walls, the ceiling, the doors, the sideboard – in fact the whole room except for the marble mantelpiece with its Persian tiles and the high dado of Spanish leather – were covered with silver leaf and then tinted and toned with lacquers in various shades, ranging from crimson to pale green and silver. The *Building News* concluded that the result was 'bright and yet subdued, producing a most satisfactory scheme of colour decoration'.[41] Gleeson White commented that 'To read a description of this room may call up a picture of glitter and overgorgeous ornament; yet one glimpse of it would prove how false were such an impression. Although not a square inch is free from decoration, the breadth of the whole is preserved, and ... it would be very hard to find another instance of equally elaborate decoration that was so cunningly kept within the proper restraint ... the result is the reverse of gaudy, and as harmonious as a fine piece of ancient metal with the patina of age upon it.'[42] Lewis F. Day described the room in a similar vein:

The colour-scheme is a daring experiment, justified by complete success ... the brightness of the silver has been so softened by lacquer, deepened here to gold colour, there to copper, glazed to bronze or brighter green, and occasionally to ruby red, that it goes for little more than a rather higher note of the prevailing sober colour of the walls below. The danger of anything like glare or glitter has been most skilfully parried, and this really rather gorgeous decoration is restful and reposeful enough in effect, not merely for a room to dine in, but for one in which even a modest man might comfortably live.[43]

Plate 7.7 Holland Park: the dining room, with Webb's sideboard and fireplace. Gesso decoration by Walter Crane
Victoria & Albert Museum

The opulence of the room was further enhanced by the soft furnishings. The chairs were upholstered in red velvet by Morris & Co. at a cost of £30 12s. 8d., matching the curtains supplied by the firm at a cost of £88 8s. 6d. The firm also supplied a mahogany dining-table inlaid with ebony for the sum of £38.

The chief architectural features of the morning-room, located on the first floor above the billiard room, were its large semicircular bay window and fireplace with overmantel and grate designed by Jeckyll. The overmantel was comparatively simple, inset with panels of red Japanese lacquer, 'admirably suited for a background to the rare red-and-white Nankin vases, which form its principal ornament. In the deep green marble of the mantlepiece are embedded a number of blue-and-white Nankin saucers, with quaint but admirably harmonious effect.'[44] The bay window ran the full width of the room. It was glazed in small panes of clear glass, and provided splendid views across Holland Park.

Much of the work on the morning-room (which is also described as the sitting-room or studio in some of the contemporary accounts) was undertaken towards the end of the 1880s. On 18 June 1888, Morris & Co. wrote to Alecco Ionides to inform him that:

By Mr Morris' request we send you estimate for carpets and parquet flooring for the Morning Room. Mr Morris would advise a Hammersmith Carpet for this room, one large one and a good rug for the window as plan enclosed, the coloring of the centre he would propose to make a deep rich red ground broken by foliage, and a rich blue border, the small rug would have the same coloring.

The Hammersmith carpet was Morris's *Little Flower* design; it was 10' 8" x 14' 9" and cost £74. The watercolour design which Morris prepared for his client is illustrated in Linda Parry's *William Morris Textiles*. The Hammersmith rug (*Little Tree*) for the bay window was 8' 11" x 11' 1" and cost £17. Parquet flooring for the morning-room cost £26 12s.[45]

To modern eyes, this seems the most cluttered of the principal rooms. Lewis F. Day remarked that

the main colour of the walls is a low-toned green, but there is little left bare of pictures and what-not. This is the room of contrasts, not to say contradictions. A dish of Japanese dragons in raised lacquer is hung as a pendant to one of Spanish lustre, and a Graeco-Roman elephant in bronze is found in close proximity to one in brass, patterned all over with subordinate beasts and ornament in a manner peculiar to Persian Art. Yet it is one of the cosiest and most reposeful rooms in the house. It is here that Mr Ionides finds place for his bookcases, his bureau, and such-like furniture necessary to personal comfort, all of which are in the English version of the style of 'Louis-Seize', to which we give the name of Sherraton [sic].[46]

A large tapestry occupied the upper portion of one entire side of the room. This was *The Forest*, one of Morris's most successful tapestries. Webb was responsible for the birds and animals and some of the foreground decoration, to which J.H. Dearle is also believed to have contributed. Morris was responsible for the overall design of the panel, the splendid background of acanthus leaves and the poetic description. Parry notes that 'Morris arranged Philip Webb's animal designs in a most charming manner, peeping from behind tendrils and leaves, and, although caught momentarily motionless, they are still full of vitality and movement.'[47] It was probably woven by William Knight, Morris & Co.'s most gifted weaver in the 1880s. The tapestry, which was exhibited at the Arts and Crafts Exhibition of 1887, was hung together with a subsidiary panel by Dearle. It was sold to the Victoria & Albert Museum by the family in 1926.

Contemporaries understandably focused upon the splendours of the principal rooms, yet it is clear that careful attention was paid to lesser rooms, lobbies and servants' quarters. The use of Morris & Co. Axminsters on the stairs and corridors, the servants' hall with its antique blue china arranged 'on shelf upon shelf' around the walls, the Morris papers in the bedrooms, and even the pictures and prints in the up-to-date bathroom, all added to the general effect.

Though much of the decorative scheme was under the personal control of William Morris, 1 Holland Park was very much the owner's achievement, not that of the justly celebrated people whom he commissioned. Reviewers were generally in agreement about the success of the whole, though a few critical notes can be detected. An article on Webb's contribution to domestic architecture in the *Architectural Review*, for example, stated that 'one would almost wish that the same spirit had been present throughout, instead of the eclecticism that pervades', but concluded that there was a fairly harmonious welding of 'the severe simplicity of the architect with the sumptuous decoration' of Jeckyll, Crane and Morris.[48] Indeed, one wonders how far Morris was in sympathy with Holland Park's 'sumptuous decoration'; it was, after all, very different from the simplicity which Morris at heart preferred.

Plate 7.8 Holland Park: the morning-room, showing *The Forest* tapestry and Jeckyll's fireplace *Victoria & Albert Museum*

There is some evidence to suggest that during the course of the 1880s he began to withdraw from active participation in the work at Holland Park, leaving much of the work to J.H. Dearle, who was to succeed him as Morris & Co.'s chief designer, and to Frank Smith, the manager of his Oxford Street shop, with whom he entered into partnership in 1890. Morris's desire to disengage was yet more evident during the opulent decoration of Stanmore Hall in 1888–96 for the Australian mining magnate William Knox D'Arcy.[49]

In general, though, contemporaries were impressed with the sense of *Gemütlichkeit* which prevailed at Holland Park. The house did not overawe the visitor, but rather impressed with its comfort and charm. Lewis F. Day concluded that 'It is one great charm of the whole house that it strikes one unmistakably as a place to live in. It is stored full of beautiful things; but they take their place, and are not, as it-were, on exhibition; it has none of the air of a museum … Here everything is so choice that there is not much to choose between them, and nothing asserts itself. One is struck not so much by the richness of it all as by its beauty, and the taste with which, out of elements one would have thought sometimes incongruous, a congruous whole has been evolved.'[50]

In recent years, historians and designers alike have come to recognise the vitality and richness of the decorative arts in the Victorian era. Those Victorian interiors which have survived, more or less intact, through the intervening decades of neglect, to remind us how the wealthy and cultured lived are prized as a vital contribution to the cultural legacy of nineteenth-century Britain. Sadly, 1 Holland Park is not amongst them. For all its deserved celebrity in the 1880s and 1890s, it soon faded into obscurity. Alecco's family moved to Esher after his early death in 1898, and his widow sold the house ten years later to trustees for the sixth Earl of Ilchester, the owners of Holland House. Its subsequent history was not a happy one. Its Morris ceilings were white-washed over in the 1920s,[51] and it was badly damaged by bombing in the Second World War. It was included in the sale of Holland House and its grounds to London County Council in 1952. When the house was demolished in the following year, it was claimed that nothing of value remained in the interior from its great days in the 1880s.[52] Fortunately, we still have the Lemere photographs, numerous contemporary articles and, best of all, the surviving works of Morris & Co., to remind us of 1 Holland Park in its late Victorian heyday.

NOTES

1. This essay originally appeared as 'The Ionides Family and 1 Holland Park', in the *Journal of the Decorative Arts Society*, Vol. 18 (1994), pp. 2–14.

2. M. Arnold, 'Culture and Anarchy: An Essay in Political and Social Criticism', in R.H. Super (ed.), *The Complete Prose Works of Matthew Arnold* (Ann Arbor, MI, 1965), Vol. V, p. 105.

3. A.C. Ionides, Jr, *Ion: A Grandfather's Tale* (Dublin, 1927), Vol. 1, pp. 4–5; J. Atkins, 'The Ionides Family', *Antique Collector* (June 1987), p. 90.

4. *Survey of London*, Vol. XXXVII (1973), pp. 123–4.

5. W. Crane, *An Artist's Reminiscences* (1907), p. 218.

6. Victoria & Albert Museum (hereafter V&A), Box 86 kk III (xiv). For Morris's correspondence, see N. Kelvin (ed.), *Collected Letters of William Morris*, 2 vols. (Princeton, NJ, 1984–87).

7. The Bank of London was established in 1855. With its failure in 1866 it was amalgamated with the Consolidated Bank. L.S. Pressnell and J. Orbell, *A Guide to the Historical Records of British Banking* (Aldershot, 1985), p. 7.

8. *Commercial Directory of London* (1855); D. du Maurier (ed.), *The Young George du Maurier: Letters, 1860–67* (1951), p. 57.

9. See Hove Museum and Art Gallery, *From Primitives to Pre-Raphaelites: The Art Treasures of Constantine Ionides, Hove's Greatest Collector* (Hove, 1992), unpaginated.

10. A.C. Ionides, *Ion*, Vol. 2, pp. 17–18.

11. J.W. Mackail, *The Life of William Morris* (2 vols., 1899), Vol. 1, p. 290.

12. See, for example, Kelvin (ed.), *Letters*, Vol. I, pp. 172, 178, 216, 294, William Morris to Aglaia Coronio, 25 Nov. 1872; 11 Feb. 1873; 5 March 1874; 28 March 1876.

13. The collection comprised 1,138 pictures, prints and drawings, together with a further 20 items which were added following the death of his widow in 1920. Victoria & Albert Museum, *Catalogue of the Constantine Ionides Collection* (1904, 2nd edn 1925), pp. iv–vii; Hove Museum and Art Gallery, *From Primitives to Pre-Raphaelites*.

14. C.A. Ionides, *Ion*, Vol. 2, p. 20; S. Jones, 'The Liberal Connoisseur: Constantine Alexander Ionides and his Collection', *V & A Album*, Vol. 1 (1982), p. 199; Hove Museum and Art Gallery, *From Primitives to Pre-Raphaelites, passim*.

15. L. Ionides, *Memories* (Paris, 1925).

16. *Stock Exchange Members, 1885–86* (1886), p. 58.

17. See, for example, Burlington Fine Arts Club, *Illustrated Catalogue of Specimens of Persian and Arab Art, exhibited in 1885* (1885). Numerous items were loaned by A.A. Ionides to the exhibition.

18. George du Maurier to T. Armstrong, October 1864, quoted in Atkins, 'The Ionides Family', p. 91.

19. L.F. Day, 'A Kensington Interior', *Art Journal* (May 1893), p. 144.

20. E. Aslin, *The Aesthetic Movement: Prelude to Art Nouveau* (1969), pp. 93–4; L. Ionides, *Memories*, p. 15. There is an excellent colour illustration of the wardrobe in Atkins, 'The Ionides Family', p. 93.

21. For a summary of Webb's work by George Jack, who worked in his office, see the *Architectural Review* (July 1915).

22. V&A, Box III.86.kk.(xiv); also see William Morris Gallery, Walthamstow, Box 15a.

23. V&A, Box 86 kk III (xiv), Estimate from Morris & Co. to A.A. Ionides, March 1880. Further visits were made in subsequent years. See, for example, Kelvin (ed.), *Letters*, Vol. II, p. 111, to Aglaia Coronio, 23 May 1882.

24. We are indebted to Linda Parry for this information.

25. See Morris & Co., *The Morris Exhibit at the Foreign Fair, Boston, 1883–84* (Boston, MA, 1883), p. 7.

26. L. Ionides, *Memories*, pp.21–2. For other quotations, see G. White, 'An Epoch-Making House', *Studio*, Vol. XIV (1898), p. 107.

27. G.LL. Morris, 'On Mr. Philip Webb's Town Work', *Architectural Review*, Vol. 2 (1897), p. 206.

28. The *Carbrook* carpet is illustrated in L. Parry, *William Morris Textiles* (1983), p. 94.

29. White, 'An Epoch-Making House', p. 107.

30. The use of metal foil and lacquer was not an entirely new technique. For example, it had been used by Morris, Marshall, Faulkner & Co. for some of the items shown at the 1862 Great Exhibition – though not in the heavy, lavish ways popular in the 1880s.

31. K.A. Lochnan, 'Wallpapers', in K.A. Lochnan, D.E. Schoenherr and C. Silver (eds), *The Earthly Paradise: Arts and Crafts by William Morris and His Circle from Canadian Collections* (Ontario, 1993), pp. 137, 139.

32. I. Spencer, *Walter Crane* (1975), p. 115.

33. Quoted in Parry, *William Morris Textiles*, p. 152.

34. Kelvin (ed.), *Letters*, Vol. II, p. 177, to Alfred James Hipkins, 17 March 1883. Hipkins had presented a paper at the Society of Arts on 'The History of the Pianoforte'.

35. White, 'An Epoch-Making House', p. 107.

36. L. Parry, 'Textiles', in Lochnan, Schoenherr and Silver (eds), *The Earthly Paradise*, p. 170; *idem*, *William Morris Textiles*, p. 95.

37. Morris, 'On Mr. Philip Webb's Town Work', Vol. 2 (1897), p. 206.

38. Day, 'A Kensington Interior', p. 142.

39. Spencer, *Walter Crane*, p. 114.

40. Crane, *An Artist's Reminiscences*, p. 218.

41. *Building News*, 21 Dec. 1883, p. 999.

42. White, 'An Epoch-Making House', pp. 107–10.

43. Day, 'A Kensington Interior', p. 142.

44. Ibid., p. 144.

45. V&A, Box 86 kk III (xiv), Estimate from Morris & Co. to A.A. Ionides, 18 June 1888.

46. Day, 'A Kensington Interior', p. 144.

47. Parry, *William Morris Textiles*, p. 111.

48. Morris, 'On Mr. Philip Webb's Town Work', p. 206.

49. Morris had little sympathy with D'Arcy's requirements. In a letter to Georgiana

Burne-Jones, Morris described Stanmore Hall as 'a house of a very rich man – and such a wretched uncomfortable place'. P. Henderson, *The Letters of William Morris to his Family and Friends* (1950), pp. 322–3, to Georgiana Burne-Jones, 10 June 1890.

50. Day, 'A Kensington Interior', p. 142.
51. L. Ionides, *Memories*, pp. 21–2.
52. *Survey of London*, Vol. XXXVII (1973), p. 124.

8

William Morris and the Royal Commission on Technical Instruction[1]

B Y THE EARLY 1880s, William Morris was a well-known and much respected figure. Morris & Co. had entered its heyday, and Morris's public lectures ensured that his social criticism and views on design reached an ever-widening audience. One mark of his growing reputation was the development of a close and rewarding association with the South Kensington Museum, as the Victoria and Albert was known until the last year of the nineteenth century. The Museum had been set up with the proceeds of the 1851 Great Exhibition 'for the express purpose of allying art and industry and improving design in manufactured goods'.[2] Morris's relationship with the Museum dated from 1864 when the recently founded Morris, Marshall, Faulkner & Co. contributed panels to an exhibition of contemporary stained glass. Three years later, Henry Cole, South Kensington's first Director, and Francis Fowke, the architect of the museum buildings, commissioned the firm to decorate the Green Dining Room – one of its first major secular commissions.

By the early 1880s, William Morris was frequently consulted by the Museum on the acquisition of textiles, carpets, tapestries and embroidery. He was formally appointed as one of its Art Referees in 1884.[3] His work for the South Kensington Museum, which continued until the year of his death, is by no means the least of his legacies to succeeding generations. For, as Ray Watkinson has remarked, 'it was on his advice, under the guidance of his enormous knowledge, practical as well as historic and aesthetic ... that scores of objects were bought by, or given to, the Museum; and so, to us'.[4]

Morris regarded the collections as invaluable sources of reference for the designer. Barbara Morris and Linda Parry, amongst others, have demonstrated how critically Morris's maturing skills as a designer drew upon frequent visits to the Museum to study objects and the rare books in the library.[5] Additionally, he served, from the late 1870s, as an examiner for the South Kensington School of Design, where his own daughter May attended classes in embroidery.[6] In 1882, when the Royal Commission on Technical Instruction heard evidence at the Museum, Morris, not surprisingly, was called as an accomplished and well-informed witness.

The Royal Commission, under the chairmanship of Sir Bernhard Samuelson MP, a Cleveland ironmaster, was one of several that examined the state of Britain's education system in the course of the nineteenth century. They were a response to rising concern over international competition and the apparent superiority of French, German and American scientific and technical training. Most concern was expressed about training in the applied sciences, but there was also anxiety about the lack of educational opportunities for artists and designers, and about the standards of industrial design.

Concern over the training of artists and designers first came to the fore in 1835, when the Liverpool MP William Ewart proposed a Select Committee on Arts and Manufactures 'to inquire into the best means of extending a knowledge of the Arts and of the principles of design among the people (especially the manufacturing population) of this country'. Ewart was heavily influenced by Benjamin Robert Haydon, one of the earliest advocates of schools of design, who was fiercely critical of the Royal Academy's failure to develop its educational functions.[7] In its Report, published in 1836, the Committee set out an alarming tale of the deficiencies of British workmanship. Whereas France and Germany had established art educational systems adapted to the needs of industry, in Britain it was largely true that 'art education was still in the hands of the drawing master whose task it was to educate the sons and daughters of the rich'.[8] The efforts of the Mechanics' Institutes were singled out as a notable but limited exception to the rule.

The publicity generated by the Select Committee's work spurred the government into action. A School of Design was established at Somerset House in 1837. William Dyce, appointed Superintendent in August 1838, was largely responsible for shaping its policies. A somewhat enigmatic figure, he was undeniably correct in asserting the need to make art education more widely available. He emphasised in his writings the importance of the relationship between the style of an object and the use to which it was put. He also 'made the bold suggestion that the school should become an actual workshop for the production of patterns which would be supplied to manufacturers'.[9] In practice, though, the School struggled under his leadership. His ideas on design itself were limited – his teachers concentrating upon ornament rather than design – and the emphasis was on paper and patterns rather than working with real materials. There was, nevertheless, some success in extending provision to the manufacturing towns. Between 1842 and 1852, 21 provincial schools of design were created in Manchester, Birmingham, Glasgow and elsewhere.

Further state intervention came around mid-century, amid concerns that the School of Design was not working well. Financial provision remained very limited, and in the provinces businessmen were not convinced of the benefits of their local schools of design. In 1852, the Duke of Aberdeen's government promised a comprehensive scheme for art and science education. The outcome was the establishment of the Department of Science and Art. The main objectives of its Art Division were: 'the promotion of elementary instruction in drawing and modelling; special instruction in the knowledge and practice of ornamental art; the practical application of such knowledge to the improvement of manufactures.'[10] Sir Henry Cole became the first Secretary for Art, taking sole charge of the Department of Science and Art in 1858. Under his leadership, the Department began by reorganising and granting aid to existing art schools, which became subject to regular inspection and payment by results. The Department set up training courses and examinations for those intending to teach its classes. By the time of Cole's retirement in 1873, the Department could point to a record of substantial achievement. There were now 120 schools of art spread across the UK. In addition, 180,000 boys and girls were being taught drawing in elementary schools, and there were 500 night schools for teaching drawing to artisans.[11]

Despite these efforts, the spectre of foreign competition continued to threaten; and to some it grew more menacing as the years passed. Underlying this perception was the undeniable fact that industrial growth rates in the UK in the last third of the nineteenth century compared badly with those of Germany and the United States. While it was hardly surprising that Britain's growth rate should have lagged behind those of newer industrialisers, the sharpening of foreign competition coupled with the onset of the 'Great Depression' in the early 1880s certainly did much to concentrate attention on the question of technical education in Britain.

The catalyst for renewed activity was the 1867 Paris Exhibition. Unlike the Great Exhibition of 1851, when Britain and her Empire had carried off the honours in all but a handful of the hundred or so departments, the Paris Exhibition provided highly disconcerting evidence of the success of her rivals. British manufacturers were triumphant in only ten of the 90 categories of exhibit. As John Scott Russell wrote in 1869, 'by that Exhibition, we were rudely awakened and thoroughly alarmed. We then learnt, not that we were equalled, but that we were beaten – not on some points, but by some nation or other on nearly all those points on which we had prided ourselves.'[12] The experience of 1867 led Russell and a growing number of like-minded individuals to conclude that a more systematic, state-led approach to technical instruction was required. The proselytisers included well-informed industrialists like Isaac Lowthian Bell and William Siemens with first-hand experience of conditions on the Continent. Other leading figures were Thomas Huxley, Lyon Playfair, first head of the Department of Science and Art, and Henry Roscoe, who graduated from the Universities of London and Heidelberg before becoming Professor of Chemistry at Owens College, Manchester in 1857.[13] Their opposition to the anti-vocational liberal education advocated by J.S. Mill was so forceful and influential that 'what they were saying rapidly became the banalities of almost any speech on university or industrial matters from the 1880s to the 1900s and now appears a kind of common-sense orthodoxy scarcely worth reiterating. Indeed, it is now the old orthodoxy of the liberal education that needs a special defence.'[14]

Further recognition of the competitive dangers facing the United Kingdom came in the Reports of the Royal Commission on Scientific Instruction and the Advancement of Science, chaired by the Duke of Devonshire (1872–75), and when Samuelson's Royal Commission on Technical Instruction followed at the beginning of the next decade (1881–84) its brief was explicitly a comparative one: 'to inquire into the instruction of the industrial classes of certain foreign countries in technical and other subjects, for the purpose of comparison with that of the corresponding classes in this country.'

Apart from Samuelson himself, the other members of the Royal Commission were Swire Smith, a Bradford woollen manufacturer; John Slagg, an MP and cotton magnate; the pottery manufacturer and MP from Burslem, Staffordshire, William Woodall; Philip Magnus, the Director and Secretary of the City and Guilds of London Institute; and

Henry Roscoe. It heard evidence from many of the leading industrialists and educationalists whose voices had been raised in the debates over technical instruction. Morris's fellow-witnesses included William Siemens, the President of the Midland Institute; Godfrey Wedgwood, the senior partner in Wedgwood & Sons; the ironmaster Isaac Lowthian Bell; Philip Cunliffe-Owen, the Director of the South Kensington Museum; and T.H. Huxley, the Dean of the College of Science. Amongst the other witnesses were numerous artisans, and representatives of mechanics' institutes, trade schools, the City and Guilds of London, and other institutions involved in technical education. Another expert who supplied information to the Commission was Thomas Wardle, who had shared Morris's dyeing experiments of the mid-1870s. Wardle submitted a long and at times pessimistic written report on the silk textiles industry in Britain.[15]

The Commission, like its predecessors, spent much of its time considering scientific education rather than instruction in art and design.[16] But while the greatest competitive threat in many areas came from Germany, in the case of high quality textiles it was France which, since the early decades of the nineteenth century, had posed the greatest challenge. The lead established by English manufacturers in the later decades of the eighteenth century had been lost in the great trade recession which followed the Napoleonic Wars, and 'Lancashire had to look to Lyons or to Paris for their inspiration'.[17] It was widely believed that the superiority of French designers in silk, printed cottons and lace was founded upon their Schools of Design. The Lyons school had been founded in the mid-eighteenth century, and was expressly intended to train those draughtsmen who prepared patterns for the region's silk industry. This in turn influenced printed cottons, which tended to follow trends in the more expensive silk. Later, in 1833, the Mulhouse printers, who constituted Manchester's main rivals, set up their own school of design.[18] Concerns about foreign competition were not confined to silks and cottons. In hosiery, A.J. Mundella had acquired a firm in Chemnitz, the centre of the successful Saxon industry, in the 1860s. His English manager swiftly concluded that Saxony's advantage over Nottingham was primarily due to Chemnitz's polytechnic school, which trained the more skilled of its workmen. When the manager, H.M. Felkin, published his findings in a book, *Technical Instruction in a Saxon Town* (1881), it created widespread public interest, and was largely responsible for the appointment of the Samuelson Commission.[19]

William Morris was called as a witness because, besides acting as a consultant and assessor for the South Kensington Museum, he was regarded as a successful businessman and authority on the design and manufacture of high-class textiles. As a well-known and much-respected figure, Morris's views on art, design and manufacturing were taken very seriously by the members of the Commission, who questioned him at length on the deficiencies of domestic products, and the steps which might be taken to improve the competitive position of British manufacturers. The printed version of his evidence covers 11 closely printed pages.[20]

He began with the observation that English designs lacked the mastery of style exhibited by their French counterparts, especially in good quality textiles. This was an increasingly important segment of the market in which French goods were generally presumed superior to British. However, he denied that the French necessarily had a better appreciation of beauty and colour than the English, adding that 'so long as a thing is in a definite style, it seems to satisfy the ordinary French mind, even though it is obviously ugly'. As regards wallpapers, for example, he asserted that 'on the whole English designs were more original and better in design than the French, at any rate since the last 12 years'. Likewise, he did not think that printed fabrics were a strong point of the French, although he conceded that 'they have an enormous variety in the way of woven stuffs for furnitures, and their cleverness in adapting material and shifting things about is very great. ... I do not much admire the goods myself, but they are clever things, and showy, and very cheap.'

While Morris recognised the cleverness of French designs, he did not accept that emulation of the French approach to design was the best way for Britain to 'establish a trade and a reputation for goods of a high class'. He thought it better 'as a matter of competition ... not to attack the French on their ground at all, but to try to produce our own styles'. Moreover, he was highly critical of the fact that French designers, based in Paris, were not fully conversant with the manufacturing techniques and materials used in provincial industrial centres like Lyons:

I think it rather a thing to be deprecated that there should be a class of mere artists like some of these Paris designers, who furnish designs, as it were, ready made, to what you may call the technical designers, the technical designers having next to nothing to do with the drawing, but having what you may call the grinding work to do. The designer learns about as much as is necessary for his work from the weaver, in a perfunctory and dull sort of manner, and the result is not so satisfactory as it would be if a different system were adopted.

For Morris, the division of labour was a particular cause for concern since it was through this, and the deskilling that generally accompanied it, that work became joyless. Thus Morris, like Ruskin before him, looked back to the medieval period, when the labour of the artisan was a source of interest and pleasure, and resulted in products which were fitting and beautiful. The freedom to take full responsibility for the manufacturing process – and indeed, the freedom to make mistakes – ennobled the worker, and satisfied his creative needs. This was, of course, to become a central theme of much of Morris's socialist writings. In *Commonweal*, for instance, he wrote that in capitalist production, 'the creation of surplus values being the one aim of the employers of labour, they cannot for a moment trouble themselves as to whether the work which creates the surplus value is pleasurable to the worker, or not'.[21]

But there was another reason why William Morris opposed the division of labour: unlike most of his socialist contemporaries, who concentrated their attention upon its effect on the workforce, Morris was also concerned about its impact on the quality of the product. Thus, in his evidence to the Royal Commission on Technical Instruction, Morris argued that 'division of labour does a good deal to cheapen goods, but on the other hand I think it does a great deal to deteriorate them'. He concluded that 'it is not desirable to divide the labour between the artist and what is technically called the designer ... I think it would be better, when it could be managed, that the man who actually goes through the technical work of counting the threads, and settling how the thing is to be woven, through and through, should do the drawing.'

When Sir Bernhard Samuelson, seeking clarification, asked him whether he considered that the designer should acquaint himself with the exigencies of the machine and the material in which the design was executed, Morris replied: 'Yes, I speak as strongly as I can upon that. I think that is the very foundation of all design.' Sterility in design might be avoided through a deep knowledge of the manufacturing process. Only in this way could the designer make a design which took full account of the nature of the material and the capabilities of the production process.

In his evidence, Morris also emphasised the commercial importance of originality and beauty. Originality was the linchpin of the Morris business; to a remarkable degree, the identity of the firm was a reflection of his own personality, thought and aspirations. He rarely employed outside designers because 'it is so very difficult to get a due amount of originality out of them; the designs which one gets are so hackneyed, and there is the same sort of idea harped on about for ever and ever'. The emphasis on invention and originality was one which conferred competitive advantage in a fiercely contested market. That Morris understood the importance of a reputation for originality and quality is underlined by the observation that 'beauty is a marketable quality, and ... the better the work is all round, both as a work of art and in its technique, the more likely it is to find favour with the public'.

Mere originality, however, was not enough; the designer should have an understanding of the best historical examples which might form a rich fund of ideas and inspiration. He believed that 'however original a man may be, he cannot afford to disregard the works of art that have been produced in times past when design was flourishing'. Moreover,

he is also bound to supplement that by a careful study of nature, because if he does not he will certainly fall into a sort of cut and dried, conventional method of designing, which is the bane of most these French designs that we are talking about, and the only way for a person to keep clear of that, especially one in the ordinary rank and file of designers, is to study nature along with the old examples. It takes a man of considerable originality, to deal with the old examples, and to get what is good out of them, without making a design which lays itself open distinctly to the charge of plagiarism. No doubt the only help out of that is for a man to be always drawing from nature, getting the habit of knowing what beautiful forms and lines are; that I think is a positive necessity.[22]

Having clearly set out his views on the foundations of good design, Morris went on to advise the Commission on how to meet the challenge of the French in markets for high-class goods. Most important of all, he believed, was 'an education all round of the workmen, from the lowest to the highest'. This education should begin with elementary instruction in the three Rs, which he believed had a considerable influence on the ultimate success of the workman: 'I often have great difficulty in dealing with the workmen I employ in London, because of their general ignorance.' Training in drawing was important to give an understanding of form – Morris objected to what he called 'mere mechanical finish' – and he believed that 'everybody ought to be taught to draw just as much as everybody be taught to read and write'. Thus he was in sympathy with the efforts of the Department of Science and Art to provide grants for elementary schools where they taught drawing in addition to the three Rs.

At a more advanced level, he was strongly supportive of the provincial schools of design which had been set up under the auspices of the Department of Science and Art. Like many contemporaries, he was firmly of the opinion that Britain's textile industries had suffered in competition with other countries from the absence of school training in the designing of patterns. Furthermore, this training 'should be obtainable in the several centres of industry; that is, a man should not be obliged to have to come to London to learn his work, but should be able in some way or other to do all that was necessary in the way of study in his own town, wherever it might be.'

But, while in general he approved of the courses of instruction which the provincial schools provided, there were a number of areas in which improvements might be made. For example, he was concerned that the provincial schools of design should avoid training students as picture painters. He was induced to make the remark as a result of having visited a school where a great number of still lifes were exhibited. Though some of them were very fair, 'that sort of study certainly did not help the students very much in design'. This, though, he did not consider to be indicative of the general emphasis followed by the provincial schools, but 'a matter of accident owing to the master having a turn in that direction'. He might perhaps have added that it was often as much a consequence of the students' preference as their masters'. One of the perennial tensions experienced by the provincial schools was that the students often wanted to 'become artists' against the wishes of those who had founded the schools and saw for them a strictly vocational role.

Morris also suggested improvements in the conduct of national design competitions. Under the system established by Henry Cole, the work of the provincial school students was assessed by inspectors, and the assessments were used as the basis of a system of payment by results. The inspector awarded local medals, and all work was sent to London for examination. The best was selected to compete in national competitions for medallions and prizes. Morris, who had served as one of the national judges since the late 1870s, felt that not enough attention was given to the turning out of the actual goods themselves; 'we cannot give prizes for the things started out, we can only give prizes for the designs. I think it would be a very good thing to give prizes for the goods themselves. Prizes ought to be given for general excellence and appropriateness of design, and for careful and artistic execution.' This, he believed, could easily be achieved.

Another theme taken up by Morris was the relative merits of practical training in schools of design versus the workplace. Clearly, something needed to be done, for 'the old system of apprenticeship, by which workmen learned their craft, is a good deal broken down now, and nothing as yet has taken its place'. As the workshop training provided in most trades was insufficient, Morris suggested that the schools of design ought to afford opportunities for people to learn the practical side of designing. Students following courses of formal training should have ready access to workshops where they might become conversant with manufacturing methods. For example, it would be possible to introduce Jacquard looms for figure weaving, as they did not take up a vast amount of room: 'it might seem that there would be no very great advantage in putting a Jacquard loom into an art school, but it would be a great advantage for one who was learning designing to see weaving going on. I think it essential that a designer should learn the practical way of carrying out the work for which he designs; he ought to be able to weave himself.'

Morris was far from dogmatic in his assertions, recognising that there might be operational difficulties in providing practical experience in the schools of design. Yet, if the difficulties could be overcome, the student was likely to benefit for two reasons. One lay in the fact that the learner would be not so much hurried over the work as he would be in the factory. The other was that 'in workshops it is often the interest of these who have to teach him to keep him back instead of advancing him'. In calling for more practical training, Morris was highlighting one of the principal deficiencies of the schools of design. In the National Art Training School at South Kensington, for instance, no workshop training of any kind was provided between 1877 and 1886.[23]

Morris regretted the tendency for the designer to cease formal studies after entering employment. He agreed with Samuelson that general art instruction should be continued in night schools and the like; 'it would be most desirable; I think that it is the only way in which he would keep his mind fresh, upon the subjects that he would be taught there.'

Perhaps the most important of all Morris's recommendations to the Royal Commission concerned the educational role of museums. Since the training of designers should include the opportunity to examine very closely 'good old examples', Morris insisted upon the importance of museum collections, not just in London, but in each of the manufacturing centres of the land. This he considered 'a positive necessity … I do not see how they could get on without it'. For example, in the case of the lace manufacture of Nottingham, the student certainly ought to have easy access to good old examples, or drawings, or prints of old lace. Morris emphasised that there were 'many books printed between 1530 and 1630 full of designs of lace, and things of that sort'. What was true for the lace industry was equally true for other trades. Moreover, the designer should have access not only to examples of his own craft, but also the other crafts which had a bearing upon it, 'because a man must not be narrowed to studying only his own special manufacture; he would get too dull and mechanical if he did.'

It is difficult for us to appreciate today exactly how hard it must have been in Victoria's reign to gain access to the best historical examples. A great deal of progress had, of course, been made. Early museums tended to be collections of curiosities, the products of travel, and so on. They were not meant for training, and the scholarship behind them was speculative, antiquarian, and non-scientific. All this was beginning to change as the nineteenth century unfolded, and so too were people's perceptions of what museums had to offer. The emerging concept of the museum as an educational tool was important, and the South Kensington Museum and the Natural History Museum were the great exemplars. Even so, one wonders how accessible good historical examples were to the average designer in the closing decades of the nineteenth century, especially those geographically distant from the metropolis.

Morris drew a clear distinction between metropolitan and provincial collections. The South Kensington Museum 'should contain complete collections in all styles, and when an opportunity occurred for purchasing private collections, any gaps in the metropolitan collection should be filled up at the expense of the nation.' In the provincial museum, on the other hand, 'you want types of good work, not a mere multiplication of articles'. It did not matter if it were small, provided that its collections were representative, and appropriate to the needs of the locality. Morris did not think that the provincial museum 'need set itself to what is called collecting, or need try the sort of things which a private man with a long purse may do. Here the things are only wanted for educational purposes, and not as curiosities.'

Morris then considered how these provincial museums might be provided for. Samuelson, from the chair, enquired whether he believed that the benefit to the nation would justify substantial state aid being given to the localities, for the formation of such collections. Morris was sceptical of this approach: 'I would rather that the localities should establish such museums for themselves. I do not see why they should not; it concerns their own trades, and I think they might do it for themselves, more or less. At the same time I think national aid might be given to them to a reasonable extent, if they were seriously trying to make good museums of their own.'

With regard to the provision of articles for provincial museums, Morris said that he would give all the aid to such museums that could be given without robbing 'the great existing museum' at South Kensington. 'I must say, I think it would be a great mistake to do anything that was really like breaking up the collection here. People who want to study the objects, know that they are to be found here, and they can get at them ... The things have a certain value in a great collection, which they would not have in a small one.'

Nor was he at all in favour of the system of circulation, which had been developed at South Kensington since the 1850s. The Circulation Department provided a selection of the collections, ranging from glass, ceramics and metalwork to textiles and wallpapers, supplemented by photographs and drawings of rare exhibits. Special loans to exhibitions of industrial and fine art which were organised in various localities – mostly those centres of manufacturing which possessed design schools – and objects were available for copying by electrotyping, plaster casting, photography and other methods. The Circulation Department was undoubtedly successful – its exhibitions were popular, and helped to raise the necessary capital and local interest to establish a number of provincial museums. Morris's remarks were prompted by the decision in 1880 to extend the loan scheme to municipal museums, especially those in manufacturing districts. This resulted in objects being removed from the collections displayed at South Kensington for a year at a time.[24] Although it was generally felt at South Kensington that the advantages to the provinces outweighed the drawbacks, Morris did not agree, remarking that he could not help 'looking upon the thing rather from a collector's point of view':

I must confess I do not think it is a good plan. In the first place these things are extremely precious and if destroyed can never be replaced; the risk in transit, though it may not be absolutely great, still is a risk, and should only be run when there is a strong necessity for it. There is another objection to the system of circulation of these objects. A museum, to be of any great use to those who are studying in it as artists or as designers, must be arranged in a permanent manner, so that one can come day after day to see the same thing; so that a man who is a lecturer can take his class to see the museum and give a lecture on such and such an article, or that a manufacturer, like myself, can take a designer to the museum and say, I want a thing done in such and such a way.

Morris's view was very different from many of his contemporaries. Thomas Wardle, for example, strongly supported the loan, for a year at a time, of objects from South Kensington, remarking that 'a fixed collection soon becomes uninteresting. Nothing is more stupid than a local museum.'[25] Here, of course, Wardle was expressing the frustrations of a man who had experienced the shortcomings of a small local museum; Morris, on the other hand, spoke as a man who had South Kensington at hand for study and reference, and as a source of pleasure.

Rather than expanding the circulating collections, Morris wanted towns to acquire their own. While he did not want the metropolitan collections to be plundered of essential items and lose their claim to comprehensiveness, he firmly believed that any superfluous items might be transferred to the provinces on a permanent basis. 'My experience in using the museum here, and perhaps I have used it as much as any living man, is that the museum has got rather more things than it knows what to do with. ... I know there are things stowed away in chests which might be sent to provincial museums.' Similarly, any items acquired by the nation from private collections that were not wanted to fill up gaps in the metropolitan collection might be sent to the provinces.

Taking a concrete instance, the Commissioners asked how he would deal with the large collection of Indian fabrics at South Kensington. Morris replied, 'there are, I should think, a good many things amongst those Indian specimens which, though not perhaps actually and literally duplicates, may almost be considered as duplicates, and I think there would be no harm in sending some of those things away. I think the museum might spare them.' Similarly, he noted that 'there is an enormous quantity of blue pottery-ware in the Persian collection, and very fine it is, but it runs alike to a certain extent, and some of the specimens might be spared'.

Morris was also an emphatic supporter of copying important objects for provincial museums – this aspect of the Circulation Department's work was one he approved of: 'when any objects were acquired by the nation for the central museum, those objects ought, where possible, as a rule, to be copied, and the copies ought to be distributed amongst the provincial museums; in many cases they would be almost as valuable for study as the originals.' He did, however, recognise that accurate reproductions were easier to make in some media than others. In metal-work, for example, he had seen reproductions made at the museum, 'and no doubt they are very good as far as they go, but they do not quite supply the place of originals as pieces of execution. Metal ware is so much a matter of execution.' In such cases, a few good genuine examples, supported by drawings, might be better.

Finally, Morris asserted that such museums would not only benefit designers and workers: 'certainly, I do not wish myself by any means to limit the technical education wholly to workmen and people of that sort'. The public also needed a technical education: 'I think it is most desirable from my point of view, that the public should know something about it, so that you may get a market for excellence and not for appearance.' Just as Morris's own firm, from its inception, had sought to 'shape the market', so too schools of design and museums had a duty to educate the public.

The Royal Commission's report was not particularly radical, and indeed in some respects it was distinctly complacent about British practice. In particular, it was hostile to the extension of state inter-vention, despite its prevalence on the Continent, arguing instead that local funds should be sought to finance a substantial increase in provision. Nevertheless, there were some highly critical comments. Samuelson's report repeated many of the recommendations of the earlier Taunton and Devonshire Commissions, stressing 'the need to improve primary and secondary education as the prerequisite to a sound system of scientific and technical instruction',[26] and emphasising that there was an urgent need for a more substantial and widespread provision of technical instruction of all kinds. The report concluded by remarking that English entrepreneurs and educationalists had 'yet to learn that an extended and systematic education up to and including the methods of original research is now a necessary preliminary to the fullest development of industry'.[27]

The Royal Commission on Technical Instruction did much to

publicise the cause of technical education in Britain and helped shape political opinion, paving the way for the 1889 Technical Instruction Act. This empowered local authorities to raise money for technical education. The 1890 Local Taxation (Customs and Excise) Act diverted funds (the so-called whisky money) for the same purpose. The process culminated in the Education Act of 1902, which placed all national education in the hands of county councils and county borough councils, and set up local education authorities with sub-committees for technical education.[28]

Much of the Royal Commission's General Report, as noted earlier, focused upon the question of scientific education. Yet it did seek, too, to address the issues raised by Morris, such as the relationship between design and industry, the importance of practical experience, and the roles of the school of art and design – knotty problems which have remained the subject of intense debate down to the present day. The Commissioners' conclusions and recommendations echoed many – but not all – of Morris's arguments.[29]

To ensure that there was a suitable foundation for higher-level studies, the Commissioners accepted Morris's pleas that the rudiments of drawing should form part of everyone's education, and recommended that drawing should be made compulsory in elementary schools along with reading, writing and arithmetic. Like Morris, too, they emphasised that 'amongst the most important means of stimulating industrial art education and of spreading a knowledge and appreciation of art through-out the country, is the foundation of local museums of applied art of such a character as is best adapted to advance the industries of the districts in which they are situated … We are of the opinion that the connection between these museums and the local schools of art should be of an intimate character.'

However, they did not agree with William Morris on the drawbacks of South Kensington's Circulation Department. The Commissioners concluded that 'we must express strong approval … of the system of circulating amongst the local museums collections of works of art from the national collections at South Kensington'. Like Morris, however, they recognised the strength of the argument that state aid might best be applied to central institutions and their collections, while recommending that reproductions be supplied to the provincial museums gratis or at a low cost. They also recommended that 'contributions be made provincial industrial museums of original examples tending to advance the industries of the districts in which such museums are situated'.

Another recommendation which resulted from a suggestion by Morris was that the Department of Science and Art should break with its principle of encouraging design *per se*. In future, it should pay more attention to the suitability of the design to the material in which it was to be executed, awarding grants 'for specimens of applied art-workmanship in the materials themselves, as a test of the applicability of the design and as a reward for success in overcoming the technical difficulties of the manufacture'.

They welcomed this suggestion from Morris because, while the Commissioners had many positive things to say about the training available under the auspices of the Department of Science and Art, they were highly critical of the lack of attention paid to industrial design. They concluded that art teachers lacked an adequate knowledge of manufactures, and proprietors of industrial works were unsympathetic to the work of the schools. As a result, industrial design 'has not received sufficient attention in our schools and classes. In fact, there has been a great departure in this respect from the intention with which the "Schools of Design" were originally founded, viz., "the practical application of a knowledge of ornamental Art to the improvement of manufactures." Large grants of public money for teaching art to artizans in such classes can scarcely be justified on any other ground than its industrial utility.'

One immediate result of this criticism was that the Director of the Art Division of the Department of Science and Art, Thomas Armstrong, set forth to reintroduce craft work to the Art Training Schools. Armstrong, who was a close friend of Morris, invited Walter Crane to give a series of lectures in 1886 at South Kensington. As Crane noted in his memoirs, 'I undertook a series of lectures or demonstrations in various crafts allied to decorative design in which I had personal experience, such as gesso and plaster relief-work, sgraffito, tempera, painting, stencilling, designing for embroidery, repoussé metal work ... I believe they were the first lectures of the kind at South Kensington – fore-runners of the time when craft classes became part of the ordinary college course on design.'[30]

Thus Morris's views certainly were taken seriously by Samuelson and his fellow Commissioners, and they are reflected in the long and detailed General Report which resulted. Yet is probably true to say that Morris's main influence on contemporary thought was not through official channels, but through the work of a younger generation of architects, designers and craftsmen which, from the 1880s onwards, sought to implement the principles enunciated in his lectures and confirmed by his example. The societies which they established, such as the Art Workers' Guild and the Arts and Crafts Exhibition Society, had clear educational goals. The Art Workers' Guild in particular was committed to public art education. Its members included Walter Crane, R. Catterson Smith and William Richard Lethaby. Crane was Director of the Manchester School of Art, later becoming the first Principal of the Royal School of Art in 1898. He never ceased to crusade on behalf of the decorative arts, design education and craft-work. R. Catterson Smith, who worked with Morris on illustrations for the Kelmscott *Chaucer*, went on to become headmaster of the Birmingham School of Arts and Crafts.[31] Lethaby, as one of the main forces behind the Technical Education Board and first Principal of the Central School of Arts and Crafts, was perhaps the most influential Morrisian standard-bearer.[32] Morris's ideas on art, design and politics had a profound impact on the development of Lethaby's own thinking, which in turn inspired successive generations of students, including the likes of Eric Gill and Edward Johnston and many other leading twentieth-century designers.

NOTES

We are indebted to Ray Watkinson for his comments on an earlier draft of this article.

1. This essay was originally commissioned for a special issue of the *Journal of the William Morris Society* on Morris and Education, Vol. XI No. 1 (Autumn 1994), pp. 31–43.
2. B. Morris, *William Morris and the South Kensington Museum* (1987), p. 5.
3. Since 1867, the Lords of the Committee of the Council on Education had appointed a number of Art Referees to advise them on purchases for the South Kensington Museum. B. Morris, *Inspiration for Design: The Influence of the Victoria & Albert Museum* (1986), p. 100; L. Parry, *William Morris Textiles* (1983), pp. 85, 103.
4. R. Watkinson, 'Introduction', in Morris, *William Morris and the South Kensington Museum*, p. 4.
5. See, for example, Morris, *William Morris and the South Kensington Museum*, pp. 7–15; Parry, *William Morris Textiles*, pp. 53–4, 64–5, 126.
6. *Second Report of the Royal Commissioners on Technical Instruction* (Parliamentary

Papers, c.3981, 1884 XXXI). See Morris's evidence, Q.1595.

7. On Ewart, see G.W. Shirley, *William Ewart* (Dumfries, 1930); W.A. Munford, *William Ewart, M.P.* (1960). On Haydon, see Q. Bell, *The Schools of Design* (1963), especially pp. 38–50.

8. Bell, *The Schools of Design*, p. 48.

9. Ibid., p. 81. On Dyce, see M. Pointon, *William Dyce, 1806–1864: A Critical Biography* (Oxford, 1979), especially pp. 43–60; S. MacDonald, *The History and Philosophy of Art Education* (1970), pp. 116–28.

10. *Calendar and General Directory of the Science and Art Department, being a Supplement to the Thirty-Second Report* (Parliamentary Papers, c.4254, 1884/85 XXIX), p. 19.

11. Sir Henry Cole, *50 Years of Public Work* (1884), Vol. 2, p. 388. Also see MacDonald, *History and Philosophy of Art Education*, pp. 157–87.

12. J. Scott Russell, *Systematic Technical Education for the English People* (1869), p. 86.

13. Roscoe was the most important link between industry and the provincial colleges which were to become the new civic universities; as Sanderson has remarked, 'it is quite impossible to do justice to or to exaggerate the importance of Roscoe as the new model of the English industrially orientated scientific professor, as a conceiver of the idea of a civic university serving local industry, and as a founder of modern chemical education in this country.' M. Sanderson, *The Universities and British Industry, 1850–1970* (1972), p. 84.

14. Ibid., p. 7. On J.S. Mill's views, see his *Inaugural Address delivered to the University of St Andrews, 1 February 1867* (1867).

15. *Second Report of the Royal Commissioners on Technical Instruction* (Parliamentary Papers, c.3981, 1884 XXXI), *passim*. Wardle's report, in which he refers to 'the steady growth of the silk industry abroad, and its unhappy decadence in England', is on pp. 29–106.

16. This is an emphasis which is also reflected in the historical literature relating to technical instruction in Britain. See, for example, G.W. Roderick and M.D. Stephens, *Education and Industry in the Nineteenth Century* (1978); *idem* (eds), *Where Did We Go Wrong? Industrial Performance, Education and the Economy in Victorian Britain* (Lewes, Sussex, 1981); Sanderson, *The Universities and British Industry*; M. Argles, *South Kensington to Robbins: An Account of English Technical and Scientific Instruction since 1851* (1964). Nevertheless, these sources do provide valuable introductions to the topics considered here.

17. S.D. Chapman, 'The Textile Industries', in Roderick and Stephens (eds), *Where Did We Go Wrong?*, p. 134.

18. Ibid.

19. Ibid., p. 135.

20. Morris's evidence is in Parliamentary Papers, c.3981, 1884 XXXI, pp. 150–61. All subsequent quotations come from here unless otherwise stated.

21. *Commonweal*, June supplement, 1885.

22. As always, Morris practised what he preached. Thus his textile designs, which at first were naturalistic and free-flowing, underwent a radical change in 1876 as a result of his discovery of medieval woven textiles at the South Kensington Museum. Subsequent designs, with a few exceptions, tended to be more formal

and symmetrical – such as his *Mohair Damask* of 1876, a design for woven wool and mohair which was based on a linen fabric believed to have been printed in the Rhineland in the fifteenth century. Other designs drew upon woven silks and damasks from medieval Spain and Italy. The link was less direct in the case of printed fabrics, but the medieval example was still a potent influence. See P. Floud, 'Dating Morris Patterns', *Architectural Review*, Vol. CXIII (July 1959), pp. 14–20; P. Thompson, *The Work of William Morris* (1967), p. 105.

23. MacDonald, *History and Philosophy of Art Education*, pp. 294–6.
24. On the Circulation Department, see Morris, *Inspiration for Design* pp. 56–64.
25. Parliamentary Papers, c.3981, 1884 XXXI, p. 79.
26. M. Le Guillou, 'Technical Education, 1850–1914', in Roderick and Stephens (eds), *Where Did We Go Wrong?*, p. 179.
27. Parliamentary Papers, c.3981, 1884 XXIX, p. 525.
28. See, *inter alia*, Roderick and Stephens, *Education and Industry in the Nineteenth Century*, pp. 72–3, 156; Argles, *South Kensington to Robbins*, pp. 30–33; H.C. Dent, *1870–1970: Century of Growth in English Education* (1970), pp. 27–80. M. Sanderson, *The Missing Stratum: Technical School Instruction in England, 1900–1990s* (1994), pp. 1–20.
29. The following paragraphs are based upon Parliamentary Papers, c.3981, 1884 XXIX, pp. 519–38.
30. W. Crane, *An Artist's Reminiscences* (1907), p. 300.
31. MacDonald, *The History and Philosophy of Art Education*, pp. 292–3.
32. See G. Rubens, *William Richard Lethaby: His Life and Work, 1857–1931* (1986), especially pp. 173–98.

9

John Ruskin and the Ethical Foundations of Morris & Company, 1861–96[1]

D URING THE course of the 1850s, John Ruskin's investigations into art and architecture gradually led him towards social criticism and political economy. The first stirrings occur in *The Seven Lamps of Architecture* (1849). In 'The Lamp of Life', Ruskin began to evolve a new understanding of the nature of men's work, and what it meant for society. Like Carlyle before him, Ruskin was insistent that it was through work that man fulfilled himself. For Ruskin, however, it had to be creative labour, which drew upon the workman's intellectual and moral strengths as well as his physical powers. Such ideas were further developed in *The Stones of Venice* (3 volumes, 1851–53), where they are drawn together in the famous chapter entitled 'The Nature of Gothic'. Here Ruskin set out his belief that the architecture and art of a particular society express the values of its entire culture. According to Ruskin, architecture and its attendant arts should be judged according to the amount of freedom of expression allowed to the individual workman. He contrasted the arts and crafts of the Middle Ages and the relationships they engendered favourably with the industrial society of the nineteenth century, which seemed to him to place more restrictions on the work-man than any preceding age had done. Modern society was thus indicted for having alienated and dehumanised workers, forcing them to perform monotonous and soul-destroying tasks. This led Ruskin into a critique of contemporary society, industrialisation and economic thought which culminated in the publication of four essays in August–November 1860 in the *Cornhill Magazine*, then under the editorship of Thackeray. In these essays, published in book form in 1862 as *Unto this Last: Four Essays on the Principles of Political Economy*, Ruskin argued that Britain's industrial society was morally degenerate and pernicious in that it drove the labouring class into cultural and material poverty. The thinking of the Political Economists, which supported the new liberal industrial order, he saw as correspondingly flawed, particularly because it lacked any credible moral element. Delivered in the sermonising tone so characteristic of Ruskin, these essays are highly coloured by the injection of a series of moral pronouncements which give them a strong ethical tone, at the expense of strictly consistent reasoning. And, while much of *Unto this Last* is devoted to destroying the claims of the 'science' of Political Economy, Ruskin goes on to offer a number of points of guidance for the business community. Though he fully accepts the need for a hierarchical society, governed by an educated élite, he encourages merchants and manufacturers to adopt a value system aimed at social harmony rather than individual profit. His writings are in essence an appeal to business leaders to behave in a socially responsible, paternalistic fashion according to his own moral prescriptions. In this way, British society might be regenerated.

These arguments were greeted by a storm of protest, and they alienated many of those members of the commercial and professional classes who had responded so positively to his readings of famous works of art and architecture in *Modern Painters* and *The Stones of Venice*. The result was that Ruskin's readership contracted sharply in the middle decades of the century. Many of the thousand copies of *Unto this Last* which were printed in 1862 remained unsold ten years later, and the controversy also affected sales of his other works. In retrospect, however, *Unto this Last* stands as 'the great central work of Ruskin's middle years'.[2] Gradually, it became a major success. By the early twentieth century, 100,000 copies had been sold, and there were also several pirated editions which had commanded a ready sale in America.

William Morris, writing in 1892, could assert that it was the ethical and political side of Ruskin's work, rather than the artistic, which would prove the most durable:

It is just this part of his work, fairly begun in the 'Nature of Gothic' and brought to its culmination in that great book 'Unto this Last', which has the most enduring and beneficent effect on his contemporaries, and will have through them on succeeding generations.[3]

'The Nature of Gothic', he believed, would come to be regarded as 'one of the few necessary and inevitable utterances of the century':

For the lesson which Ruskin here teaches us is that art is the expression of man's pleasure in labour; that it is possible for a man to rejoice in his work ... that unless man's work once again becomes a pleasure to him, the token of which change will be that beauty is once again a natural and necessary accompaniment of productive labour, all but the worthless must toil in pain.[4]

There is no doubt that Ruskin was the principal – though by no means the only[5] – influence upon Morris's formative years, and through-out his life Morris 'retained towards him the attitude of a scholar to a great teacher and master, not only in matters of art, but throughout the whole sphere of human life'.[6] From Ruskin, Morris took two funda-mental principles: his belief in the importance of the decorative arts, and his views on work and business morality. During his career, Morris worked hard to put Ruskin's ideas into practice – and indeed to extend them in important ways. The ways in which William Morris sought to give practical expression to these ideas are examined here. The vehicle for this practical expression was the Morris firm – established in 1861 as Morris, Marshall, Faulkner & Co., and reconstituted as Morris & Co., under his sole ownership, in 1875.

THE MORRIS ENTERPRISE

First of all, Morris's reading of Ruskin was a major factor determining his choice of career and consequently the formation of the Morris firm. At the time, in the late 1850s, when Morris met Ruskin and was studying his major works, he was tormented by the need to find a satisfying and fulfilling career. Having given up the Church and architecture, he was struggling to become a painter at the instigation of Dante Gabriel Rossetti, and in his view he was failing. Eventually, he turned to a career in the decorative arts, and it was here, as we know, that he found his true *métier*. But this was not a natural career for a young man from a wealthy commercial family, not least because the decorative arts were generally considered to be the 'lesser arts'.

The decorative arts were not, however, without their champions. G.E. Street, one of the leading figures of the Gothic Revival, to whom Morris had himself been articled, insisted that a good architect should understand the principles of decoration, and have a full knowledge of the relevant crafts.[7] One might mention too the work of Pugin, Owen Jones and Christopher Dresser, all of whom stressed the need for good design. Even more influential was the 'Art Manufactures' group led by Henry Cole.[8] But it was Ruskin who emerged as the most influential advocate of the decorative arts. In a lecture on 'Modern Manufacture and Design', published in *The Two Paths* (1859), he rejected the idea that decoration was an inferior or subsidiary art-form, instructing his audience to get rid of 'any idea of Decorative art being a degraded or separate kind of art. Its nature or essence is simply its being fitted for a definite place; and, in that place, forming part of a great and harmonious whole, in companionship with other art.' Contrary to general opinion, 'so far from decorative art being inferior to other art because it is fixed to a spot … it may be considered as rather a piece of degradation that it should be portable'.[9] Ruskin's advocacy must have been particularly gratifying to William Morris as he took the decision to embark on a career as a designer. Morris, Marshall, Faulkner & Co. was conceived as a vehicle to bring together a group of 'artists of reputation', who should use their talents in decorative art. As the firm's 1861 prospectus pointed out, there were considerable advantages to association; a group of artists working together could offer a much more complete service than they could as individuals.

Moreover, Ruskin not only legitimised decorative art, he also made the case, in his various writings, for the artist, designer and craftsman to be seen as one. Artists should design. Designers should make things. 'In each several profession, no man should be too proud to do its hardest work. The painter should grind his own colours; the architect work in the mason's yard with his men; the master-manufacturer be himself a more skilled operative than any man in his mills.'[10] This was vitally important, for 'no person is able to give useful or definite help towards the special applications of art, unless he is entirely familiar with the conditions of labour and materials involved in the work'.[11]

The principle that the artist or designer should be 'entirely familiar' with the processes and materials involved in the work made a great impression on Morris. While Cole's Art Manufactures group was concerned purely with designing for established manufacturers, Morris and his partners determined to involve themselves in the production and marketing of their designs, bridging the perceived gulf between designer and producer. And, while all the partners contributed towards the supply of designs, it was Morris who devoted most time and effort to gaining a working knowledge of the techniques and processes needed to produce the firm's wares. This was particularly true of stained glass, the most important product in the early years of Morris, Marshall, Faulkner & Co. While other partners contributed many splendid cartoons, Morris's contribution to the history of stained glass making in Britain derives largely from his complete mastery of the manufacturing process. Almost from the beginning, he played the central co-ordinating role in the business. He was responsible for interpreting the design, selecting the glass, and overseeing the assembly and installation of the finished window. The whole process was later described by George Wardle, general manager of the firm between 1870 and 1890. The scheme or general plan of the window was settled by Morris in consultation with the client. He would then distribute parts of the job to selected artists for them to produce the required artwork. Once the cartoons were ready, he examined the stock of glass, or 'pot metal' as it was known, and told the foreman of the glass painters which pieces to use. The various parts of the design were then handed over to the painters, 'whose work as it went on Mr Morris was able to watch, though he usually reserved any comments until the painter had done all he thought necessary'. Once the figure or picture had been burnt and leaded up, it might be accepted, retouched, or, if seriously flawed, rejected and the part begun again. When all parts of a window were ready, Morris turned to its appearance as a whole. In cramped workshops this was no easy matter, for it was seldom possible to assemble an entire window for examination. But 'here again Mr Morris showed how quick was his perception and how tenacious his memory. In passing all the parts of a large window one by one before the light he never lost sight of the general tone of the colour or of the relation of this part and that to each other.' All important work he would look at again after it was in place.[12]

Nor is it coincidental that William Morris should have carried on pursuing the artist/designer/craftsman ideal long after his erstwhile partners had given up. Ruskin's sentiments were frequently echoed by Morris, after years spent mastering the diverse crafts that formed the business of his firm. For example, his evidence to the Royal Commission on Technical Instruction in 1882 echoes Ruskin's strictures on the indivisibility of the artist and the designer: 'my view is that it is not desirable to divide the labour between the artist and what is technically called the designer.'[13] Here, too, he repeatedly emphasised that a full understanding of the manufacturing process for which the designer was working was 'the very foundation of design'.[14] Only in this way could the designer properly fit his design to the nature of the material and to the capabilities of the production process. Morris's own work practices invariably followed the prescriptions he set out for others. In all his many activities – painting, pattern design, weaving, dyeing, printing – he applied a common method of working, beginning with systematic research and exploration of the topic, and then passing on to identification of the best practice or suitable models; experimentation to identify through personal experience the problems involved; and modification of ideas, techniques or methods to bring his own work to fruition. Once a process was thoroughly investigated and understood, however – and here he differed from many members of the Arts and Crafts movements who followed in his footsteps – he would not continue with it. Instead, he delegated the work to others, passing on to fresh challenges.

So what Morris brought from Ruskin to his own firm was the conviction that the decorative arts were serious arts; a belief in the indivisibility of design and production; and a commitment to produce designs appropriate to each product.

FORGING THE MARKET

An important sphere of Ruskinian thought which influenced Morris deeply relates to those things worth producing and how they should be presented to the world. Ruskin was not a passive figure. He actively encouraged manufacturers to abandon the production of ugly dross and to lead by example in the creation of standards of good taste in manufactured goods, thereby 'forging the market' and educating public taste:

your business as manufacturers, is to form the market, as much as to supply it. If, in shortsighted and reckless eagerness for wealth, you catch at every humour of the populace ... you may, by accident, snatch the market; or, by energy, command it; you may obtain the confidence of the public, and cause the ruin of opponent houses; or you may, with equal justice of fortune, be ruined by them. But whatever happens to you ... the whole of your life will have been spent in corrupting public taste and encouraging public extravagance. ...

But, on the other hand, if you resolve from the first that ... you will produce what is best, on an intelligent consideration of the probable tendencies and possible tastes of the people whom you supply, you may literally become more influential for all kinds of good than many lecturers on art, or many treatise-writers on morality.[15]

Ruskin's vision of the socially responsible businessman, as one who put purpose before profit, and education before convenience, was accepted as an ideal by William Morris. He set for himself the very highest standards in design and manufacture; he preferred to set new trends rather than merely follow fashions; he never wasted an opportunity, at exhibitions or in publicity materials, to educate the public. And in his own public pronouncements, in the late 1870s and early 1880s, he took up a position very similar to that of Ruskin. His beliefs were epitomised in the famous clarion cries of the 1880 lecture on 'The Beauty of Life': 'Art made by the people and for the people, a joy to the maker and the user' and 'Have nothing in your houses which you do not know to be useful, or believe to be beautiful.'[16] Adulteration, shoddy goods and profit-mongering were all topics about which he felt deeply, as he revealed when addressing a group of designers and craftsmen in 1878:

I know that the public in general are set on having things cheap, being so ignorant that they do not know when they get them nasty also ... I know that the manufacturers (so-called) are so set on competition to its utmost, competition of cheapness, not of excellence, that they meet the bargain-hunters half way, and cheerfully furnish them with nasty wares at the cheap rate they asked for, by means of what can be called no prettier name than fraud.[17]

He went on to recommend to his audience that they themselves accept the honour of:

educating the public ... so that we may adorn life with the pleasure of cheerfully *buying* goods at their due price; with the pleasure of *selling* goods that we could be proud of both for fair price and fair workmanship; with the pleasure of working soundly and without haste at *making* goods that we could be proud of.[18]

Here, in essence, was the business philosophy of Morris & Co. Two basic ideas were accepted by Morris: the emphasis on originality and quality of the product range; and the duty to shape public taste.

First, Morris believed that the maker of any object should strive for originality in design. Originality in design pleases and elevates life, whereas uninspired goods reduce the quality of life. 'Never encourage imitation or copying of any kind except for the sake of preserving great works', Ruskin exhorted in 'The Nature of Gothic' – a sentiment with which Morris concurred wholeheartedly. Coupled with originality of design were high standards of manufacture. This led to the constant search for best quality materials and methods in dyeing, weaving, tapestry and other media which characterised the mature firm of the

1870s and 1880s; and where outside suppliers could not meet Morris's high standards production was internalised.

The emphasis on invention, originality and high quality was *the* central feature of the Morris business, and one which conferred competitive advantage in a fiercely contested market. It was for this reason that the firm's advertising placed considerable emphasis upon its chief designers, Burne-Jones and Morris himself. It was no coincidence that the firm's gradual decline began when it could no longer call upon their remarkable skills. The importance of a reputation for originality and quality is asserted in Morris's evidence before the Royal Commission on Technical Instruction in March 1882 when he remarked that 'beauty is a marketable quality, and ... the better the work is all round, both as a work of art and in its technique, the more likely it is to find favour with the public'.[19] Moreover, Morris argued that the firm's products were in fact value for money. In *A Joy Forever*, Ruskin asserts that 'as a rule of art economy, original work is, on the whole, cheapest and best worth having.' In a similar vein, Morris never tired of advertising the originality, quality and durability of his goods, which in the end made them 'cheap'. The 1861 prospectus boldly declared that 'good decoration, involving rather the luxury of taste than the luxury of costliness, will be found to be much less expensive than is generally supposed',[20] and this emphasis on 'the luxury of taste' remained a characteristic theme of the firm's publicity in the 1880s and 1890s.[21] A brochure of 1882, for example, which lists the main products and services offered by Morris & Co., identifies uniqueness, beautiful design and colouring, hand manufacture, the use of high quality materials, and in-house manufacture as the desirable features of Morris products.[22]

Secondly, from the earliest days of Morris, Marshall, Faulkner & Co., Morris accepted the responsibility, as a manufacturer, for moulding public taste. In April 1861, Morris expressed to F.B. Guy the belief that his was 'the only really artistic firm of the kind',[23] and the prospectus was equally dismissive of the commitment of rival firms to quality and originality. Other inventive and enterprising firms were understandably affronted by Morris, Marshall, Faulkner & Co.'s sweeping dismissal of the quality of contemporary work. The designer Lewis F. Day, for instance, recalled having heard about 'a set of amateurs who are going to teach us our trade' when he joined Lavers & Barraud around 1866.[24]

Not surprisingly, the mission to influence public taste and lead the market proved harder than Morris and his partners optimistically assumed in the first flush of their enthusiasm. Nevertheless, Morris persevered throughout his career as a designer and producer. Many of his best lectures of the late 1870s and early 1880s, such as 'Making the Best of It' and 'The Lesser Arts' seek to educate producers and consumers in the way Ruskin had urged. Dealings with individual customers also provided plenty of opportunities for Morris to influence consumer taste. Until the later 1880s, when J.H. Dearle took over as the firm's consultant on interior design and decoration, Morris was always available to advise customers on decorative schemes and expensive purchases.[25] Morris's honest and often forthright opinions appear to have done little to deter customers. Of course, there were exceptions: George Wardle, in his 'Memorials', enjoyed telling the story of how a customer commented adversely on the brightness of some Hammersmith carpets. Morris informed the customer that if he wanted dirt, he could find it in the street. No sale resulted.[26]

All in all, Morris did much to give practical effect to Ruskin's exhortations to raise standards and shape the market. He fully accepted that manufacturers had responsibilities beyond merely commercial ones. He certainly strove for originality in design, high standards of manufacture and the education of consumers. But he could not afford to aim for absolute perfection. As he wrestled to develop and market his products, compromises had to be made.

Goods were sold that did not entirely meet with Morris's approval. He had for some years been reluctantly obliged, in the absence of alternatives, to make use of chemical dyes; he did not like it, for artistic reasons, but for commercial reasons he had to. During the 1870s, Morris's long series of experiments with natural dyes at Sir Thomas Wardle's works at Leek, Staffordshire, began to bear fruit, but the use of indigo, technically by far the most intractable of the traditional dyes, continued to cause problems. In October 1876, Morris noted that dyeing silk with the indigo process was still unreliable, because the colours were not fast, and decided to continue with modern chemicals for the time being. He told Wardle that 'it seems more than a pity to lose our order as we shall do if we put it off much longer: so I propose to get this silk dyed by you in the fastest modern way possible'.[27] Wardle continued to experiment but never achieved satisfactory results, and Morris was obliged to abandon his plans to begin indigo dyeing on a commercial scale until he could set up his own dyeworks at Merton Abbey in 1881. At times, to avoid disappointing customers, other fabrics were accepted which did not reach his high standards. In 1881, for example, when Wardle accused him of rejecting goods which were only slightly substandard, he replied that 'I assure you positively that I have been so far from rejecting pieces on slight grounds, that I have often accepted them when I knew that they were not up to the mark.'[28] There were also occasions when the firm fulfilled decorative schemes which were not in keeping with Morris's own prescriptions. One instance was the decoration of Stanmore Hall in Middlesex. Morris had little sympathy with the 'sumptuous decoration' required by its owner, an Australian mining magnate, and was content to leave J.H. Dearle to oversee the work.[29] One wonders, too, what Morris thought about the firm's readiness in the 1880s and 1890s to meet the demand for furniture in the Queen Anne style – a period with which he had little sympathy.[30]

Whilst Morris always insisted upon originality of design, market pressures forced him to abandon the notion of uniqueness of product which characterised Morris, Marshall, Faulkner & Co. in its early years. In the 1870s, as Morris made strenuous efforts to ensure the financial success of the firm, he recognised that the possibilities for expansion on the basis of a fresh design for each commission were limited. Instead, he began to develop a complete range of decorative products for the secular market, such as wallpapers, chintzes and woven fabrics, which could be reproduced as the level of demand required. Serial production and the use of outside manufacturers were to play a major part in the firm's increasing prosperity in the 1870s.

Ownership of a large and growing stock of designs of enduring appeal was of vital importance to Morris & Co. Favoured designs could be repeated time and time again over many seasons. Morris designs for printed fabrics, most of which dated from the later 1870s or the early 1880s, retained their popularity until the First World War and beyond; out of 35 designs by William Morris, all but two were still available in 1912. *Daisy*, one of Morris's earliest wallpapers, long remained a firm favourite, achieving good sales through to the end of the nineteenth century.[31]

These compromises were symptomatic of a conflict between artistic integrity and commercial necessity, and the result of this tension was a unique enterprise, fighting as much against the market as working with it. It was also a business bounded in size and scope by the market for the goods it produced. While the Victorian middle class was growing rapidly from the 1870s, the number of people who could afford the firm's creations was always relatively few.

BUSINESS PRACTICE

The limited size of the Morris business, however, was also a matter of choice. Ruskin had much to say on the evils of scale and monopoly. He recognised that the path to personal fortune was through mass production: 'It is only through some method of taxing the labour of others that he [the manufacturer] becomes opulent. Every increase in his capital enables him to extend his taxation more widely ... to direct, accordingly, vaster and yet vaster masses of labour, and to appropriate profits.' He recommended capitalists not to seek undue size and profits. They should not try to monopolise markets or use unfair business tactics, 'not yielding to temptations of precarious gain'.[32] Ruskin went further and recommended manufacturers to adopt the self-sacrificial values of professional people like clergymen and army officers. This meant that they should apply all their 'energies to producing ... in a perfect state, and distributing ... at the cheapest possible price where most needed'. Moreover, they should be scrupulous in their dealings with other businessmen and the public, safeguarding quality and helping the weak. 'A man who has stoutness of thought and swiftness of capacity ... should not use his intellect to take the bread out of all the other men who are in the same trade with him.'[33] As always, Ruskin's moral prescriptions about business practice are aimed at the individual – unlike Marx, Ruskin was firmly of the opinion that individual actions count.

It is difficult to know how seriously Morris took these words. Certainly, Morris never sought to become the omnipotent paternalist recommended by Ruskin in *Unto this Last*. On the other hand, though, he was always an opponent of monopoly. At times, he was even ambivalent about those who sought to copy the firm's products. An instance is recounted by George Wardle. One of the firms which produced Kidderminster carpets for Morris & Co. sold copies to the large furnishing firm of Maples in Tottenham Court Road. When Morris remonstrated with Sir John Maple, the latter acknowledged the source of the design, but added that 'he thought it was fair that the sun should shine a little on him also'. Morris, to Wardle's astonishment, recognised the justice of the reply, and left.[34]

Moreover, Morris deliberately rejected the possibility of growth on many occasions. In a letter to the Austrian socialist Andreas Scheu, written in 1883, he admitted that he had had 'considerable success' in business, but added that 'if I had yielded on a few points of principle I might have become a positively rich man'.[35] Profit maximisation never became a prime objective of Morris & Co. Inevitably, Morris's insistence on perfecting production techniques and maintaining high quality had some effect on profitability. Nor was growth in terms of capital or numbers employed important to Morris. The maximum capital employed by the firm during his day was only £34,194[36] and the firm never employed many more than 100 people.[37] The Merton Abbey works could be considered as a number of craft enterprises – stained glass, dyeing, weaving, etc. – each of which only employed a handful of men. Typically, expansion of the labour force only came about as Morris developed new arts and processes. The choice of technology also contrived to limit the size of the Morris enterprise. Morris used techniques like block printing for chintzes and high warp tapestry weaving because, in his view, they provided the best quality, and thus he was more than willing to accept the limitations on output which they imposed.

Sometimes, too, the principles which William Morris had espoused led him to turn business away. A good example is provided by the firm's experiences following the establishment of the Society for the Protection of Ancient Buildings. Morris included in his moral concern not only the quality of the product, but also the use to which the product was put. In 1876–77, his anger began to rise at the drastic restorations then being carried out on many medieval buildings; for the Victorians, as well as rebuilding and repairing genuine dilapidations, felt justified in 'correcting' medieval work which was still sound. Architects like Sir Gilbert Scott were insistent that buildings should be of a single coherent architectural style (preferably Decorated Gothic). This belief put at risk a good majority of England's medieval churches, which were an amalgam of different styles, and had been extended or modified many times during their existence. Admittedly, the later additions were sometimes of a poorer quality than the early work, but even so they provided a historical record of centuries of devoted care and continuous use.

Morris, of course, was not the only person concerned about the consequences of restoration. Pugin and Ruskin were both highly critical of the restorers, while the *Athenaeum*'s art critic, F.G. Stephens, had published a number of articles criticising restorers, and Scott in

Plate 9.1 The dyehouse at Merton Abbey; small vats used for dyeing embroidery and weaving yarns *William Morris Gallery*

particular.[38] But Morris's commitment to 'put Protection in the place of Restoration'[39] had important implications for the firm's stained glass business. Morris & Co. announced that it would no longer supply glass for medieval buildings which were undergoing restoration or improvement.[40] This did not amount to a complete ban on work for old churches. Morris & Co. continued to supply windows to those with earlier work by the firm, and those which were not considered 'monuments of ancient art'. Even so, this was a costly decision, for the announcement was ill-understood by many potential clients, who considered Morris glass to be well suited to ancient buildings.[41] The rumour spread – apparently fostered by some of Morris & Co.'s rivals – that the firm had given up making stained glass altogether. Morris was obliged to restate his position in a series of advertisements in the *Pall Mall Gazette*, *Athenaeum* and *Saturday Review*, but his business was none the less affected for some time. The number of commissions undertaken by the firm almost halved between 1877–78 and 1880.[42]

Needless to say, Morris & Co. was scrupulous in its dealings with other businessmen and the public, as Ruskin demanded, though there were some instances of disorganisation and late completion of work in the early years of the firm.[43] Considerable care was taken in the preparation of invoices; every item, including consultancy fees and travel expenses, was meticulously listed, and the firm's terms of trade were plainly set out.[44] In the Oxford Street shop, the name, dimension and price of each item was clearly marked. This was relatively unusual, for at that time it was still the practice in high-class shops to avoid labelling goods. However, Morris was not alone in having high trading standards. Ruskin undoubtedly exaggerated the extent of commercial corruption – for the most part, Victorian entrepreneurs were well aware that it made good sense to trade fairly. Ruskin was nearer the target in his analysis of labour and social organisation of labour under capitalism.

THE FIRM AS SOCIAL ORGANISATION

Ruskin recognised that business firms were communities in their own right, and he had much to say on the way these communities should be organised. He was appalled by the joyless nature of factory labour. In one of those great outbursts which are so characteristic of his writings, he lamented:

The great cry that arises from all our manufacturing cities, louder than their furnace blast, is … that we manufacture everything there except men; we blanch cotton, and strengthen steel, and refine sugar, and shape pottery; but to brighten, to strengthen, to refine, or to form a single living spirit, never enters into our estimate of advantages.[45]

As noted in the introduction, Ruskin believed that creative work, which was intellectually and morally fulfilling as well as physically demanding, was of great importance to man. 'It would be well if all of us were good handicraftsmen of some kind', he said, 'and the dishonour of manual labour done away with altogether.'[46] And the notion that 'art is the expression of man's pleasure in labour … it is possible for a man to rejoice in his work' became central to Morris's system of thought.[47]

But for most people, they believed, this possibility was being destroyed by industrialisation – first by the craft system of eighteenth-century proto-industrialisation and subsequently by the extension of factory production. 'The slavery of England is a thousand times more bitter', said Ruskin, '… than that of the scourged African.' His hostility to the Industrial Revolution was largely based – as was Morris's – on the belief that mass production was pernicious. Through the division of labour, mass production ensured that no worker could identify with the finished product. This is reminiscent of Marx's idea of alienation – though Morris and Marx went further than Ruskin in recognising that the pernicious force was not industrialisation itself, but capitalism.

Three particular causes for concern were identified. The first of these was the division of labour, since it was through this, and the deskilling that generally accompanied it, that work became joyless. Thus Ruskin looked back to the medieval period, when the labour of the artisan was a source of interest and pleasure, and resulted in products which were fitting and beautiful. The freedom to take full responsibility for the manufacturing process – and indeed, the freedom to make mistakes – ennobled the worker, and satisfied his creative needs. While Morris's medievalism was less pervasive than that of Ruskin (and a good deal less pervasive than critics and admirers alike often assumed), he likewise placed a high value upon the virtues of the guild system of the late Middle Ages. In particular, he was attracted by the existence of a direct relationship between producer and consumer, and the local nature of craftsmanship. The division of labour, which he saw as one of the principal evils of the factory and machine age, had not yet taken place.

Secondly, goods should not be over-finished. 'Never demand an exact finish for its own sake, but only for some practical or noble end', said Ruskin in 'The Nature of Gothic':

Observe, you are put to a stern choice in the matter. You must either make a tool of the creature, or a man of him. You cannot make both. Men were not intended to work with the accuracy of tools, to be precise and perfect in all their actions. If you will have that precision out of them ... you must unhumanise them. On the other hand, if you will make a man of the working creature, you cannot make a tool. Let him but begin to imagine, to think, to try to do anything worth doing; and the engine-turned precision is lost at once. Out come all his roughness, all his dullness, all his incapability; shame upon shame, failure upon failure, pause after pause: but out comes the whole majesty of him also.[48]

Fitness for purpose was a guiding Ruskinian principle, which was frequently reiterated by Morris in his own writings. It was partly for this reason that Ruskin and Morris shared a dislike of the eighteenth century's quest for perfection and repeatability. This was epitomised by Josiah Wedgwood's desire that his workers should produce a uniform, consistent product, and his belief that this was indispensable to his success. As he wrote to his partner, Thomas Bentley, he was 'preparing to make such *Machines* of the Men as cannot err'.[49]

Finally, the awful conditions in which so many working people spent their lives contrived to make their work joyless and uncreative. 'Beautiful art can only be produced by people who have beautiful things about them, and leisure to look at them' said Ruskin; 'and unless you provide some elements of beauty for your workmen to be surrounded by, you will find that no elements of beauty can be invented by them.'[50] It was a theme to which Morris returned in 'The Lesser Arts' (1877), when he raged against the spread of squalid, cheaply built suburbs around Britain's great cities: 'How can I ask working-men passing up or down these hideous streets day to day to care about beauty?' he asked.[51]

In all this, Morris was a convinced Ruskinian and it is here that his mentor's influence can be felt most strongly. His work processes were civilised and not over intense; hours of work and wages were a little above the norm for work of that kind; he did break down the barrier between master and men by working long hours as a craftsman himself; the weak were not exploited; and the work was carried on in pleasant surroundings after the move to Merton in 1881 – a move which was itself inspired by considerations of the kind highlighted by Ruskin.

Yet Morris was acutely aware that the employment he offered fell short of both his and Ruskin's ideal. He felt himself caught up in a commercial system which, for one reason or another, prevented him from sharing with his employees the pleasures of the creative process. This he explained in a letter to the American poetess and socialist Emma Lazarus in April 1884:

except with a small part of the more artistic side of the work I could not do anything or at least but little to give this pleasure to the workmen; because I should have had to change their method of working so utterly, that it should have disqualified them from earning a living elsewhere: you see I have got to understand thoroughly the manner of the work under which the art of the Middle Ages was done, and that it is the *only* manner of work which can turn out popular art, only to discover that it is impossible to work in that manner in this profit grinding Society.[52]

There was, however, another reason why it was impossible: while William Morris took on board many of Ruskin's prescriptions, he did not in practice give them equal weight. The most important was the emphasis on the quality of the product – it was this, above all, that determined whether (or when) the production of a particular item was internalised, or whether (in some cases) it was always manufactured by subcontractors. In the pursuit of quality, William Morris adopted some practices which were at odds with other Ruskinian objectives.

At Merton, some attempts were made to give the workmen opportunities to exercise their creative abilities, but there were strict limits to this. Morris employed older technologies mainly because they gave him, as designer and manufacturer, the close control over the production process which he felt he needed. His technological choices were made, first and foremost, for artistic and commercial reasons, rather that for reasons of social philosophy. In fact, many of his workers had very little personal influence over the production process: their choices were few, the division of labour quite fine. From Jacquard loom weaving to vegetable dyeing, the work was arranged to satisfy Morris, leaving the individual worker barely elevated in status from his or her counterpart elsewhere. Those who viewed Morris as a medievalist and anti-industrialist may perhaps have been surprised by his willingness to adopt the Jacquard loom. It was, after all, widely used in the fearsome mills of the industrial north, and, even if the weaver had any aesthetic judgement, he could not use it; for the punched cards controlled the whole operation. But, against this, it produced good quality results; it speeded up production and produced goods of a greater consistency than the older types of hand-looms. Even Morris & Co.'s tapestry weavers often had little freedom to interpret a design; most worked on backgrounds and draperies, leaving the difficult parts such as hands and faces to the most skilled.

Conditions at Merton were, of course, far preferable to those of countless other workers at the time. Nevertheless, Morris himself was frank enough to admit that they fell short of Ruskin's full prescription.

THE REWARDS OF LABOUR

It is often said of Morris that he cannot have been a true socialist because he paid himself much more than his fellow workers received. He certainly did. By the 1880s, as he turned to socialist action, his earnings from the firm had far outstripped his earlier income from his family's mining interests, and he had become a very wealthy man. Morris recognised the paradox, and admitted that there was some justification for the sniping of the press. A frequent criticism was that he had not sought to distribute the firm's profits amongst its employees. His correspondence with Georgiana Burne-Jones and Emma Lazarus indicates that he was uneasy about the situation he found himself in, and felt constrained to explain why he rejected profit-sharing as a social solution:

I ought to say why I think mere profit sharing would be no solution to the labour difficulty: in the first place it would do nothing towards the extinction of *competition* which lies at the root of the evils of today: because each *cooperative* society would compete for its corporate advantage with other societies, would in fact so far be nothing but a joint-stock-company – in the second place it would do nothing towards the extinction of exploitage, because the most it could do in that direction would be to create a body of small capitalists who would exploit the labour of those underneath them quite as implacably as the bigger Capitalists do: ... in the third place the immediate results would be an increase of overwork amongst the industrious, who would of course always tend upwards towards the small capitalist class abovesaid: this would practically mean putting the screw on all wage-earners, and intensifying the contrast between the well to do and the mere unskilled; ... Thus, you see, so accursed is the capitalist system under which we live, that even what should be the virtues of good management and thrift under its slavery do but add to the misery of our thralldom, and indeed become mere vices, and have at last the faces of cruelty and shabbiness.[53]

Plate 9.2 Jacquard looms at Merton Abbey *William Morris Gallery*

Thus his defence was expressed in part in Marxian terms: individual acts were meaningless. However, the defence offered to contemporaries was also Ruskinian in tone. Ruskin believed that people should be paid at different rates according to levels of skill and experience. In 'The Nature of Gothic', he argued that 'the distinction between one man and another [should] be only in experience and skill, and the authority and wealth which these must naturally and justly obtain'.[54] What mattered in his view was the avoidance of extremes of wealth and that money should be put to work to good purpose:

Inequalities of wealth, unjustly established, have assuredly injured the nation in which they exist during their establishment; and unjustly directed, injure it yet more during their existence. But inequalities of wealth, justly established, benefit the nation in the cause of their establishment; and, nobly used, aid it yet more by their existence.[55]

Businessmen, moreover, could justly expect to earn more than workers. 'When you have fully achieved the superiority which is due to you, and you have acquired the wealth which is a fitting reward of your sagacity, if you solemnly accept the responsibility of it ... then wealth is not the net of a spider, entangling and destroying: but wealth well used is the net of the sacred fisher who gathers souls of men out of the deep.'

In this important respect, as in others, the firm was run on Ruskinian, rather than Marxian, lines. Indeed, this principle was firmly established from the very inception of Morris, Marshall, Faulkner & Co. Rates of pay for similar jobs varied according to the level of skill brought to bear. So, for instance, Burne-Jones, Rossetti and Brown could expect to be paid more for stained glass cartoons than Morris or Marshall. Despite the commercial success of some of his cartoons, Morris always remained diffident about his abilities in figure drawing, and of course never acquired a reputation to match some of the other partners as painter and cartoonist. On 15 April 1863, for example, the minute book noted, 'distribution of the 4 major prophets for Bradford East window. Ezekiel and Daniel to Rossetti for £3. Isaiah and Jeremiah to Morris for the small sum of £2.'[56]

Morris's abilities were thought to lie elsewhere. Unlike the other partners, he had some experience of business finance and management acquired during his dealings with West Country mining interests. He had, furthermore, already demonstrated his drive and ability to organise in his work for the *Oxford and Cambridge Magazine* and his contribution to the painting of the Oxford Union in 1857.[57] Thus it was in recognition of proven experience, and not merely the fact that he had time to spare, that he was made manager of Morris, Marshall, Faulkner & Co. at the not inconsiderable salary of £150 a year.

Later in his career, as he turned to socialism, Morris was not unduly embarrassed by his wealth: it was earned through his own labour; it was needed to support his family; redistribution would have brought little extra to his colleagues; the cash could be used in part to finance his activities on behalf of socialism. And, while most workers were paid on a piece-rate basis, he did set up a limited profit-sharing scheme for key personnel. As he told Georgiana Burne-Jones in 1884:

Some of those who work for me share in the profits formally: I suppose, I made the last year or two about £1,800. Wardle about £1,200, the Smiths about £600 each; Debney & West £400 – all share directly in the profits: Kenyon the colour-mixer, & Goodacre the foreman dyer have also a kind of bonus on the goods turned out.[58]

For the most part, though, he continued to pay workers at different rates according to skill and experience very much along Ruskinian lines.

CONCLUSION

There is no perfect correspondence between the business notions of John Ruskin and the practice of William Morris. Yet, equally, it is evident that Morris stuck to many of his mentor's ideas with remarkable tenacity; making compromises surely, but limiting the effects of these. And the operation of the Morris business, in turn, especially those aspects relating to design, craftsmanship, work organisation, working conditions, scale and the market, owed much to Ruskin.

All this was not enough for Morris. In 1883, he wrote: 'both my historical studies and my practical conflict with the philistinism of modern society have forced upon me the conviction that art cannot have real life and growth under the present system of commercialism and profit mongering.'[59] Equally, there could be no good life for the working people. He turned to Marxism and politics in pursuit of a social rather than an individual solution to the evils of the age. Socialism could not be achieved by the actions of individuals, no matter how able and well-meaning they might be.

We must conclude that in his business dealings Morris was profoundly influenced by his study of Ruskin's key works of social criticism and political economy; and that he extracted from this study certain general principles which were used to guide the Morris firm in all its aspects. During the 1870s, Morris came to realise, through personal experience, that Ruskinism could not solve the problems of society at large. In recognising this, he searched actively for an alternative model of social change, which he found in Marxism. However, while Marxist ideas guided his political actions, it is evident that Ruskin was the dominant influence on Morris the businessman, and his firm continued to operate along Ruskinian lines. So it was that Morris was able to reject the charge that he was hypocritical in proclaiming socialism whilst practising capitalism: Marxism told him that the individual responsibility approach of Ruskin was futile as a basis for the regeneration of society – but better by far to be a Ruskinian than an out-and-out profit-monger.

NOTES

1. This essay first appeared under the same title in the *Journal of Business Ethics*, Vol. 14 (1995), pp. 181–94.
2. J.D. Rosenberg, *The Darkening Glass: A Portrait of Ruskin's Genius* (New York, 1961), p. 117.
3. W. Morris, preface to the Kelmscott Press edition of J. Ruskin, *The Nature of Gothic* (1892), p. v.
4. Ibid., p. i.
5. For a discussion of other influences, see C. Harvey and J. Press, *William Morris: Design and Enterprise in Victorian Britain* (Manchester, 1991), Chap. 1.
6. J.W. Mackail, *Life of William Morris* (1899), Vol. I, p. 226.
7. G.E. Street, 'On the Future of Art in England', *Ecclesiologist*, Vol. XIX (1858), pp. 232–40.
8. See Sir H. Cole, *Fifty Years of Public Work* (2 vols, 1884).
9. J. Ruskin, *The Two Paths* (1859), in E.T. Cook and A. Wedderburn (eds), *The Complete Works of John Ruskin* (39 vols, 1903–12) (hereafter *Complete Works*), Vol. 16, p. 320.
10. J. Ruskin, 'The Nature of Gothic', in *The Stones of Venice*, Vol. II (1853), p. 169.
11. Ruskin, *The Two Paths*, in *Complete Works*, Vol. 16, p. 319.
12. British Library, Add. Mss. 45350, G. Wardle, 'Memorials of William Morris' (1897), ff. 15–16.
13. *Second Report of the Royal Commissioners on Technical Instruction* (Parliamentary Papers, c.3981, 1884 XXXI), Q.1589.
14. Ibid., Q.1466. Also see QQ.1640, 1645, 1647.
15. J. Ruskin, *Unto this Last*, in *Complete Works*, Vol. 17, p. 344.

16. W. Morris, 'The Beauty of Life' (1880), in M. Morris (ed.), *The Collected Works of William Morris* (hereafter *Collected Works*), Vol. XXII, 51ff.

17. W. Morris, 'The Lesser Arts' (1877), in *Collected Works*, Vol. XXII, p. 22.

18. Ibid., pp. 22–3.

19. *Second Report of the Royal Commissioners on Technical Instruction*, Q.1580.

20. Mackail, *Life*, Vol. I, p. 56.

21. See, for example, William Morris Gallery (hereafter WMG), File 11a, Morris & Co., circular, n.d., c.1881.

22. Victoria & Albert Museum, Box I.276.A, Morris & Co., brochure, 1882.

23. N. Kelvin (ed.), *The Collected Letters of William Morris*, Vol. I (Princeton, NJ, 1984), p. 37, to the Revd Frederick B. Guy, 19 April 1861.

24. L.F. Day, 'William Morris and his Art', *Easter Art Annual of the Art Journal* (1899).

25. See, for example, WMG, File 11a, Morris & Co., circular, n.d., c.1881. On Dearle's assumption of responsibility for consultancy work see, *inter alia*, Kelvin (ed.), *Letters*, Vol. II (Princeton, NJ, 1987), pp. 407–8, to Jenny Morris, 24 March 1885.

26. Wardle, 'Memorials', ff. 10–11.

27. Kelvin (ed.), *Letters*, Vol. I, pp. 327–9, to Thomas Wardle, 31 Oct. 1876.

28. Ibid., p. 22, to Thomas Wardle, 18 Feb. 1881.

29. In a letter to Georgiana Burne-Jones, Morris described it as 'a house of a very rich man – and such a wretched uncomfortable place: a sham Gothic house of fifty years ago now being added to by a young architect of the commercial type – men who are very bad'. P. Henderson, *The Letters of William Morris to his Family and Friends* (1950), pp. 322–3, to Georgiana Burne-Jones, 10 June 1890. For a description of the house, see *The Studio* (Sept. 1893), quoted in A. Vallance, William Morris: His Art, his Writings and his Public Life (1897), pp. 124–5.

30. M. Girouard, *Sweetness and Light: The Queen Anne Movement, 1860–1900* (New Haven and London, 1977), *passim*; R. Little, 'Furniture', in K.A. Lochnan, D.E. Schoenherr and C. Silver (eds), *The Earthly Paradise: Arts and Crafts by William Morris and his Circle from Canadian Collections* (Toronto, 1993), p. 176.

31. Vallance, *William Morris*, pp. 87–8.

32. Ruskin, *Unto this Last*, in *Complete Works*, Vol. 17, p. 36.

33. Ibid., pp. 37–41.

34. Wardle, 'Memorials', f. 12.

35. Kelvin (ed.), *Letters*, Vol. II, p. 229, to Andreas Scheu, 5 Sept. 1883.

36. Public Record Office, IR59 173.

37. Walthamstow Public Library, Mrs J.W. Mackail Gift, William Morris to Georgiana Burne Jones, 1 June 1884.

38. See, for example, B. Ferrey, *Recollections of A. Welby Pugin* (1861), pp. 80–1; J. Ruskin, *The Seven Lamps of Architecture* (1849), *passim*. Even the much-maligned architectural profession had mixed feelings about restoration; the author of Butterfield's obituary in the *RIBA Journal*, for example, commented that 'we are wrapt in wonder that he could appreciate so much and spare so little'. *RIBA Journal*, Vol. VII, pp. 242–3.

39. From the Society for the Protection of Ancient Buildings' manifesto (1877), which was written by Morris and has been reprinted in every annual report down to the present day. Quoted in Kelvin (ed.), *Letters*, Vol. I, pp. 360–1.
40. WMG, File 11a, Morris & Co., Circular, 9 April 1877.
41. Wardle, 'Memorials', ff. 23–4. This belief about the suitability of Morris glass for old buildings, in fact, had always rested upon a misunderstanding: the principles of its manufacture were medieval in inspiration, but essentially the character of Morris glass was modern. The designs of Ford Madox Brown were distinctly unmedieval, and the pictorial style of Burne-Jones anticipated the aesthetic work of the 1880s and 1890s.
42. A.C. Sewter, *The Stained Glass of William Morris and His Circle* (New Haven, CT, 2 vols 1974–75), Vol. II, pp. 234–40.
43. The effective scheduling of projects, for instance, seems at times to have been neglected. One illustration is Morris, Marshall, Faulkner & Co.'s failure to complete its work on time at Jesus College, Cambridge, in 1866. See Kelvin (ed.), *Letters*, Vol. I, pp. 46–50, to E.H. Morgan, 27 Nov. 1866; 3 Dec. 1866; 26 March 1867. Also see D. Robinson and S. Wildman, *Morris & Co. in Cambridge* (1980), pp. 37–9.
44. Kelvin (ed.), *Letters*, Vol. II, p. 591, to Julius Alfred Chatwin, 2 Nov. 1886.
45. Ruskin, 'The Nature of Gothic', in *The Stones of Venice*, Vol. II, p. 165.
46. Ibid., p. 169.
47. W. Morris, preface to the Kelmscott Press edition of *The Nature of Gothic* (1892), p. v.
48. Ruskin, 'The Nature of Gothic', in *The Stones of Venice*, Vol. II, pp. 161–2, 166.
49. A. Finer and G. Savage (eds), *The Selected Letters of Josiah Wedgwood* (1965), pp. 82–3.
50. Ruskin, *The Two Paths*, in *Complete Works*, Vol. 16, p. 338.
51. Morris, 'The Lesser Arts', in *Collected Works*, Vol. XXII, p. 16.
52. Kelvin (ed.), *Letters*, Vol. II, p. 275, to Emma Lazarus, 21 April 1884, printed in the *Spectator*, Vol. 32 (1886), p. 397.
53. Ibid. Also see Kelvin (ed.), *Letters*, Vol. II, p. 283, to Georgiana Burne-Jones, 1 June 1884.
54. Ruskin, 'The Nature of Gothic', in *The Stones of Venice*, Vol. II, p. 170.
55. Ruskin, *Unto this Last*, in *Complete Works*, Vol. 17, p. 47.
56. Hammersmith and Fulham Archives Department, Morris, Marshall, Faulkner & Co., Minute Book, 15 April 1863. Also see 10 Dec. 1862, 28 Jan. 1863, 1 April 1863.
57. Mackail, *Life*, Vol. I, pp. 91–3, 121–4, 157.
58. Kelvin (ed.), *Letters*, Vol. II, p. 283, to Georgiana Burne-Jones, 1 June 1884.
59. Ibid., p. 230, to Andreas Scheu, 15 Sept. 1883.

10

William Morris and the Making of an Earthly Paradise

A CCORDING TO Mackail's biography, Morris as a small child already showed, in his tastes and activities, strong signs of characteristics which remained constant throughout his life; but in his anxiety to establish the status of his subject as child prodigy (precocity being the natural harbinger of genius), he tells us that Morris had read widely in Sir Walter Scott's *Waverley Novels* by the time he was four years old. No doubt older readers of Scott, whether or not they have four-year-old children, will find little difficulty in dismissing this alarming story as implausible, to say the least. But Mackail, though not always a totally scrupulous biographer, would hardly have gratuitously invented anything so fantastic. It seems most likely that he was happy to relate a largely apocryphal tale originating with Morris's close friends and relatives. Morris himself is on record as claiming merely to have read a great many books – 'good, bad, and indifferent', in his own words – by the time he was seven. It is quite conceivable that by the age of 11 or 12 he had actually read some of the easier works of Scott, such as *Ivanhoe*, or *The Talisman*, or even *Quentin Durward*; but what appears not in doubt is that in his later, mature years it seemed to Morris that Scott had been a life-time literary companion. In other words, he could hardly remember what it was like not to have read the works of Scott. They had become second nature to him; it must have seemed as if he had known them all his life.

The implications of all this are not small. Scott was a writer of historical fiction, much of it, though by no means all, set in the Middle Ages. Whether Morris was drawn to Scott through a natural affinity with the Middle Ages, or whether familiarity with Scott created an affinity in Morris, is conjectural; what does matter is the fact that once Morris had outgrown his infant incapacity to see much beyond his own immediate affairs, he was thenceforth fascinated and delighted by the medieval world. This was a taste which began, presumably, in the purely artistic sphere, in the medieval buildings of England (not just the great cathedrals and churches – though these may well have been in his thoughts when he was, briefly, seriously contemplating a career as a priest – but lesser buildings too, if, stretching the point, ordinary houses as late as the seventeenth century are taken as not essentially differing from much earlier ones), in medieval manuscripts, tapestries and embroidery, and, as stated, in the works of Scott, who may thus be regarded as the first notable influence in the shaping of the mature Morris's Utopian vision. It is not surprising that the society he imagines in *News from Nowhere* is distinctly medieval in terms of style – buildings, furniture and clothing; nor that his later romances use a variety of the English language deliberately designed to suggest antiquity.

This has been taken by some modern critics of Morris as being a symptom of a fundamental weakness in Morris's intellectual system: a backward-looking, regressive view of human history and civilisation, standing in fatal and unconstructive opposition to all the great achievements of the age, indeed, against all that his age stood for, its spirit. In consequence, it was a view that would never find forward-looking remedies to the undoubted problems that progress inevitably brought with it. The result, so runs the argument, was that when Morris finally embraced socialism, it was a woolly kind of socialism, dedicated to recreating a vague medieval Paradise, that had never existed, and would never exist.

These accusations, the fruit of prejudice rather than hard research and knowledge, are not sustainable. For they entail a supposition that an age can be seen as something homogeneous and consistent; and that opposition to it, or more accurately, to its ethos or spirit, is mere eccentricity, more or less damaging according to the extent of its influence. But it is reasonable to doubt whether there was any such universal ethos in the nineteenth century. For if there is such a thing as the spirit of an age, it can only be defined in terms of how that age feels about itself, how it understands itself, and what its aspirations are. That is particularly hard to establish in the case of the Victorians. It was a time when weighty and distinguished opinions were often to be found on opposite sides of most debates. It is impossible to establish what a truly Victorian view of any issue might be, when contradictory views on each are obviously and equally Victorian. There is no need to look further for examples than, on the one hand, the employers of children as virtual slave labour, and, on the other, reformers such as Shaftesbury. This multiplicity of views, characteristic also of the present age, was not so marked in previous ages. It can be argued that towards the end of the eighteenth century an immensely long period of consensus was drawing to its close. Most satire, for example, up to but not including the works of Jonathan Swift, was directed not at the structure and fabric of society, but at the incompetence or corruption of individuals. Their functions in society were considered valid; their performance all too often was not. One of the very few exceptions to this may be the medieval attacks by Langland and Chaucer on the ecclesiastical office of Pardoner; but the scandalous nature of this office in itself was a widespread perception of the late Middle Ages; it did not require particularly acute and original social criticism to show up such obvious corruption for what it was.

But the age of consensual certainty had given way, slowly at first, then with an ever-increasing momentum, to an age of scientific enquiry. The Industrial Revolution, though that remains for many people the most spectacular achievement – for good or ill – of the period, was only one manifestation of a wider intellectual revolution which, whatever its ultimate origins, seems to have gathered an unstoppable momentum towards the end of the eighteenth century, and continues unchecked today. Nor was this new spirit of enquiry confined to the scientific world. It had spread its scope to cover such areas as political and economic theory, and has to be seen as operating in the terrific clash of old assumptions and new ideologies that culminated in the French Revolution; while the work of Darwin showed that a pure science like biology could fuel debate in the remote territory of theology. In consequence, anyone with intellectual pretensions in almost any field would find a variety of often conflicting theories to choose from, and even to develop. Consequently, by the time Morris was 30, the likes of Darwin and Marx in particular had seen to it that the only alternative to intellectual conflict was intellectual opting out.

Morris is thought of nowadays as one of the more important names in the early history of the socialist movement. But that is with the benefit of hindsight. It was not until Morris was almost 50 that it would be proper to call him a socialist. Before that, he was more or less a conventional Liberal, and it is hard to discern much that was in any way political about Morris at all. The Morris of 1860, for instance, when he was 26 years old, seems to have been preoccupied with art, to the virtual exclusion of practical politics, even though it cannot be denied that his views on art and craft had political implications. Nevertheless, he had not yet formed the broad ethical system which is the basis of any fully developed political theory. Indeed, Morris's advance towards socialism was as complex and idiosyncratic a process as might have been expected of a man of his nature. It is tempting to suggest that it actually began with Sir Walter Scott, since Morris, for all the diversity of his activities, was never inclined to compartmentalise his mind, but rather tried to find some sort of unity in this diversity. At all events, when Morris writes or speaks on virtually any topic, it is in a voice that is always recognizably his, and recognizably consistent. Even the beautiful and fascinating natural environment in which Morris spent his early years had some effect on his later political outlook. But the mere possession of a medieval taste and a love of nature could lead anywhere, and less probably to socialism than to many other creeds. A great many other ingredients had to be added before the complexion of his mind reached its final, mature quality.

There were several writers who attracted Morris in his early adulthood, of whom the most enduring in his influence was John Ruskin. The theories of art and work that dominated Morris's thinking in his development of the firm were essentially Ruskin's, and underwent few modifications as Morris grew older. The two had much in common, for Morris did not have to be told by Ruskin of the virtues of medieval art. But, though he might have arrived at Ruskin's conclusions as to the implications of these virtues without Ruskin's help, he did not have to, and for this reason Ruskin remains a key figure in the history of Morris and the firm. But before considering Ruskin, acknowledgement of a somewhat guarded nature must be accorded to another powerful influence on the young Morris. This was Thomas Carlyle. He was one of the first writers to present an articulate case against the new kind of civilisation that the Industrial Revolution was creating in early nineteenth-century England.

Carlyle, whose views express a deep, original and almost totally reactionary philosophy, greatly admired the hierarchical structure of medieval society, and the order which this structure imposed on it. It should not be thought, though, that Carlyle was no more than a rigid authoritarian. What he saw and deplored was a displacement of a hierarchy based on human relationships by another based on cash. Hierarchies were not in themselves to be deplored, unpleasant though they may be for those of the lowest rank. But there was a chain of personal contact in the medieval system which provided – in theory, at any rate – links of a direct kind between the highest and lowest in the land. No such contacts characterise a system which allows one section of society to regard and treat other sections as having no value except as a means of making money for the privileged section – the so-called 'cash nexus'. This, Carlyle felt, with a good deal of passion, demeaned all concerned, and by corrupting human relationships would sooner or later corrupt society as a whole.

On the whole, though, Carlyle's solutions were not of a kind to appeal to the mature Morris. Carlyle was deeply influenced by his Puritan upbringing. He believed that religion was in his time largely a matter of form rather than of content, and that a regeneration of faith was necessary for the survival of society. This kind of thought was more likely to irritate than impress a practically-minded man like Morris: there never was a Golden Age of faith to look back on, and in no period in history, no matter what beliefs men and women have professed, have daily affairs, private or public, been noticeably conducted in the spirit of the Sermon on the Mount. Nevertheless, it is possible to accept a diagnosis without also accepting the prescribed cure. This selective approach was in the end roughly the one Morris adopted. Of course, it was not directly through reading Carlyle that Morris became a socialist. It was rather that ideas absorbed from Carlyle served him as parts of the structure of his own socialist world view; but not until the success of the Morris firm allowed him the time to look away from the workshops at Merton and become active in the wider world.

In any case, the motivation which led to the setting up of the firm had very little to do with Carlyle, and a great deal to do with John Ruskin. Throughout his adult life Morris drew on Ruskin almost as other men draw on sacred texts. Even when age and experience forced reservations on him, he never writes of Ruskin with anything less than the greatest respect. When he was forced into compromises with market forces in his own business, he came to realise that Ruskin alone did not have a complete answer to the problems of nineteenth-century society. But of all the really central tenets of the Ruskinian model, the only one which Morris fully discarded was the belief that the benevolence of individuals could combine to better the world. The guru's influence remained none the less fruitful, nowhere more so than in Morris's chosen field of the crafts. It was Ruskin's understanding, endorsed by Morris, that the Industrial Revolution was not so much a potential disaster as an actual one, certainly for the arts, and highly probably for society in general. The two men were not alone in their aversion to the new methods of mass production, which, on Ruskin's analysis, was the cause of something quite close to Marx's notion of alienation: workers in a factory where mass production was the only or main method of working felt no affinity with the product, no pride in it, no respect for it, and no satisfaction in producing it. Furthermore, though this was a matter of less concern to Marx, the goods themselves were of less value than hand-crafted goods, because in their mechanical precision, each being a mere duplicate of the others, they lacked individuality, the character and warmth that the authentic human touch inevitably imparts. There is something both profound and appealing about this far from clinical aesthetic system. After all, if in the greatest art we are led to expect no imperfections, or perhaps the right word is irregularities, we are presumably looking for an art which conceals, not reveals, the truth; because nothing that is perfect is a true representation of the human spirit.

Another of Ruskin's ideas which must have particularly gratified Morris was the elevation of the decorative arts to a status comparable with that of art and architecture.[1] Morris was, after all, planning a career as a craftsman-designer, and it had become clear early in that career that for all his fine talent as a designer he would never be in the top rank as a painter of pictures. Morris found in Ruskin inspirations of a thoroughly practical kind – above all, the notion that the decorative arts were important because they created the visual environment in which men and women lived. This point is one that might particularly interest our own age, since it was not simply a matter of aesthetics. It has its roots in the Romantic movement, which swept Europe towards the end of the eighteenth century, and which arose out of a revulsion against the rather smooth and mannered complacency of the so-called Enlightenment. In this Romantic movement, we may detect also the beginnings of an anxiety about the environment and what human activity – industrial activity – was doing to it. This anxiety has resurfaced over the past 20 years or so in a form so intense as to amount almost to panic. But even in the early to mid-nineteenth century, Wordsworth and Blake, and later, of course, Ruskin, Dickens, Kingsley, and many others, joined in the concern. But a reading of any of these authors will suggest that their real fear was not of the physical destruction of the earth's ecology. Among the well-known figures of the time, only Thomas Malthus seems to have faced up to that possibility, and then only one aspect of it

– the population explosion – and it is unclear, without much research, how many people took him seriously. The danger more generally perceived was to the human psyche, or, in contemporary language, to the human soul. They thought it self-evident that living amid squalor, ugliness, stench and din was bound to be bad for people. It may be retorted that this is indeed self-evident, and therefore hardly worth saying. Such enlightenment, however, was not – is not – universal. The wealthier classes of Victorian England seem to have contemplated the pervasive misery of their fellow-citizens with stoical equanimity, until some of the misery made its way into the water supply, and began to lay low the rich alongside the poor by means of cholera.

It appears, therefore, that ugliness and filth are happily tolerated by those who do not have to suffer them, until they become an identifiable physical threat; and that the wiser instinct which on sensing danger does not ask for proof is a rarer quality than might be hoped for. That instinct was particularly strong in Morris. It may even serve to account for his admirable artistic taste, on which, as he himself said, 'the whole of [his] business depends'.[2] It seems to lie at the heart of Morris's dislike of chemical dyes, which had in his time replaced the traditional organic dyes, universally used from ancient times right up to the early nineteenth century. Of the aniline dyes, he said that all the colours they produced were 'hideous' in themselves, whereas the old dyes were all beautiful.[3] This raises, for the philosopher at least, a minor question of aesthetics. For though Morris's taste in the matter of colour will meet no challenge here, it is hard to know how he arrived at his judgment, except through some sort of process at least akin to instinct. How can one colour legitimately be considered more beautiful than another? It is at least possible that something in the mind responds to the nature of the dyestuffs themselves. After all, some of the old dyes, such as cochineal, are actually edible; and none – to our knowledge, at least – are poisonous. The chemical dyes, on the other hand, are disagreeably derived from toxic substances, such as cyanide and coal-tar. Perhaps something of these unfriendly origins expresses itself in something cold and inhuman about the end product; they are, quite simply, unnatural, which for Morris was a term of condemnation, whether applied to art or to society.

This may seem a minor matter. It did not seem minor to William Morris. He spent a great amount of time in research and experiment, spread over several years, in an eventually successful attempt at mastering the technically very tricky process of indigo dyeing, simply in order not to have use chemical dyes such as Prussian blue. His dislike of them is a striking aspect of his artistic scheme from which may be inferred the crucial Morrisian view of the relationship between art and nature: 'For, and this is at the root of the whole matter, everything made by man's hands has a form, which must be either beautiful or ugly; beautiful if it accords with Nature, and helps her; ugly if it is discordant with Nature, and thwarts her.'[4] In this passage, the capital N, together with the personification 'helps' or 'thwarts' her, might suggest that Morris saw nature much as Wordsworth did, in the almost mystical, reverential mode of high Romanticism. But this seems unlikely, since such personifications were quite conventional. His response to nature was much more realistic and robust than Wordsworth's. He was, after all, a practical man, who made use of the products of nature to earn his living. To him, nature was the dye obtained from the root of a plant; how the carver responded to the grain of the wood; the harmony of the chosen colours with the texture of the fabrics. Of course, he enjoyed the beauty of natural landscapes, but in a matter-of-fact way. There is, for instance, nothing remotely sentimental about his reaction to the proposals for the development, or despoiling, of Epping Forest, which he had known so well as a boy. Nature, then, is no more nor less than things produced by normal natural processes, and good art allows these processes due expression in the finished product.

There are two questions here: to what extent did Morris set out to create a business in accordance with Ruskin's principles and to what extent did he succeed? It will be seen that the second question immediately implies that the barest answer to the first has to be, to some extent, however minimal. In fact, Morris went quite a long way along the Ruskinian road. He fully accepted Ruskin's teaching that manufacturers had responsibilities beyond purely commercial considerations. Manufacturers were to 'form the market'; that is, to lead by example in the creation of standards of good taste in manufactured goods. If they shirked this responsibility, said Ruskin, they might well become very rich, but at the cost of knowing themselves to be corrupters of public taste.[5] Nobody could have striven more mightily than Morris to put this dictum to practical effect. Nobody was less likely than Morris to say, 'this will do'. For it would not do, not unless it was absolutely right, or as right as it was possible to be. But the proviso, as right as possible, is necessary, all the same. After all, Morris was a businessman. He quite simply could not afford to be an absolute, out-and-out perfectionist, no matter how much he would have desired it. Of course, this by no means makes Morris a corrupter of public taste; it does show how hard it can be to maintain artistic ideals when faced with the ever-present, insistent, nagging requirement that things be sold.

There were also occasions when Morris was quite ready to exploit recently developed technology, such as the Jacquard loom. For present purposes, it needs only to be stated that this invention, introduced in 1804, was everywhere in action throughout the heavily industrialised North of England, and was typical enough of its time. It speeded up production significantly. It also produced perfectly satisfactory results; no reasons presented themselves for not adopting it, except for its associations with the grim towns of northern England, whose teeming slums were the wonder and horror of Europe, until Europe caught up with England, and created slums of its own to house its own industrial workers. Mere associations, however, no matter how vivid, did not provide solid grounds for rejecting the Jacquard loom. Ruskin's answer might have been that mechanisation of any kind puts an undesirable distance between worker and product. But Morris had come to see that to shun mechanisation completely would be to succumb to the competition and simply go out of business.

Nor can it really be argued that conditions at Merton Abbey were those of the ideal factory, as Ruskin would have understood the term – a place of light, artistic satisfaction, learning and pleasure, in utter contrast to the appalling conditions prevalent elsewhere. For whereas there is no doubt that actual working conditions at Merton were a great deal better than most employers at the time offered, and could even be described as pleasant, they still fell short of the elusive Ruskinian ideal. Morris, for a start, took overall control of the entire operation from the artistic side, so that the workers had little or nothing to add creatively. They worked at piece rates – that is, they were paid according to what they produced, not for their hours. The rates of pay were not such as to allow pleasantly short working days; in fact, Morris's workers were only somewhat better off than others with similar employment elsewhere, though of course being only somewhat better off was certainly more to be desired than not.

Considering how well Morris eventually did from the firm, it is greatly to his credit that he both acknowledged and deplored these facts. So what way out of this maze of problems did he devise? What view did he form of this unacceptable modern society, with its shoddy products, its dehumanised working classes, and its rejection of principles, both artistic and moral? At first, he contented himself with simply rejecting society in its turn. He said and wrote many times that his dominant passion was a hatred of modern civilisation. This was inevitable, indeed quite rational, given his particular cast of mind; but it took rather a long time for his hatred to find a direction and a focus.

That this was a process, and not a question of sudden conversion, is illustrated by the Icelandic connection. Morris had started studying the Icelandic sagas in the original language in 1868, and was so captivated by them that he visited the land of their origin three years later. Nowadays, of course, this remarkable and admirable country is among the world's wealthiest. In those days, it was not. Its inhabitants were pressed – sometimes very hard-pressed – to scratch the most meagre of livings from a rugged, barren, volcanic land, and yet it did not seem to Morris to be a gloomy or unhappy place. And Morris, as he himself observed, learned 'that the most grinding poverty is a trifling evil compared with the inequality of classes'.[6] But this was not the Morris of 1871 speaking. In 1871, it is likely that he would scarcely have been capable of formulating such a thought in such words. In fact, the letter from which the quote is taken was written in 1883; and the slightly Marxian reference to 'classes' strongly suggests that this lesson was a long time sinking in. No doubt Morris had seen something and felt something in Iceland, but he did not fully appreciate what that something was until socialism allowed him to place it in a context.

Some indication has already been given as to why Morris did not arrive at socialist commitment until about 1883. It may be true that the holders of socialist views had not organised themselves into a movement much before then; it may be true that Morris simply had not worked out his ideas about society as a whole before then – he did say as much himself, that he had been kept back in this respect by poetry and art. It is certainly true that by 1883 the firm was a highly profitable and well-run concern, requiring far less of Morris's own time, while still providing him with a good income. He was, therefore, secure, and had time to spare to look up from his own affairs, and to consider how things stood with the world at large, and how they ought to stand.

And what he saw was the late Victorian world. He saw a society in which Carlyle's abhorrent 'cash nexus' prevailed, so that ordinary men were treated as money-making machines. A world in which cheap, unpleasant, technology was drowning the Ruskinian aesthetic in a flood of shoddiness; in which men could take no pleasure or pride in their 'useless toil'. He had seen that before, but now he saw more. He saw massive injustice and inequality, and that, because vested interests held all the power in the state, and would not voluntarily give them up, power would in the end have to be taken from these vested interests by force. And that meant, if civilisation were to be saved from moral, spiritual and artistic decline, there would have to be a revolution. Of course, the only credible revolutionary groups active at the time were the various branches of the socialist movement. If Morris had been Kingsley, or Carlyle, he might have had difficulties swallowing the idea of socialism. But it is clear from his political output that advocating socialism was something both easy and congenial to him; it came naturally, as it were, insofar as politics can ever be a natural activity.

There was good reason for this, beyond a strong sense of natural justice. His investigations into socialism led him to integrate an older belief into the new system. This was that competition, of all the forces at work in a capitalist society, could be most clearly indicted on the charge of debasing the arts, and not merely art in general but the decorative arts – Morris's arts – in particular. It is not hard to see why: the ruthless process of cost-cutting, which normally meant, besides low wages, that producing goods of high quality was no longer seen as affordable. He also saw that socialism could not be achieved within small organisations, however well-meaning their owners might be. He never came near to suggesting that Morris & Co. should be run on socialist lines, and to the end the firm did business in accordance with the orthodoxies of the time. As has been observed, his workforce was better treated than most, but this was closer to the fine Victorian tradition of paternalism than to socialism. In his time, he received a good deal of criticism for this, from specious critics who liked to think that this rather wealthy man's idealism was really the mask of a hypocrite.[7] Morris himself was fully aware of the irony of his position: a revolutionary Communist (as he called himself) who made a living feeding the tastes of the 'swinish rich' (as he called them). But while there may be irony, there is no contradiction. After all, nothing can be purer than the motives of a man, who, having done very well out of a system, believes that the system should be overthrown, to his own detriment financially, and to the benefit of others; and who proves his sincerity by vigorous campaigning for the cause of that overthrow, at great expense both of his own time and his own money.

These, then, were the realities, as Morris saw them. But what of the vision, the future, the Utopia? After all, if the term Christian may used with equal validity of an upper-class, sybaritic, Tory member of the synod of the Church of England, and a wild-eyed, filthy, tangle-haired hermit in his desert cave, what extremes and variants may not lie hidden under the blanket designation Socialist? What kind of socialist was Morris?

In the first place, it may seem surprising that the preceding brief outline of the influences on his thinking does not contain the name of Marx. The reason is that Morris began his study of Marx at the age of about 49, and therefore entered the list late on. In any case, the young, for all their occasional arrogance, have a paradoxical relish of heroes, and are glad to acknowledge them as influences, whereas a man of nearly 50 insists on his dignity, and controls the intake of new ideas through the regulating power of his own mature wisdom. Of course, an understanding of Marx remained a necessity for anybody who aspired to a leading position in the contemporary socialist movement; but Morris came to Marx not in search of a socialist Bible, but for confirmation of what he already felt to be right, a stocking up of his intellectual armoury. It is almost certain that Morris did not need Marx or anybody else to tell him that the exploitation of labour by capital was iniquitous. There is, however, no doubt at all that he acquired from Marx the historical theory of the revolutionary process, as he shows very clearly in his account of an imaginary English revolution in *News from Nowhere*. Elsewhere in the book, he is very much his own man; it is here, and in the earlier work, *A Dream of John Ball*, that we can discover the essence of Morris's socialism.

There is something of a symmetry about these two fantasies, one moving back to the time of the suppressed Peasants' Revolt of 1381, the other forward to a period after the successful Socialist Revolution of the 1950s. It is as though an historical wheel has turned full circle – except that the end product, while in many ways resembling the starting-point, has been purged of its ancient poisons: cruelty, barbarism, illiteracy, injustice, war, disease and famine. The Peasants' Revolt was in essence a vigorous response to certain government measures widely seen as oppressive and unfair. (Commentators on more recent events in British history have enjoyed noting that one of these measures was a capitation or poll tax.) Even if it had succeeded, even if the peasants had forced the authorities to remedy their grievances, it would probably have had little

Plate 10.1 Kelmscott Manor, Oxfordshire, Morris's house on the banks of the Thames; it provides the setting for the concluding chapters of *News from Nowhere* *William Morris Gallery*

impact on the course of history; either the government would have taken care not to be quite so provocative – until the next time – or it would have been well and truly ready to clamp down very firmly in the event of any repetition.

But that was not especially important to Morris. What mattered was the challenge that ordinary people had mounted against an arbitrary and tyrannical authority and, above all, the resolution and comradeship which the events implied. This is called solidarity, in the language of modern socialism. Morris called it fellowship. It is interesting to look again at one of the more commonly quoted passages from *A Dream*, to illustrate how easy it was for Socialism to adopt the imagery and language of religion.

Forsooth, brothers, fellowship is heaven, and lack of fellowship is hell: fellowship is life, and lack of fellowship is death: and the deeds that ye do upon earth, it is for fellowship's sake that ye do them, and the life that is in it, that shall live on it forever, and each one of you part of it, while many a man's life upon the earth shall wane.[8]

This is the centre of Morris's Socialism. Just as nature is central to art, and craft is central to work, so fellowship is central to society. And a distinction is to be drawn between fellowship and the more modern concept of solidarity. For this is always solidarity against something – the class enemy, or imperialism, or Fascism, or treachery; whereas it is the great ideal of fellowship to be all-embracing. And here Morris found an early example of the thing itself, displayed by a mob of rough, unorganised, uneducated but heroically indignant men and women, with no claim to any sort of sophisticated wisdom, but with every claim to know what injustice was, and filled with an implacable hatred of it. This may not be history, although there is no reason to be unduly cynical about the motives of the rebels, and no reason to doubt their courage. But it does not have to be history. For Morris, the Peasants' Revolt served as an admirable metaphor for countless other fighters against injustice, all those who insisted that mankind should have freedom, Diggers, Levellers, Chartists and the like; and its suppression for countless other acts of tyranny, some not so remote in time, such as Peterloo (1819), or Bloody Sunday, 13 November 1887, when troops attacked unarmed demonstrators near Trafalgar Square.

The spirit of revolution, then, has to be seen as something of great antiquity in terms of the human life-span; but in terms of its own development as something just coming to maturity. The great question remained: what would it be like when the spirit of revolution had finally prevailed? Everybody has his or her own idiosyncrasy, and no doubt every revolutionary has his or her in some way distinctive vision of an ideal world. This is a problem, for whenever a revolutionary proposes a particular world order, it will clearly come as near as possible to a personal idea of perfection. If this order has to be set up against other people's ideas, and perhaps imposed on them, there is an immediate suggestion of a kind of tyranny, however benevolent its form.

As it happens, back in 1890, there was no pressing danger – in Britain at least – that any revolutionary would have to undergo the nerve-jangling ordeal of having his theories put to the test. Then, as now, Morris's Utopian vision, *News from Nowhere*, represented no menace of tyranny, just an intriguing exposition of what Morris hoped the future might bring. But in the world which he imagined perhaps the most striking aspect of the new society was the freedom of every man and woman to control the course of his or her own life. This is a freedom both precious and elusive, possessed in any age by no more than a handful of individuals. It is the antithesis of tyranny to wish to see it extended to everybody, as far as nature and justice allow. That it was important to Morris is unsurprising. For he more than most *had* been able to take control of his life. From early adulthood he had shaped a career, created his firm, developed and exploited his talents to the full, and, it must be said, made himself rich enough to be in his last years as independent an actor on the political and social scene as he could ever have wished. It is likely that after leaving school he never once had to take an order from anybody, apart, perhaps, from some court official during his occasional brushes with the law. Yet it is not every privileged person who wants privileges to be universal. After all, as Adam Smith pointed out from what modern Conservatism claims is the other side of the argument, if everyone is privileged equally, then no one is: there can be no status within an equal society. But a society without status or privilege is just what Morris wanted. It is the spirit of magnanimity which informs all that is best in socialist thinking, and it is a spirit that cannot be effectively denigrated, even by socialism's most cynical and unscrupulous critics.

This, then, is the ethic of Nowhere. Morris also built himself, so to speak, into the actual fabric of the place as well, for he has depicted it as a society whose activities are to a large extent underpinned by his own beloved crafts. Nothing else was to be expected, but, to stress once more how diverse socialist ideals can be, Nowhere was conceived in part as an answer to a book called *Looking Backward*, by the American socialist Edward Bellamy. Bellamy's Utopia was a highly centralised world of high technology with huge urban landscapes dominated by giant sky-scrapers – a scientific workers' paradise which says much for Bellamy's powers of prophecy. But if Bellamy was able to foretell with some accuracy the environment in which we live now, it is one which must have struck Morris as being just as bad as the system it was to replace. His own prophetic nature concerned a very different matter: not what was to be, but what ought to be. So he created Nowhere, in the God-like way that authors have, out of images from his own happy experiences; medievally beautiful images, without the taint of medieval squalor; images of satisfaction, even joy, in work; a world where pretensions have been mocked out of existence; where scholarship is valued, but not insisted on; and where no one has cause to feel superior to his neighbour – a world which would be, in Thomas Hardy's words, 'a pure delight, a beauty spot, where all is gentle, true, and just, and darkness is unknown'.[9] Hardy, not a noted optimist, thought that such a world was an impossibility. He may well have been right. But William Morris thought otherwise, and for this deserves honour. For after the unlamented death of the deformed, Stalinist socialism that prevailed so long in eastern Europe, the ideas of such men as Morris still provide the humanity and moral insight that should re-establish the good name of an essentially decent and idealistic creed.

NOTES

1. See J. Ruskin, *The Two Paths* (1859), in E.T. Cook and A. Wedderburn (eds), *The Complete Works of John Ruskin* (39 vols., 1903–12), Vol. 16, p. 320.
2. N. Kelvin (ed.), *The Collected Letters of William Morris*, Vol. I (Princeton, NJ, 1984), pp. 275, to Thomas Wardle, 5 Nov. 1875.
3. W. Morris, 'The Lesser Arts of Life' (1882), in M. Morris (ed.), *The Collected Works of William Morris* (24 vols., 1910–15), Vol. XXII, p. 257. Also see *idem*, 'Of Dyeing as an Art', reprinted in *Arts and Crafts Essays, by Members of the Arts and Crafts Exhibition Society* (1893), pp. 196–211.
4. Quoted in A. Briggs (ed.), *William Morris: News from Nowhere and Selected Writings and Designs* (1984 edn.), p. 85.
5. J. Ruskin, *Unto this Last*, in *Complete Works*, Vol. 17, p. 344.

6. Kelvin (ed.), *Letters*, Vol. II (Princeton, NJ, 1987), p. 229, to Andreas Scheu, 15 Sept. 1883.
7. On Morris's critics, see E.P. Thompson, *William Morris: Romantic to Revolutionary* (New York, 2nd edn 1977), pp. 308–10, 316–27.
8. W. Morris, *A Dream of John Ball* (1886–87), *Collected Works*, Vol. XVI, p. 230.
9. *The Unborn*, in S. Hynes (ed.), Thomas Hardy (Oxford, 1984), p. 122.

Postscript: The Work of the William Morris Society

THE LIFE, work and ideas of William Morris are as important today as they were in his lifetime. The William Morris Society exists to make them as widely known as possible.

The many-sidedness of Morris and the variety of his activities bring together in the Society those who are interested in him as designer, craftsman, businessman, poet, socialist or who admire his robust and generous personality, his creative energy and courage. His views on creative work, leisure and machinery, on ecology and conservation, on the place of the arts in our lives and their relation to politics, as on much else, remain as challenging now as they were a century ago. He provides a focus for those who deplore the progressive dehumanisation of the world in the twentieth century and who believe, with him, that the trend is not inevitable.

The Society provides information on topics of interest to its members and arranges lectures, visits, exhibitions and other events. It encourages the reprinting of his works and the continued manufacture of his textile and wallpaper designs. It publishes a journal twice a year, free to members, which carries articles across the field of Morris scholarship. It also publishes a quarterly newsletter giving details of its programme, new publications and other matters of interest concerning Morris and his circle. Members are invited to contribute items both to the journal and to the newsletter. The William Morris Society has a world-wide membership and offers the chance to make contact with fellow Morrisians both in Britain and abroad.

Regular events include a Kelmscott Lecture and visits to exhibitions and such places as the William Morris Gallery, Red House, Kelmscott Manor and Standen. These visits, tours and short residential study courses enable members living abroad or outside London to participate in the Society's activities. The Society also has local groups in various parts of Britain and affiliated Societies in the USA and Canada.

The Society's headquarters are at Kelmscott House, Hammersmith, Morris's home for the last 18 years of his life. Kelmscott House was named after Morris's country home, Kelmscott Manor: in the coach house alongside, Hammersmith carpets were woven and later the Hammersmith Socialist Society met there.

For further details, write to:

> The Hon. Membership Secretary
> Kelmscott House
> 26 Upper Mall
> Hammersmith
> London W6 9TA

Index